Sylvester Stallone

Sylvester Stallone
A Life on Film

ADRIAN WRIGHT

ROBERT HALE · LONDON

© *Adrian Wright 1991*
First published in Great Britain 1991

ISBN 0 7090 4428 3

Robert Hale Limited
Clerkenwell House
Clerkenwell Green
London EC1R 0HT

Photoset in Ehrhardt in North Wales by
Derek Doyle & Associates, Mold, Clwyd.
Printed in Great Britain by
St Edmundsbury Press, Bury St Edmunds, Suffolk.
Bound by Hunter and Foulis.

Contents

List of Illustrations		7
Acknowledgements		9
Introduction: Legend		11
1	Never Like the Waltons	15
2	Sasha	24
3	Early Films	33
4	Sleeper	45
5	Whistling Past the Graveyard	58
6	The Worst Reviews Since Hitler	69
7	Sequel	80
8	Eye of the Tiger	90
9	Enter Rambo	104
10	Fairy-Tales with Music	113
11	Again, with a Vengeance	124
12	Brigitte	133
13	O.T.T.	144
14	Jogging Through Dante's Inferno	156
15	Transitions	167
Conclusion: Past Magic		178
Bibliography		182
Filmography		183
Index		189

Illustrations

Facing page

Looking out on a career that Rex Reed called 'as mysterious as cot death' 80

The four Lords of Flatbush: Paul Mace, Stallone, Henry Winkler and Perry King 80

Coping with the threat of marriage from Maria Smith in *The Lords of Flatbush* 81

Stallone's own creation Rocky Balboa, before the Big Time 81

Rocky and the faithful Adrian: Stallone with Talia Shire in *Rocky II* 81

Rocky at home in the ring 96

Stallone surrounded by Rocky memorabilia 96

Directing *Rocky III* 97

Despite the thoughtful gaze, Stallone spent years trying to convince cinema-goers he was not as slow as Rocky 97

Preparing to talk about the weather in *F.I.S.T.* 128

Meeting his fans during *F.I.S.T.*, but soon admirers would be kept at arm's length 128

The Carboni brothers of *Paradise Alley*: Stallone with Armand Assante and Lee Canalito (in foreground) 129

With Sasha and Travolta, celebrating *Staying Alive* 129

Stallone and Travolta struttin' at the time of *Staying Alive* 129

Stallone's other immortal: John Rambo 144

Images of violence that went round the world with Rambo 144

Peace at last. With Richard Crenna at the close of *Rambo III* 145

Still coming up with the action: Stallone in *Lock Up* 145

As so often before in his career, fiction and reality met in *Rocky V*, with son Sage playing Rocky Junior 145

Acknowledgements

I have to thank the staffs of various institutions for their willing assistance, especially the British Film Institute, the National Film Archive, British Equity and American Equity. For their helpfulness, I am also indebted to the staffs of the British Library, Norfolk County Library, and Jane Rees of the *Guardian*.

Among the actors who talked to me about Mr Stallone, many wished to remain anonymous, but I must especially thank Michael Cochrane, Daniel Massey and Tim Pigott-Smith for sharing their memories with me. Maurice Roeves generously plundered material from his own autobiography to provide me with his reminiscences of working with Mr Stallone, for which I am very grateful.

In researching material for this book, I have made a careful study of every film Mr Stallone has appeared in, except for the elusive *A Party at Kitty and Studs*, and I have to thank the various people who made the viewing of these films possible. Other friends and colleagues brought material to my notice which I might otherwise have missed, among them Lynn Jacobs and Miriam Robbins.

I am grateful to Cambridge University Press for permission to use extracts from *Indelible Shadows: Film and the Holocaust* by Annette Insdorf. For critical reviews of Mr Stallone's films, as well as for production details, I have made extensive use of the excellent *Monthly Film Bulletin* published by the British Film Institute; the reviews contained there are usually carefully judged. The opinions of other critics and journalists regarding Mr Stallone often provide fascinating insights – whether they agree or disagree with those of the author – and I acknowledge their contributions. There is an obvious debt to two earlier biographies of Mr Stallone, which I acknowledge: *Stallone! A hero's story* by Jeff Rovin (Pocket Books, 1985; New English Library, 1987), and *Sylvester Stallone: an illustrated biography* by Marsha Daly (Zomba, 1985).

For their kind hospitality in London when I was researching the book, my warm thanks must go to Betty and Robert Bates. I am also indebted to Michael King for his patience and technical assistance, making it possible for me to look my word processor in the face. And, lastly, I owe a great debt to Terry Dunning, for his ever-willing assistance, critical interest, and unflinching encouragement.

Introduction: Legend

In Hollywood, nothing succeeds like excess.

Excess, so far as cinema is concerned, may indeed be what legends are made of and, in writing about any great film star, the biographer may end up with a book that seems like a re-run of the life of the purely fictional Hollywood star Belle Poitrine, as related by Patrick Dennis in his devastating pastiche of stars' autobiographies *Little Me*.

To qualify as such a film star, certain prerequisites are demanded. The story should ideally begin with rags and end with riches – or, even more fascinatingly, proceed to riches and go back to the rags. The climb to fame, and the achievement of that elusive lucky break, should have an element of ruthlessness about it. The sudden access of fame, when it arrives, should be phenomenal. The legendary film star does not, of course, depend on critical approval. More than a little lambasting will probably do his career no harm at all, and may even enhance it.

It goes without saying that the lifestyle must be rich and extravagant.

Hopefully, sex will play a major part in the story, with discarded lovers and partners worked through in the full glare of media publicity.

The most enduring of movie stars will always have a high quota of drama in his real life, as well as those he lives out on the screen. And when all these individual qualifications have been counted, the star who wishes to live in legend will only do so if there is a strong, though sometimes intangible, bond between him and his public.

Sylvester Stallone, without question, has all the qualifications. He comes weighed down with them, but he also brings something quite different into American cinema. The giants among the leading men of Hollywood – James Dean, Clark Gable, Cary Grant, John Wayne, and all the rest – each, in his own way, made a contribution, personifying various types of American manhood, but in a generalized, all-purpose sort of way. Stallone has done this, but has also created two specific characters, Rocky Balboa and John Rambo, who each represent apparently very different, yet sometimes similar, portraits of American masculinity and culture. These inventions (and Rocky was completely Stallone's own) have played out their lives in a series of films that have achieved startling commercial, and sometimes even critical, success, creating two epics that have run a remarkable span of time.

Throughout this process, Stallone has not merely been the actor hired to speak the words, but has also contributed as writer (for all the Rocky films) and director (for three of the Rocky films), functions he has also fulfilled on several other movies, with varying degrees of success. Stallone, in a very real way, has been able to chart his own life through that of Rocky, while Rambo may be said to chart – however crudely – his country's conscience. In so many of his movies, Stallone has been able to act out his own life on screen, in a way very few other artists have found possible.

There was a time when Sylvester Stallone seemed about to become the new darling of the critics: 'The next Mitchum, Brando and Pacino rolled into one,' said *Time*, soon after his star had first ascended. Thomas Schatz, Professor of Communications at the University of Texas, discovered 'a little Henry Fonda in the guy, a little John Wayne, a little Clint Eastwood. But it's difficult to think of a precedent for him'. The fact that Stallone the actor was being compared to these luminaries of Hollywood becomes all the more extraordinary when set against his own insistence that 'I only wanted to be a writer. That's my profession.'

It is doubtful that many of his millions of fans would agree with that, or come to accept it. And, even more than most of his contemporaries in cinema, Stallone has become so identified with his own screen characters that the division between reality and fantasy has often become seriously blurred. On meeting him, Gerald Ford, Jimmy Carter, Edward Kennedy and Ronald Reagan all addressed him as 'Rocky'.

There have, of course, always been highly contrasted attitudes towards Stallone. His *Rocky* co-star, Talia Shire, speaks of him as 'an intellectual caveman'. A spectator, watching him filming *Paradise Alley*, announced 'He's a little squirt.' Shortly after the onset of his first great success, a fellow actor said, 'He's become such a bastard that even his dog Butkus turned on him and bit him.' Before long, rumours circulated that the 5ft 10in Stallone refused to work with anyone taller than himself, and didn't allow anyone on his set to use the bathroom. He even, apparently, had his name baked into biscuits.

Throughout, Stallone himself has never been without his own positive thoughts on what his role in the film world has been. 'I think,' he has said, 'the primary objective of creative art – of film art – is to create simplistic stories that touch everyone and affect their lives through giving them heroes, through answering questions ... People don't want to go to the movies to think, and they don't want to go to see realism.' Has this, then, been the bedrock of Stallone's success, a phenomenon that the sharp-tongued Rex Reed has described as 'more mysterious than cot death'?

In the life of the ideally legendary film star, the focus should, of course, occasionally move away to the supporting players and here, again, Stallone does not disappoint. Permeating the story, from the beginning to the present, is the figure of his mother, who has carved out her own extraordinarily high-profile career without ever displaying any particularly definable talents. Her celebrity is so pronounced that when I told friends I was writing a book about Sylvester Stallone, they asked why I wasn't writing a book about his mother.

If Jacqueline hovers over her son's life like a benevolent harpy, there are also Sasha and Brigitte – two classically cast supporting actresses – as well as a gaggle of other beautiful women. Between them, Sasha and Brigitte would have the most tremendous influence on Stallone's life, with Brigitte as his Nemesis. At the time of his parting from her, Stallone began to face up to the fact that all was not as he would wish in his life and career. Disillusionment, another highly necessary qualification for the legendary film star, had set in.

Glancing back in the late 1980s, Stallone could see other actors racing to overtake his position of supremacy – sometimes actors, like Dolph Lundgren, whom he had helped to early success. At the same time, the public's perception of what a macho hero should offer was changing. The cinema-goer looked to Arnold Schwarzenegger, Bruce Willis, or Mel Gibson.

Now, perhaps more strongly than ever before, Stallone realized the other major difficulty of his career – the gap between his intelligence and his reputation as a mumbling, brain-damaged hulk. Stallone had long ago been forced to come to terms with this, but he wanted his public to come to terms with it as well.

This, then, is the story of a writer, actor and director who has unquestionably become a legend in his own lifetime, even if that legend has not always been taken particularly seriously. This is the story of Sylvester Stallone, in all his manifestations: the story of Sly, Rocky, Rambo, the Italian Stallion, baby Binky, adolescent Michael – stories and lives that have coalesced and played themselves out ... on film.

1 Never Like the Waltons

Hell's Kitchen, New York, was never a very good address, but for anyone destined to get to the top from the bottom, was probably an ideal place to be born.

Two policemen are supposed to have given the stretch of slum between 30th Street and 57th Street West of 9th Avenue its picturesque place name, as they looked on one steamy night at a brawl that had started up in the neighbourhood.

'This place is hot as Hell,' said one.

'Hell's cool,' said the other. 'This place is Hell's Kitchen.'

Frank Stallone had come to America from Sicily as a young boy with his parents, and grew up with a strong sense of family values, matched with a fierce ambition to better himself, to earn money as an amateur singer, and to remain a good Catholic. Frank's father had been a hairdresser, a trade that many of the family had turned a hand to, and which Frank himself would eventually embrace with considerable success.

At Billy Rose's Diamond Horseshoe Club, Jacqueline Labofish, glorifying in her professional capacity as a Longstemmed Rose – in effect a cigarette-girl-cum-singer – was nursing her own undimmable ambitions. Much of the considerable success that would come to her would be courtesy of her elder son's fame, but there is every reason to believe she would have won through completely on her own merits.

When Jacqueline and Frank married, however, their ambitions showed no sign of taking off, and the best they could afford for a home was a cramped tenement apartment at the edge of Hell's Kitchen, on 9th Avenue. By late 1945, Jacqueline was pregnant and became a rather implausible Longstemmed Rose. Frank went on cutting hair, his hopes of becoming an entertainer having faded, though life with Jacqueline often had the hallmark of true theatre. Their eldest son was later to describe his parents' marriage as 'a war between the black and the red ants' and sometimes it is possible to understand the problems Frank may have endured. When Jacqueline's labour pains were down to five minute intervals she still refused to get into a taxi to take her to the hospital, firmly stating her intention to eat a loaf of bread before catching a bus there.

Lack of money directed her to the charity ward of the West 44th Street hospital (not far from the famed Actors' Studio) where she was delivered of a baby on 6 July 1946. Forty-four years later, officials at the hospital discovered the Stallones had never picked up the bill for services rendered.

Forceps were used to effect the delivery. In the excitement of the occasion, the boy was welcomed as perfectly formed. Jacqueline's predilection for perfection was obvious from the name she had selected for the child – Tyrone, after one of her favourite movie stars. But Italian family pride had beaten her to it, for by the time Jacqueline had come out of labour, Frank had already given the names which were to appear on the birth certificate. The first name, though not Tyrone, was unquestionably that of a very famous film personality, if not quite of the type Jacqueline had hoped to emulate: Sylvester was the name of the Warner Bros cartoon cat, forever haplessly in pursuit of Tweetie-Pie. His name was one of the first burdens Sylvester Gardenzio Stallone would have to come to terms with.

Back home with the baby, Frank and Jacqueline noticed that the baby's left eye drooped, and returned to the hospital which admitted that during delivery the use of forceps had obviously damaged the child, severing one of the major facial nerves and, in effect, paralysing one side of the face under the eye and around the lip, chin and tongue. Nothing, apparently, could be done to remedy the disfigurement, but the baby was loved and nicknamed 'Binky', possibly the least masculine name that, in adulthood, the boy would have to endure. 'Binky' would somehow, over the years, transmute to Michael, to Sly, to Rocky, to Rambo, to Cobra, to the Italian Stallion.

Money was short, and Jacqueline returned to strutting her stuff as a soubrette, while Frank's busy attempts to build the family fortune continued. Sylvester could not adequately be cared for at home because of the ambitious pursuits of his parents, and was farmed out to a child-minder in Queens. In fact, she became something of a surrogate mother since his parents only took him home with them at weekends. It was not a beginning which augured particularly well for the child's future.

When, in 1950, another son was born to Frank and Jacqueline, Sylvester's problems were at once lessened and compounded. Frank Jnr was born perfectly formed, and found the parental favour his elder brother had somehow been denied. Frank Jnr's very existence took some of the pressures off Sylvester, but his pent-up emotions were already boiling over when, at the age of four, he qualified as a highly promising vandal by spraying the neighbours' cars with red paint. It had been a mere adventurous fantasy to Sylvester, but to his father it was a bad deed to be heavily dealt with. The boy also developed a penchant for urinating in plug sockets.

Frank Jnr proved to be into more socially acceptable pursuits, and from his earliest years was encouraged in a love of music by his parents. They bought him a saxophone, which he enjoyed playing. Later Frank and Jacqueline extended the opportunity to learn the instrument to Sylvester, hoping the strenuous facial movements involved would help him to overcome his disabilities. They were disappointed when Sylvester showed no interest in, and no talent for, the instrument. To Sylvester, it was merely an idea that had been thought up to help his brother, and then been passed carelessly down to him. It didn't begin to solve any of his own emotional isolation. In his desperation, and craving for genuine affection and friendship, he took to raiding his father's purse so he could buy treats for the neighbourhood kids. Friendship, it seemed to him, could be bought.

When Sylvester was five, funds allowed the family to move to the far more salubrious district of Silver Springs in Maryland, Washington, where they took over a three-storey house. Frank's determination to better himself had another boost at this time, for he opened a hairdressing salon and soon owned a group of such establishments. These were profitable enough for him to buy a farm where there was room to breathe and raise ponies to be used in polo matches. It was Sylvester's first nod with what would become one of his favourite sports.

But at seven years of age, his world was still largely centred on make-believe. No boisterous childhood would be complete without the worship of, or need to emulate, an out-of-this-

world-hero. Sylvester's need to identify with such a figure was
perhaps a little extreme, leading him to make a full costume of
his idol, the comic-book wonder Superboy. This consisted of a
sweatshirt emblazoned with the letter 'S' tucked into red shorts
worn, in best Superman style, over blue tights, finished off with
the obligatory cape. When his teacher pulled him out to the
front of the class and made him reveal this garb, which he had
hopefully covered with his school clothes, it was a deep
humiliation. Possibly so early an exposure to mockery went
some way to protecting him from the many shafts he would have
to endure in later years. His weedy looks, his struggling voice,
his lack of parental understanding, did nothing to help improve
his confidence, and his academic future did not look good.

Artistically, there were possible outlets for any talents he
might possess, and by the age of nine he showed interest in
painting, but his efforts were largely dismissed by the usual,
critical attitude of Frank. If there was one thing Sylvester
seemed assured of, it appeared to be a lack of emotional support
and encouragement.

'Our parents were very inconsistent with us,' said his brother
of this period. 'Sly went through much undue physical and
emotional abuse from them.'

Confirming this, Sylvester was later to confess: 'I can't lie and
say it was a wonderful childhood. It was terrible', and he has
spoken of himself as 'an unwanted kid, an abused kid', though
not abused in the worst senses we might mean today. His father
meted out physical punishment to answer his elder son's less
socially acceptable activities.

'I was swatted a few times with great power,' Sylvester
reported. 'I was sent flying, a heat seeking missile, across the
room. But I was a difficult child, so I would get difficult
spankings.'

Sylvester's willingness to stay on the rails seemed sure
enough when he eventually joined the Cub Scouts, an
organization that gave him his first opportunity to act. The lower
half of Smokey the Bear didn't seem much, however, and wasn't
enough experience to land him the title role in his school's
production of *Mr Toad Goes West*. The fact that he was rejected
for a speaking role did nothing to help his confidence, and he
looked again to Superboy and, with the coming of adolescence,
to the antics of the Lone Ranger, a character he would later pay

homage to in the closing scenes of *Rhinestone*.

If his childhood was uncomfortable, it was at least throwing up all sorts of experiences that would be played out in his later years, when Hollywood and the paying public offered him the chance, time and again, to re-open what had never been a childhood box of delights. The bored, frustrated street corner kids that crop up in *Rocky* are a reminder of that childhood, just as the roof-top race that forms the overture to *Paradise Alley* harks back to the roof jumping he indulged in as a boy. And when he wasn't jumping from roof to roof, he was jumping off them with an opened umbrella. An unlikely Mary Poppins, his fall was broken in a trough of water, and Frank could once again point to a troublesome son.

Perhaps more worrying was Sylvester's tendency to get involved in heavy physical scraps, but this was almost to be expected as a riposte against his unsympathetic home life and the ribbings he constantly suffered from his siblings. The name Sylvester was itself quite an able instrument in the hands of another child, but 'Tweetie-Pie' and 'Sylvia' were even more effective teasers, helped along by the fact that the bearer of these names had a funny voice and a droopy face.

Sylvester's fighting was also another reaction of a naturally creative child denied any outlets for his enthusiasms, though at this time Sylvester didn't actually realize what he might be enthusiastic about. It certainly wasn't the tap-dancing lessons Jacqueline had him sent to, or the painfully unproductive piano lessons he had to endure, over which Jacqueline presided with a stick in her hand. She had abandoned her own dreams of becoming a concert pianist, at least for the time being, but had hopes that one day Sylvester might work out that dream for her. However questionable her motives with regard to Sylvester's musicianship, she was at least trying to nudge her son toward some sort of positive activity. Such prodding did not end with Sylvester's childhood. When he was seventeen, and professed to have no interest in books, she paid him a dollar to read Errol Flynn's soul-baring autobiography *My Wicked, Wicked Ways*. Among the various effects this book had on him, one may have been that it did indeed encourage him to read; Sylvester would become a voracious reader.

But the gulf between the child and his parents remained. When Jacqueline took her errant son to a psychologist, she claimed that he told her the child should be institutionalized, but Sylvester remembered differently. There was nothing wrong with Sylvester, the psychologist explained; it was the parents who needed treatment.

But any parental support that might have been forthcoming further receded when Sylvester was ten years old. Frank and Jacqueline decided to part, though a divorce was not easily assimilated into Frank's religious beliefs. Both of them would find new partners over the years – several of them. For the moment, however, the future for Frank Jnr and Sylvester was considered in as much as an arrangement was made that gave over each child to each parent on an alternate yearly rota. This annual turnabout of surroundings, friends and emotional ties hardly seemed a perfect settlement or one in which the children's happiness would naturally flourish, but the bargain was struck. No matter how nervous he might be of his father, the strong familial quality of their lives together had, it seemed, to be preserved, no matter what. The scars Sylvester was left with ran deep. He once confessed to his mother that he was wary of having children of his own in case he became the father Frank had been.

Frank continued living in Maryland and Jacqueline moved to Philadelphia. In her new life Jacqueline met and married a pizza-maker called Filita (the original Crispy Pizza King) who encouraged her growing interest in the health and beauty business, an interest that bloomed when she opened a gymnasium – Barbella's – at which women were made especially welcome. Seeing the success his astute mother could make of such a project, and the seemingly limitless opportunities the body offered for the strengthening of confidence and ego, was an early and positive awakening of Sylvester's obsession with his own body. In his philosophy, body fitness not only scored physically, but marked the way to mental, perhaps even intellectual, fertility.

His father had offered encouragement – of sorts – for his son's interest in his body: 'You weren't born with much of a brain,' he told him, 'so you'd better develop your body.'

This was at once a criticism and a nudge that would in time find its way into Rocky Balboa's life. In his dismissive helpfulness, Frank had played a major part in shaping Sylvester's creed for success, a creed that would eventually achieve undreamed-of goals through Sylvester's combined strengths of mind and body.

The body part of it all was pushed further when he saw his first Steve Reeves picture in 1959. A former Mr World and Mr Universe, fellow American Reeves had already been a sizeable film name for six years as the body beautiful of colourful Italian historical extravaganzas. Never in danger of taking home an Oscar for his acting, Reeves was nevertheless a blazing example of how far a brilliant physique could get you.

For the thirteen-year-old Sylvester, the lifeless tableaux of Superboy had given way to the fully developed adulthood of the George Eastman-coloured *Hercules*. It was an energizing experience and made him want to tear the seats out of the theatre.

What he could and did do the following day was to raid a local junk-yard for something to use as weights – he eventually purloined an automobile axle. He then found that by securing cement blocks to the ends of brooms he had got himself a set of barbells.

For himself, however, any hopes of a life in show-business or, more wildly, films, seemed remote. At Philadelphia High he summoned enough courage to try for the school play and was again turned down. Rejection on any sort of intellectual level only served to push him further along the road of physical improvement. The distance between his intellectualism and physical supremacy would be at once an asset and a disadvantage in the stunning career that was, as yet, perhaps only dreamed of. For the present, at least Jacqueline was pleased to see him applying himself seriously to making the most of everything physical.

If Philadelphia (during one of the years he was with his mother) couldn't persuade him to take education seriously, neither could the Catholic school he attended in Maryland during one of his father's years, where he played practical tricks on the nuns whose sense of fun was not highly developed. Back in Philadelphia there were even fears that he might grow up a fully qualified pyromaniac after he started fires in three different schools. These establishments usually found they could do without this particular pupil. By the age of sixteen he had passed through (sometimes very quickly) over a dozen schools.

He did have a well developed body, but academically and

even socially the boy seemed intent on turning out a dud. Throwing his hands up at the past, he turned his back on school and for a while considered joining the navy or, as a last resort and in an attempt to emulate his father, leaving to work in Australia as a shepherd. He was too young for the navy, and anyway Frank had a more practical if less picturesque suggestion. The beauty business had been good to the Stallones over the years; why didn't Sylvester, like a good elder son, travel that same path? Probably partly in a desperate effort to appease his parents' criticisms of him, he agreed to sign on at beauty college, but after only a few months he walked out on his new career and went trailing back to Philadelphia.

Now, Jacqueline took a decisive decision that was certainly to improve her son's chance of achieving something in life. She had enough money, determination and belief in him to search out a private school that would take on his individual problems, and would earn their fees by giving him the urgent attention he needed at this critical time. She found the place among rolling lawns and woodland in Berwyn, Pennsylvania. The Devereux Foundation was in charge of the Manor High School, which catered for young people of both sexes aged between fourteen and twenty-one, all of whom needed assistance with a wide range of emotional and educational problems. The school's fees were steep – his stay cost something like $11,000 – but the staff to pupil ratio was encouragingly good, and Sylvester was enrolled at the school as 'Michael'. This deliberate breakaway from his given name was a sensible precaution against immediate baiting. If his confidence was to have an up-turn, 'Mike' would stand him in better shape than Sylvia or Tweetie-Pie.

Though he still refused to shine academically at Manor High, Mike's prowess at sport was allowed full play, and worked its wonders for character building. He earned a reputation as a good all-round sportsman: a promising rider, fencer, an able footballer who, in his senior year, was co-captain of the school team. There was also his interest in boxing which was keenly fostered; it channelled the aggression he had squandered in earlier years, and gave him the discipline his slack childhood had cried out for. Mike was growing into a personable young man, thanks not only to the generous sporting activities of the school but to the team of psychiatrists and psychologists that oversaw each pupil's progress. A course of speech therapy was another useful component, and the self-consciousness that the young Sylvester had felt with his voice and face became less of a problem to Mike.

Despite the evident wonders worked by Manor High staff, however, Mike was unable to muster enough sheer learning to earn graduation into college. This would have meant another life full stop had it not been for Jacqueline who now only wanted the best opportunities for her elder son. She hit on the idea of his attending the exclusive, and very expensive, American College in Leysin, Switzerland. She applied and was turned down. Undeterred, she flew out to Switzerland and confronted the College management head-on. She offered a full year's fees on the understanding that if their new pupil walked out on them before that year was up, the money would be forfeited. He would also go some way to earn his place by acting as the College boxing-coach.

No doubt the staff ended up admiring the tenacity of such a mother. Perhaps they ended up agreeing with her son's assessment of her as 'a Vesuvian in skirts. I don't know where she comes from, but I don't think she's earthly'.

At the beginning of his life she had showed no particular adoration or belief in him. Turning over childhood memories, Sylvester remembered only twice being kissed by her. For his father to forget himself so far as to kiss his son was unthinkable, but there had been one occasion when he had stroked his son's head in a sudden burst of affection. Now, the fierceness of Jacqueline's promotion of him had grown to an almost alarming degree. To what extent such faith would be repaid probably did not occur to her in her moments of decision. Returning from Switzerland, she at least knew she had given Sylvester yet another chance at life, and had cleverly waved the carrot of boxing-coach in front of him.

2 Sasha

Switzerland was, to say the least, a surprising place for Sylvester to have ended up to work out his adolescence, though it is doubtful that he fully appreciated his luck, or his surroundings.

Of Leysin, he said, 'the town was like one of those small objects you buy at the zoo for $4 and you turn it over and the snowflakes come down. I didn't want to ski. I just wanted to get loaded and play pin-ball machines.'

As for the company he kept at the American College, it was a far cry from the crowd he had mixed with before, and he put this change of luck down to his mother being a 'con artist'. In many ways, his streetwise background was an advantage when living alongside the 300 or so pupils, mostly the children of the wealthy and privileged, that made up the roll-call. These included the Shah of Iran's offspring, the heir to the Hershey fortune, and the child of the man who owned the Kimberly mines.

For a time, it looked as if Sylvester's future might be as an entrepreneur. Forming a friendship with Prince Paul of Ethiopia, Sylvester worked a fast-food industry within the college, financed by Paul, churning out burgers that were part lamb, part beef and part sawdust. Now dubbed as 'Studley', Sylvester also picked up pocket money as a monitor of the girls' dormitory, who may or may not have had his charges' best interests at heart; he charged for other boys to get a look in. His philanthropic attitude to his duties could be turned to the girls' advantage too. There was a set fee for letting a favoured male pupil through into the girls' quarters for a mutually satisfying assignation. This was no more than natural and harmless fun, and quite in line with Jacqueline's advice that a young man, and that included her son, should get as much sex as he could before marriage. More money – twenty dollars a time – could be earned by teaching other pupils how to get out of class by faking an asthma attack.

He provided a more legitimate service to the college by teaching boxing, which did wonders for his burgeoning confidence. The romance he associated with the sport was confirmed when he saw Kirk Douglas in *Champion*, though he couldn't have guessed that, many years later, he would almost co-star with Douglas in *First Blood*. There was some acting success, too, when in his sophomore year Sylvester played the role of Biff in Arthur Miller's *Death of a Salesman*, and liked 'the gratification of making words come alive'. At last, he was finding outlets for the various talents that had barely been suspected before, though at the end of his time at the college, his stated ambition was modest: he wanted to sell air-conditioners in Alaska.

He left college, but nothing particular occurred to him in the way of finding a job, and he wandered through Europe, living on the wind. In Cannes, he turned to the Tarot to discover what might lie ahead, and was told by the woman who had drawn the Death card that this signified nothing more sinister than the passing away of his first phase of life. He hitched a ride to Spain and hit the Costa Brava where he claimed to live 'on mussels for twenty pesetas and a piece of cheese'. Bored and dissatisfied, he returned to New York in 1967. He was twenty-one.

The year had more sometimes unhappy but formative experiences in waiting. He won a place as a drama student at the University of Miami, but neither tutors nor pupil seemed overjoyed about it. His mentors read his often slurred speech, his facial peculiarities, as unhelpful to a successful career. Not surprisingly, Sylvester found them unsympathetic, and the course constricting. Worse, the University football team wouldn't let him in. It looked as if he was set to major in Rejection, in which he was already pretty well qualified.

Still the rebel, he and a fellow student, John Herzfeld, turned their backs on the school's drama by writing and presenting their own productions which showed up in local basements and church halls. Determined to win approval for their efforts, they also wrote their own reviews for the University paper.

'We'd have one fucking line,' said Sylvester, 'but we'd write "John Herzfeld and Sylvester Stallone exploded on to the stage like whirling Tasmanian dervishes".'

Herzfeld had first come across Stallone at Miami getting

through a production of *The Hunchback of Notre Dame*, and trying
to correct his stammer by reciting Walt Whitman poems into a
sympathetic reel-to-reel recorder. But such enterprise, and the
devotion to such experimental drama as written by Pinter and
Ionesco, didn't go down well with the tutors, and in the autumn
of 1969, three credits away from a diploma, Sylvester was
thrown out of university. The pattern seemed depressingly
familiar. He went back to Philadelphia, to Jacqueline, who made
an astrological prediction that he would win through to success,
but it would happen in seven years time, and the success would
come, not from his acting, but from writing.

The seven years had to be lived, and he headed for New York,
where he was turned down for acting job after acting job. The
talent agent Rhoda Young, who would later be a casting director
on some Stallone films, sent him to audition for the role of a
greaser, but he was discounted by the producer who took one
look at him and told him there was a limit even to seediness.
One day a driver told him to get off his bus because he was
giving off bad vibes.

For bread money he was taken on as an usher at the Baronet
Theatre, with the bonus of a free uniform that had built in body
odour. The job was of no significance, but through it he met the
one woman, apart from his mother, who would have the most
beneficial influence over his life and career: Sasha Czach.

The red-headed Miss Czach – she became a blonde a little later
– had started life in Chester, Pennsylvania, where her father had
been an engineer. Like Sylvester, she nursed ambitions to be an
actor, and like him she had ended up ushering at the Baronet.
Their affair was sparked off by Sylvester, who walked up to her
and told her, 'I think I love you.'

From the start of their affair Sasha had complete faith in her
lover's talents, lending a support that would strengthen
throughout their time together. It was on the back of her
understanding and determination that he would succeed, and
that his eventual breakthrough would ride. As time would tell,
the dizzy heights of stardom would result in her love being
tested almost beyond endurance, and more than once.

In 1969, however, even talk of success seemed a rumour.
Sylvester was making thirty-eight dollars a week and living in a
small room at the unsavoury Sutton Hotel where, if he wanted

clean clothes, he took a bath with his clothes on (a tactic later used by the hero of *Staying Alive*).

Lessons at the prestigious Actors' Studio were out of the question. Sylvester developed his acting in front of mirrors. In future years he would stress that he had always had a perfectly natural approach to the actor's art. He would know if he could play a part or not.

'I figured if I could convince myself, I could convince anyone,' he said, as he went through the motions 'with only the cockroaches floating in the toilet bowl for an audience.'

Between shifts at the Baronet, he attended auditions for productions that were willing to take on non-union hopefuls, but none wanted to take him. At one audition, for a production of *Fortune and Men's Eyes*, a play about the homosexual adventures of a group of Canadian convicts, Sylvester read for its director, the actor Sal Mineo, but was turned down as not being a sufficiently intimidating type. Frustrated at being rejected for such a reason, Sylvester flung himself at Mineo and, squaring up to the alarmed director, asked for a second opinion. Mineo conceded that Sylvester could be frightening, but still didn't offer him the part.

During this period, Sylvester did land the part of the hideous Minotaur in a real curiosity – Picasso's only play, *Desire Caught by the Tail*, which managed to run for three weeks, hidden away in a Bronx theatre. Nobody noticed him in it. He also did extra film work for a sex comedy, *Lovers and Other Strangers*, starring Gig Young.

Meanwhile, the Baronet wasn't paying big money, but Sylvester decided there might be money to be got out of it. His earnings soared to between $300 and $600 a week when he became the theatre's unofficial ticket tout, selling tickets at inflated prices to people far-off down the queue. One day he picked a bad punter, who looked as if he might have money to spare for the privilege of jumping the other customers. It was the Baronet's boss, Walter Reade, who may have appreciated his employee's initiative, but sacked him on the spot. After leaving the fold, Sylvester continued to make a living out of the theatre by xeroxing bootlegged Walter Reade passes which he sold to students.

By May 1970, Sylvester was verging on the destitute, sleeping rough at the Port Authority Bus Terminal, his acting career at zero, his writing career not even off the ground, though he had bought a book on how to write successful screenplays. He used his last money to store his writing materials in a locker.

Desperate for an acting job that paid money, Sylvester snatched the opportunity to take a lead in his first major film; the fact that it was a pornographic movie didn't have him hesitating. He was offered a hundred dollars a day for his services as one of the stars of *A Party at Kitty and Studs*, for which he would have to appear out of his clothes.

'Why not?' he argued. 'I take them off for free at home every night.'

In fact, the film turned out a pretty tame affair, not even exciting enough for its producers to bother issuing. One scene had Sylvester sharing the shower with a girl whose favourite trick was to rescue the soap from the floor, giving her a closer look at her partner's sexual equipment. (It was an idea that would turn up again twenty years later in *Tango and Cash* with one crucial difference – the girl was replaced by another macho star, Kurt Russell.)

But *A Party at Kitty and Studs* had nothing entertaining or hard core about it, though when *Rocky* brought its young star fame, the producers turned it out again, hoping to exploit Sylvester's sudden access of stardom. They could do nothing about it being a dreary film, but did manage to give it a good title, acknowledging what they now saw as their hottest property: *The Italian Stallion*. And there could be no doubt of it. Sylvester, Binky, Sylvia, Tweetie-Pie, Mike, Studley, had metamorphosed into Stallone. To his friends, he would be known as Sly, but his public at large seemed to prefer him as Stallone.

Subsequently, Jacqueline was to claim that her son had made two porn movies, but this was inaccurate; though his next commission, in 1970, was another in which he had to appear naked, it was on stage, and very off-Broadway. At this time, nudity on stage (not counting strip joints) was an almost fashionable, though by no means commonplace, thing. In 1967, the musical *Hair* had its cast naked at the first half finale, and by 1969 the sexual revue *Oh Calcutta!* had bared the way for a few other evenings in the theatre where management could at least save on the wardrobe. Sometimes such efforts had salaciously suggestive titles. 1974 saw a revue called *Let My People Come*, and the title of the play Stallone was now hired for had its own sexual connotations: *Score*.

Jerry Douglas' play had the titillating theme of wife-swapping, and was about a married couple wanting to interchange sex with another, younger, married couple. Douglas directed, and offered Stallone a basic salary to play a telephone repairman who gets involved in the quartet's sexual imbroglio. Actress Claire Wilbur who, like the rest of the five-hander cast, had to play nude, found herself having to strip off the young Stallone on stage every night, though at least it was only in front of a few paying customers.

'He gave a good audition and also happened to have a good body,' said Douglas, who later praised his discovery as being 'creative and very professional'.

At least Douglas had the good sense to have some excellent photographs taken of his find. Today, they are about the only things left by which to remember *Score*, and show what a well-developed body Stallone could now show off. The small number of people who got to see either *A Party at Kitty and Studs* or *Score* saw far more of the actor than the millions who flocked to see him in later years would, but they had to be quick. *Score* opened on 28 October 1970 and was off after a meagre twenty-three performances, helped on its way by the unfriendly critical reception it had received.

Variety had a good word for Sylvester E. Stallone (as he had chosen to be billed) giving what it considered the best performance as the comically lecherous middle-class repairman, but the *New York Post* called it 'sheer garbage' and *The New York Times* thought it 'not very different from a pornographic paperback'. The play closed amid rumours that it was now to be made into a film, and Stallone had vague hopes of getting his role on celluloid, but it came to nothing. Another acting excursion with an off-Broadway group known as The Extension was also short-lived and didn't do anything to help his career or take money home.

Home was now above a defunct delicatessen store on 56th Street and Lexington Avenue, where he paid seventy-one dollars a month to share with rats which, he said, 'had bigger arms than me'. He attended auditions and was regularly rejected.

'It was a cruel experience,' he said later. 'I swore that if I was ever in a position of authority, I would always be nice to those who were struggling and that I would use as much undiscovered talent as I possibly could.'

But no such charity was shown to him by the talent hirers he met. He gave a fair idea of their reactions to his style: 'Jesus! His mouth, he garbles! He's got a goddam impediment.'

In fact, he did get work as an extra hidden away in *Klute*. For most of the time he worked as a bouncer, sold pizzas, gutted fish, and was taken on at Central Park Zoo where he was paid $1.12 an hour to do the most menial tasks, such as cleaning out the animals' cages. This came to an end when a lion urinated over him. There was no way any of this can have seemed rewarding at the time, but it certainly served as a trial of a character he would soon go on to create out of such experiences, for like Stallone, Rocky would have to take on demeaning, humiliating jobs to keep himself from going hungry, to preserve his dignity.

But there was still his writing, and through it the chance to fulfil Jacqueline's prophecy. Having studied the book on the writing of screenplays, Stallone almost churned them out, though, speaking after *Rocky*, he would refer to these efforts as 'drenched in negativism, nihilism, the idea that man is no good and the Hemingway philosophy that every story should end in the death of its protagonist ... Well, maybe it worked for Hemingway, but it sure wasn't paying my gas and electric'.

His determination to make something of his writing grew stronger. He bought a can of black paint and sprayed the world outside off his windows. He ripped out the phone, further cutting himself off from friends and contacts. And he fell, in a big way, for Edgar Allan Poe.

In 1982 he told William Wolf, 'Warren Beatty had a dream of *Reds*. This is my dream. I'll play Poe ... the most misunderstood of all American artists. He didn't know how to play the game and was so far advanced in his writing and thoughts of the fantasy world beyond that he was scorned as a madman rather than hailed as a visionary.'

Later, he said he could easily identify 'with Poe's tragic loss of people, his drive and his loneliness'. He wrote a screenplay based on Poe's life which, in various forms, would haunt his career for many years to come. When he was unsuccessful nobody wanted it because he was an unknown and the risk was too great. After he became famous nobody wanted it because it was light years beyond the roles that had made him a film star.

Some money did get made by the pen, however. He and

Herzfeld held writing contests with each other, turning out scripts at an alarming speed. One day, Stallone managed to come up with six scripts and even sold one, for the *Touch of Evil* series featuring Anthony Quayle. The $2,500 he earned was enough incentive to carry on, and a few other scripts were taken up though, like any other writer, Stallone soon had a bottom drawer full of still-birth projects.

One of these, *Cry Full and Whisper Empty – In the Same Breath*, can't have been much helped by its title. *Till Young Men Exit* didn't sound very cheerful either, nor *Sad Blues*, the hero of which was a pop-singer suffering from a type of heart disease that could only be cured by the eating of bananas. How far this fruit had influenced him is difficult to say, but during this period he appeared in close-up but with no lines in Woody Allen's film *Bananas* as a delinquent mugging an old lady on a subway. It gave him his first valid screen credit as an actor.

Sasha still stood by. By 1971 the couple were living together, she having left the Baronet Theatre to work as a waitress. The work was boring but at least there was a perk. She got to bring home unwanted food, providing an essential that wasn't always easy to come by from Stallone's earnings. Despite the occasional flurries of money brought in by Stallone's scripts and infrequent film work, they were living in near poverty.

Furniture at the apartment was minimal or non-existent. There was no oven, and Sasha washed dishes in the bathroom sink. As if living with him in such conditions wasn't devotion enough, she spent hours at night typing up his manuscripts and dealing as tactfully as she could with his temperamental highs and lows. He was so obsessed with his ideas and so isolated in his sense of purpose and intellectual drive, that this must have been a thoroughly testing time for Sasha.

At least one script he wrote during this period said a good deal about the sense of injustice he was nursing when it came to his career. *The Bogus Kingdom* had a fanciful plot about some resting actors who kidnap a group of influential producers and then, disguising themselves as their captives, go out into the entertainment industry and 'do good things'. It expressed a refreshing and hopeful philosophy, and was another off-beat idea to bite the dust.

In a last, almost desperate attempt to have some sort of on-screen career, Stallone worked with a friend to shoot a

16mm film called *Horses*, a feeble affair about a dead cowboy and Indian who return to the living world and, disgusted by what they see, decide it would be better to go back to the dead again. But there would soon be no further need for these home-made stabs at movie stardom. The real thing was just around the corner.

3   Early Films

When his first major film role came, it was not through any grand Hollywood contract or being snapped up by a leading studio. In fact, the picture never made much money for Stallone – certainly when compared with the sums he commanded later in his career – but it gave him an ideal platform for his talents. Many more films and much more colossal budgets later, his début lead remains one of his finest.

It would never have happened without Stephen Verona and Martin Davidson, who had been high-school seniors in Brooklyn in 1957 and had conceived the idea of making a 16-mm film based on their experiences. And Stallone didn't even audition for the movie.

A friend who was trying out for a drama college asked him to read a scene with him from *Death of a Salesman* for the adjudicating panel. Stallone's supporting performance was impressive enough for the panel to offer him a scholarship at the college, which he turned down there and then. But Stephen Verona had been sitting in on the audition and saw in Stallone the perfect actor for the role of Stanley Rosiello in his proposed film, *The Lords of Flatbush*. He sent a telegram to Stallone, who accepted the part. He was in films.

Verona and Davidson had all the enthusiasm and talent to bring the project off, but the first hurdle was raising the money to do it. Much of this had to be done almost door to door in Brooklyn, the young producers persuading prospective investors to write out cheques on the kitchen table. Because of the problems in raising a large enough block of cash to shoot the entire film, it was a stop-go production, fitted up when and as the funds became available. The initial shoot began in Brooklyn in November 1972, and filming was then taken up spasmodically over the next two years. For this commitment, Stallone was paid only about $2000, and had to keep the heavily built look he had started the picture with over the entire period of production.

Stallone's obvious involvement with the project manifested itself in various ways. The performance is testimony enough, and essential viewing for anyone keen to discover the roots of his later work; indeed, his role here can be seen almost to be a chrysalis of Rocky Balboa himself. And, as the actor worked at the characterization, so the writer added to the understanding of that character, finding ways with words to express something beyond what was already being said. So it is no fluke that Stallone's dialogue has a notably surreal tinge to it, well contained within Verona and Gayle Glecker's screenplay, but managing to plough its own strange path. The final credits acknowledged the fact that this actor was also a writer or, as Stallone himself might have put it, that this writer was also an actor. The credits would eventually reveal that 'additional dialogue' had been written by Sylvester Stallone.

The Lords of Flatbush followed the adventures of four ageing juvenile delinquents in Brooklyn in the mid-fifties, banded together in what they described as a 'social athletic club', with their greased hairstyles, leather jackets and jeans, raunchy attitudes to girls and willingness to pick fights. Chicho (Perry King), sleek-eyed, ever smooth and randy, and the lumbering Stanley (Stallone), almost ludicrously macho but uncomfortable with it, an emotionally susceptible pussycat who chews matches and pushes out his chest, are the leading lights of the quartet. Less prominent in the story are Wimpy (Paul Mace), short, scrawny and in awe of the mighty Chicho and Stanley, and the nice sensitive schmuck Butchey (Henry Winkler).

The Lords bring mayhem into the schoolroom in their last grapple with education, pick fights and seduce girls. Tension between Chicho and Stanley erupts briefly, when a playful punch slowly threatens to develop into a gladiatorial match, and this burgeoning difference in their characters is cleverly highlighted in the curious scene where Chicho visits Stanley, communing with his pigeons in their coop. Perhaps as much to the audience's surprise as to Chicho's, Stanley articulates a touching and wildly imaginative philosophy, by means of which, while staying caged in the coop, he can travel whole continents. When Chicho rejects this, we know the estrangement between them is only part of growing up, which is what the film is all about.

Stanley's earlier scenes do offer hints of his hidden depths, even when confronted by his girlfriend Frannie Malincanico (Maria Smith) in the sacred and usually masculine confines of the billiards hall.

'I'm a month late with my friend,' she tells him meaningfully. 'Stanley, I'm pregnant. That rubber band didn't work.'

Wanting to get the engagement announced in the *Brooklyn Eagle*, she watches Stanley's astounding changes of emotion as the news grips him. Throughout, Stallone brilliantly suggests his obvious fondness for Frannie, his inability to communicate it adequately, and his sudden awareness of various implications to do with fatherhood. When nothing positive seems to be coming from him in the way of reaction, Frannie, in an enforced desperation, asks if he would like her to tell his friends that he cries when he makes love to her. She is answered by more long, brooding looks from poor trapped Stanley.

Verona and Davidson's efforts to get the picture taken up by a major studio paid off when Columbia adopted it and revamped it to 35mm. A hiccup threatened to kill the picture even at this point, for it had been made strictly non-union for cheapness (a fact underlined by the messy and often unintelligible soundtrack) and the technicians' union wanted it blackballed. Columbia rode the storm and found they had a healthy success on their hands, taking $92,000 in the first two weeks of its New York première, and going on to gross a perfectly respectable $4,265,000 – indecently respectable, considering the picture had come in on a budget of a mere $400,000. So successful was *The Lords of Flatbush* that there was talk of Stallone doing a sequel that followed the married life of Stanley and Frannie, but it didn't happen. Of the four male stars, it was Henry Winkler who had been propelled into immediate stardom by being cast as Fonzie in a television comedy series, *Happy Days*, in which he enjoyed a colossal personal success.

The attractions of *The Lords of Flatbush*, and its rapid acceptance as a cult movie still much discussed and enjoyed today, is not difficult to understand. There is the charm of its performances – the four boys are irresistibly right, as are the splendid three leading ladies. Youth, energy and the genuinely hybrid quality of the enterprise work their own magic, with a sense of period cleverly evoked by Joe Brooks' sassy music. In its treatment of the transition from adolescence into manhood, it is more than often riotously funny and, ultimately, deeply touching.

Some critics resisted what *The Lords of Flatbush* had to offer, including Jay Cocks in *Time* who found the film 'pretty flimsy', but considered Stallone 'truly exceptional'. *Millimeter* found Stallone's performance 'indescribably delicious', while Geoff Brown, writing in *Monthly Film Bulletin*, thought the piece 'unexpectedly delightful' and Stallone himself 'all blow-wave and brawn ... all this aimlessness and triviality is unerringly caught, with constantly funny dialogue and attractive performances'.

The stop-start filming of *The Lords of Flatbush* meant Stallone was able to take on a second project very early during its shooting, playing what was really his first true starring role in another low budget effort, *No Place to Hide*. Here, Stallone played Jerry Savage, 'a sort of student leader, fed up with the campus revolts that never went anywhere', who hitches a lift to New York with a consignment of hippies, meets the pretty jewellery maker Laurie (Rebecca Grimes) and joins up with a group of urban terrorists, including the sexually interested Estelle (Vickie Lancaster), who have mounted a bombing campaign against the US government's Vietnam war machine. In the opening credits, we see the effects of napalm, hear songs of protest complaining at America's involvement in Vietnam, and watch as students parade with placards ('Big Firms Get Rich – GIs Die') and young men burn their draft papers.

Jerry becomes heavily involved with the terrorists' plan to target the manufacturers of the 'personal detention cells' used to incarcerate American prisoners of war, and is deaf to the protestations of peace that Laurie believes in.

'You can't pray for the kind of peace I mean,' he tells her, 'you gotta pay for it.' 'At what price?' she asks. 'Any price,' comes the reply. Jerry asks Laurie to join the cause, but she refuses. 'Only God can bring change,' she assures him. 'The God inside you and the God inside me.'

But one of the guerillas, Tom (Antony Page), is a police agent, and Estelle – having just done a sinuous belly-dance for Jerry and told him of her appalling experience giving birth to a child – is trapped by the police while planting the bomb. She falls from the roof to her death, not knowing the bomb is a harmless substitute, switched by Tom, who has left the real bomb in the gang's car. Knowing the game is up, Jerry drives the car to where he knows he will find Laurie, and leaves the car in search of her. She approaches the car and is killed by the bomb. Jerry breaks down in tears and runs off.

Despite its muddled script, fluffed lines, non-existent production values (even the crucial explosion happens off-screen, with not a hint of smoke), infuriatingly muzzy soundtrack, and the fact that most of the cast can only make a wild stab at what they think must be acting, *No Place to Hide* is of considerable interest. The performance itself is nothing remarkable. Stallone looks callow – a young looking twenty-seven-year old – and is generally mournful and uninteresting, though this is mostly due to the gloomy theme and the almost Grand Guignol feel of the film. But the easy street ambience is clearly there, as is the intelligence that is here turned against the governing warriors of Washington, showing an attitude that is interesting to compare with that displayed in the *Rambo* series.

It is possible that at least one sequence in the picture had an unconscious effect on the Stallone screen persona that was to carry through into many of his later characterizations: Jerry's tearful collapse at Laurie's death. In *The Lords of Flatbush*, although we don't see him in tears, his girlfriend threatens to tell his friends that he cries when he reaches his climax. Also, both of Stallone's most aggressively macho heroes, Rocky and Rambo, were to have spectacular emotional breakdowns. Rocky breaks down at the bedside of the comatose Adrian (*Rocky II*), collapses at the death of Mickey (*Rocky III*), and at the death of Apollo Creed (*Rocky IV*).

John Rambo's sobbing soliloquy at the end of *First Blood* – there was another at the end of *Rambo: First Blood Part II* – was of even more telling potency, used almost as a valediction to the extremes of violence that had gone before. In Stallone's professional armoury of emotions, it seems, tears underline troubled depths of character that elsewhere may have been ignored, glossed over, or merely hinted at; the last defences of manhood have been taken away. How many other cinema supermen have shown such vulnerability on screen? Victor Mature? Steve Reeves? Chuck Norris? Arnold Schwarzenegger? These epitomes of masculinity didn't exactly make a habit of crying for their audiences, and it is curious that the most blatantly and easily recognizable he-man image of them all should have such recourse to it.

Though made in 1973, *No Place to Hide* was not released until two years later, but its by then dated subject, and the obviously poor quality of the piece, resulted in a stillbirth. Its writer-director, Robert Schnitzer, had seen the potential of his young star, but had been unable to hitch it to a successful movie. When the film was dusted off and re-issued in 1980 as *Rebel* it still looked nothing like a mainstream product, and nobody seemed interested.

For Stallone, the period following *The Lords of Flatbush* was a questioning time. Taking a hard look at his career and the possibilities of other employment from his New York base, he discussed the options for the future with Sasha. There was no real doubt of it: if he was to make a successful film career, Hollywood was the place to be. Looking to the $4,000 they had saved, the immobile Stallone bought a broken-down Olds-mobile for $40. He, Sasha and the bull mastiff Butkus (later to have his own screen career as Adrian's present from the pet shop to Rocky) drove to Hollywood where they found an apartment on Hollywood Boulevard. The address sounded good, but wasn't, and Stallone's struggle, with Sasha's selfless support, resumed its energy. For a time, it seemed that only television producers were interested in using him, fitting him into series such as *Kojak* and *Police Story*, in all of which he was usually typecast as a criminal type.

The best Hollywood's film industry could offer the newcomer was a bit-part in director Melvin Frank's *The Prisoner of Second Avenue*, an adaptation of a Neil Simon comedy with a dark underbelly.

Jack Lemmon and Anne Bancroft chewed up the scenery as the long-married occupants of a high-rise apartment in a sweltering New York where the pressures of urban life threaten Lemmon with a nervous breakdown. Way down the cast list, Stallone was a woolly-hatted Central Park mugger who accosted Lemmon, only to have Lemmon mug him back. The role used up only a flash of screen time, and Stallone did not endear himself to the production team when he tried to ad lib around his few lines. Smartly told to stick to the script, he did his lines, took his pay, and left.

His second Hollywood effort, another walk-on, didn't

promise much more, and once again he was a baddie, this time threatening Robert Mitchum's Philip Marlowe in the remake of *Farewell My Lovely*. Stallone was not likely to get noticed in this one either, though he was good in an excellent cast, as the critics threw their praises directly at the star's feet. *Films In Review* announced that director Dick Richards had 'captured the atmosphere. Mitchum captures everything else'. Stallone's ego was not so well nourished, however. During the shooting of one scene, a studio executive asked a colleague why Stallone had been cast in the role of the young hoodlum. And Stallone heard the answer: 'The other guy was out of town.'

As with all other actors, there were plenty of films that Stallone tried for but didn't get, most of which ended up starring actors he would often be compared to. He didn't land *Stay Hungry* (Arnold Schwarzenegger got the role of the supercharged body-builder), or *The Godfather II* (Al Pacino carried over from its prequel to star in this one). Norman Jewison, who a couple of years later would have a not altogether happy relationship with Stallone on *F.I.S.T.*, managed without his services in *Rollerball*, though Stallone got round that one by being cast as one of the leads in *Death Race 2000*, which was in effect a sort of remake of *Rollerball*.

Trying for Sidney Lumet's *Dog Day Afternoon* didn't bring him a contract either. Al Pacino was cast as the hoodlum who holds up a bank – apparently ideal casting for Stallone. But as Pacino's character was a gay needing the money from the heist to pay for his male lover's sex-change, it turned out to be a part that might well have drastically altered Stallone's subsequent career in films, and coloured the way his public viewed him. At the time of a much later film, *Lock Up*, Stallone could see no reason why he would not play a gay role if it appealed to him.

But if better roles and more prominent billing could be found in movies less prestigious than *Farewell My Lovely*, Stallone was willing to play ball, and for his next two films he moved to the Roger Corman stable. Here there was a good chance of making stylish pictures with a speed and cheapness that often paid off with cultish and commercial success.

In 1967, Corman had made his début as a major studio director when Twentieth Century Fox had signed him to direct *The St Valentine's Day Massacre*, his first stab at making a decent film about the infamous gangster Al Capone. It didn't turn out well, and eight years on he had decided to try again with *Capone*, this time directed by Steve Carver under the Corman production umbrella. Now, Ben Gazzara was the unequivocal gangster (his cheeks apparently stuffed with more cottonwool than Anna Neagle had needed when portraying the elderly Queen Victoria), with Stallone fourth-billed in the small but pivotal part of Frank 'The Enforcer' Nitti. Among the capable cast Susan Blakely, the heroine of *The Lords of Flatbush*, provided a link with Stallone's recent past, though as the leading lady of *Capone* with her nude scenes, drunkenness and general lack of etiquette, she was far from lily-white.

The film had a strong sense of period and place, but was little more than a catalogue of killings inspired by Capone and his cohorts, with each slaying graphically shown. The dialogue wasn't the sort of thing you would overhear at a vicarage tea-party either, but often made its point.

'Give you five grand?' snarls Capone in one scene, 'I wouldn't piss up your arse if you was on fire.' And this was one of his warmer responses.

Howard Browne's screenplay (he had also written the first Corman Capone film) followed the fortunes of the monster hoodlum from ambitious no-gooder through to the triumphancy of his rule of terror. Frank Nitti becomes his most trusted henchman, but eventually does a deal with Capone's enemies who agree to let Frank take over Capone's empire if he can successfully get Capone shopped. Frank arranges for Capone to be indicted for tax evasion, and Capone is sent to Alcatraz for eleven years, after which he is released into Frank's care. Tertiary syphilis eats Capone's brain away, while Frank enjoys his position and at least understands why Capone has lost everything to him.

'This guy was so fuckin' busy pumpin' bullets in the guy across the street that he forgot somethin'. The guy you really gotta watch out for, he isn't across the street at all – he's the bum standin' on the same ladder you are.'

At the end of the film, we know that Frank will need to heed his own advice.

If *Capone* didn't make many friends of the critics, at least their barbs were meant for the film itself and not the cast, who were generally absolved from blame. *Variety* thought it 'crude': it was.

The only vaguely charming things about it were Capone's fascination with opera, and the fact that his murdering gang always put cottonwool in their ears before gunning down their victims.

Richard Coombs for *Monthly Film Bulletin* pronounced it 'an ill-at-ease effort to adapt old genres (and Corman's own undisputed past successes) to new exploitation angles', while Judith Crist for *New York* dismissed it as 'a pointless tale'. For Meg Matthews in *Films In Review* 'dependable actors ... like Sylvester Stallone are largely wasted', and the *Observer*'s verdict was that the movie was 'strong only on the heavies ... the outstanding pair are Harry Guardino and Sylvester Stallone, an even more lazy-eyed version of Al Pacino'.

Perhaps the Pacino comparison was something of a back-handed compliment, but nevertheless Stallone's coolly authoritative performance had been noted, and proved he had the maturity to bring off a serious role. It had also brought in a little money: when he signed the contract for *Capone* Stallone had been down to his last $4.

Though *Capone* had been presented as a Corman film, Stallone's next picture would have a more convincing provenance. *Death Race 2000* was in the hands of director Paul Bartel (who had been second unit director for Corman's 1974 success *Big Bad Mama*) but was drastically re-edited by Corman himself. Whoever was ultimately responsible for what was seen on screen, there is no doubt that *Death Race 2000* remains one of Stallone's most colourful roles, and his only excursion into sheer fantasy.

The film was obviously intended as Corman's riposte to *Rollerball*, which had appeared earlier that year and dealt with the use of gross violence as a political opiate, a theme picked up by Corman who based his movie on an Ib Melchior short story. As chief writer Corman hired Robert Thom, who had scripted Corman's 1974 *Bloody Mama*. Corman told Thom that 'what I wanted was something along the lines of *Dr Strangelove*: a serious comedy about violence. To me, *Death Race* was about gladiator fights in Ancient Rome or boxing today – the need the public has to experience vicarious thrills. I wanted to treat it with humour but what Paul Bartel and Chuck Griffith (co-writer) wanted to do was make it a silly comedy. A farce comedy. I wanted it to be a smart comedy.'

The black laughs were inspired by the Death Race sponsored by a futuristic US government as a way of deflecting political unrest roused by revolutionaries trying to remove the President from power, as well as being an ideal outlet for the public's thirst for deathly violence. On Euthanasia Day patients are wheeled out from hospitals to points along the route of the Race, where the five drivers can score by running over and killing pedestrians. The scoring is subtle: ten points for a woman victim, seventy for an old person. The government have their own 'plant' among the drivers, the masked Frankenstein (David Carradine in the leading role), whose body is made up from the parts of others. In fact, Frankenstein himself plans to kill the President.

As the amoral racer Joe 'Machine Gun' Viterbo ('loved by thousands, hated by millions') Stallone was consistently funny in a role that even had him punching his girlfriend; it was not a part to get the audience's sympathy. The line-up of bizarre drivers, in their fantastically designed cars, was completed by Matilda the Hun, Calamity Jane and Nero the Hero.

Joe Dante later hinted at the post-production fate of *Death Race 2000*: 'The finished film was pretty satirical. Roger re-cut it to make it more of an action film. A lot of the humour was excised because Roger felt it would alienate the audience. There are whole scenes in this movie that lead up to jokes that have been cut out of the film ... Roger went off on his own and shot some extra action scenes that did improve the picture.'

Eventually, the MPAA's threat to slap an X-rating on the film led to several of the more violent scenes being left on the cutting-room floor, but their exclusion didn't seem to affect its box-office fortunes. Audiences flocked, including many of those whose love of sheer violence the film had supposedly set out to parody, and the picture cleaned up, making $5,250,000 in the US alone – a reasonable take for a production that had come in at a mere $500,000.

According to Andrew Sarris in *Village Voice*, Bartel had directed 'on a *42nd Street* level of comic ferocity. It is just as well since only David Carradine of all the cast members seems at all beyond this sort of bear-baiting entertainment', and Sarris went on to let readers know that Stallone 'resumes the slobbish career he has taken up in *The Lords of Flatbush* and *Capone*'. Pauline

Kael, whose later criticism of Stallone often turned into an exhaustively argued thumbs-down, on this occasion found him 'rather funny as the slobbish, stupid villain', and *Time* thought his part 'well played'.

Alongside the considerable professional success he was now enjoying, Stallone's relationship with Sasha had deepened and consolidated to the point where they decided to marry. The ceremony took place on 28 December 1974. Unlike another wedding he would participate in, the details of the event were not important enough to hit the headlines. The bride wore a dress she had made herself. The groom wore the suit he had worn in *Capone*. So nervous was he when it came to the vows, that he asked if he might sit down, and was brought a chair. It was a relatively quiet affair. The bride's parents did not attend. The groom's mother did not approve. She considered her son had been intended for something better than a waitress, and that he was wasting himself on a 'girl like that'. Several years later she again made her views loudly known about another of her son's wives.

Parallel to his acting excursions, Stallone the writer was also active throughout this period. Hadn't his mother told him that ultimately success would come to him as a writer, not an actor? His persistent efforts, his application, and his professionalism were apparent in his daily schedule, waking early each morning and spending an allotted time on whatever writing project was on hand. Many years on, Stallone still follows this demanding regime. Of course he had been cheered by his script contribution to *The Lords of Flatbush* and by the infrequent scripts he had managed to sell for television, but the writing breakthrough his mother had promised him, had remained beyond his grasp.

He had good reason for thinking that this success had indeed happened in April 1975 when his screenplay for *Hell's Kitchen* (eventually to appear on screen as *Paradise Alley* with Stallone as writer, star and director) was sold for some $21,500 to the producers John Roach and Ron Suppa. This generous turn in his fortunes was to have its own comeback when Roach and Suppa consequently sued Stallone for plagiarism, maintaining that he had stolen ideas from their *Hell's Kitchen* property for the screenplay of *Rocky*. He had, but they at least had been his own ideas. This unpleasant shadow over *Paradise Alley*, plus its ultimately unappreciative critical reception, might have daunted Stallone's enthusiasm, but he had at least managed his biggest financial sale yet, and for a Hollywood production.

Besides which, in March of that year he had seen a boxing match that was to dramatically change the course of his career, and bring about the birth of a screen legend.

Rocky Balboa, almost immaculately, had been conceived.

4 Sleeper

Rocky, like many other legends, had its feet in fact. Stallone experienced the fact and went on to the fiction, but such a progress would not have been possible if he had not been in so receptive a mood by March 1975. And there was also the guiding hand of Jane Oliver, who officially may have been his agent but who also became his mentor and friend.

Life for Stallone had changed. Personally, he had progressed through marriage with Sasha, but professionally Stallone still felt he was at the starting-post. Despite his by no means inconsiderable film appearances and his clutch of good notices, there was no denying that as a writer he had failed to make anything like the impression he hoped for. The off-beat, down-beat stuff he had been turning out had proved largely unsellable and likely to appeal only to the quirkiest tastes.

Things were so desperate that at this time Stallone said, 'I was beginning to look at my dog with lust. I was going to bake the dog ... everything you can think of that goes into a real crappy melodrama was part of my life.' He realized that the mournful streak in his scripts was something of a handicap, but it took a boxing match to spur him on to his first up-tempo, blazingly hopeful and ultimately triumphant screenplay.

It was in admiration of a living legend, Muhammad Ali (Cassius Clay) that Stallone went to the Wiltern Theatre to see, via closed circuit television, the undisputed colossus of boxing take on a bread-and-butter fighter Chuck Wepner on the night of 24 March 1975. There was no money on Wepner, for what chance did he have against the indomitable Ali? Ali had the strength and easy confidence of the winner. Victory to such a man was inevitable.

The 15,000 people that had crowded into the stadium at Cleveland, Ohio, were in for a surprise. Ali did not knock

Wepner out in the opening rounds. By the ninth, Wepner was still looking strong, and knocked Ali over with a pile-driving right to his ribcage. Those that saw the champion fall to the ground divided into two camps: some said Wepner had indeed knocked Ali down, others that he had stood on Ali's foot and pushed him over. Wepner struggled on, despite cuts to the eyes, both of which were covered in blood. When at the fifteenth and final round Wepner was still standing in the ring, slogging it out with a beleaguered Ali, the crowd's admiration of the valiant underdog rose to fever pitch. Ali showered Wepner with hard blows. Wepner fell to the floor but pulled himself up on the ropes, at which moment the referee Tony Perez decided to end the contest.

That night Wepner, the no-hoper, had been the hero, and the germ of Rocky's story had been sown. The alchemy that Stallone would eventually work took this basic plot idea and brought to it all the rejection, hopelessness and bitterness that Stallone had experienced in his struggle to make it.

In June 1975 Stallone wrote *Rocky's* first draft in three and a half days, and the first link in a chain of good fortune was forged. An agent, Larry Kubik, had interested the film maker Gene Kirkwood in Stallone's work, and Kirkwood first looked at an idea Stallone had worked up about a cab driver who aspires to be mayor of Philadelphia; he turned it down. Kirkwood, who was scouting for producers Robert Chartoff and Irwin Winkler, was more interested in the *Rocky* project, but didn't think it suitable as it stood, and asked Stallone to re-write, to take some of the hard edges off the hero and alter the milieu of the original draft, which Stallone said had been 'full of desperation: filthy language and rapes in alley-ways, guys always talking about their errogenous zones in very graphic terms'. The re-writes changed all this, producing a work that he hoped would encourage 'a whole revival of sentimentality, a return to the home and the family unit'.

Winkler, whose productions had included *They Shoot Horses, Don't They?* and would go on to include *Raging Bull* (a raw movie about boxing that eschewed the ready sentimentality of *Rocky*) and *New York, New York*, recalled his first meeting with the young author of *Rocky*: 'In comes this big lug who weighed 220 pounds, didn't talk well and acted slightly punch-drunk. He said he had an idea for a boxing film. He wanted to star in it.'

A few days later, with the help of Sasha and caffeine tablets, the new draft was ready, and by July a third version had been produced. There was good reason to celebrate, and Sasha marked her husband's twenty-ninth birthday by bringing in a $1.15 cake. It was a modest purchase considering United Artists was about to offer Stallone $75,000 for his *Rocky* script. He said No.

Not surprisingly, the studio had seen the potential in Stallone's brilliant but simple playing-out of the American Dream as a vehicle for a well-established star. Such heady names as Burt Reynolds, Paul Newman and Robert Redford were spoken of, but Stallone came back at them, pointing out that *Rocky* was his work and he was going to play the lead.

At this point Chartoff and Winkler and the studio might have been forgiven for pulling out of any discussions, but United Artists persisted, upping their offer to buy the script (but not Stallone) another $50,000, but still their *enfant terrible* held out. Looking at his filmography, the studio bosses were not filled with confidence. A porn movie, some bit-parts in a few major movies, a couple of feature roles in two Roger Corman cheapies, a lead in a Brooklyn home-movie; it would be one great leap to stardom that spelt a huge risk.

But interest in the project continued. Somewhere along the line Ryan O'Neal was rumoured to have offered $350,000 to buy the package, but United Artists now pushed their offer for the script (without Stallone) to $300,000. It was tempting for a man who was hovering on the bread line.

This was serious money. If he accepted, Stallone would unquestionably have arrived as a writer, but would have to stand aside and see his first truly successful creation taken over by another, already famous, actor. If he missed out playing Rocky, it might even mean the end of a promising career as an actor. It was a dangerous time, and he and Sasha talked it over. He told her that if he held out against letting go of the script his bluff might be called and *Rocky* would be dropped. How did she feel about eating grass?

Continuing to support him, Sasha agreed he should dig his heels in. Her unflinching faith found echoes in *Rocky*'s central situation, the relationship between Rocky and Adrian. As Stallone wrote in *The Official Rocky Scrapbook*, the film was about 'two individuals – half people – two half people coming together making a whole person. Two individuals seeking love, seeking dignity and finding courage along the way. The way my wife's love gave me strength.'

It was now up to Chartoff, Winkler, Kirkwood and United Artists, if they would still consider taking Stallone as the star of the piece, to come up with a deal, and one was drawn up that budgeted the film at $1 million, with the author to be paid a basic $20,000 for the screenplay, and a weekly rate of $620 to play the title role. Against these modest payments, it was agreed that Stallone should have ten per cent of the film's profit, if any. UA also insisted that Stallone could be replaced after shooting had commenced if he proved unsatisfactory, and also demanded that Chartoff and Winkler (who would have to mortgage their homes to back the film) were liable for any costs above budget.

So far as Stallone was concerned, there could still be difficult times ahead, but the path was cleverly eased by his attorney, Jake Bloom, who got UA to agree to the exterior, and most expensive location, scenes being shot first, knowing that with these in the can the studio would be unlikely to fire its new star and have to incur more major expenses for re-shooting.

John G. Avildsen, with his reputation for producing excellent quality on modest budgets, and fresh from making *W.W. and the Dixie Dancekings* (a film Stallone had unsuccessfully tried for), was brought in as director. He seemed a sympathetic choice, for his earlier work had often shown sympathy with the undertows of the American Dream. In 1972 he had directed the Jack Lemmon movie *Save the Tiger* where the Dream was exposed as hollow and, in the same year, *The Stoolie* starring Jewish comedian Jackie Mason had shown a blunt affection for the lovable degenerates living on the fringes of modern American society. As for *Rocky*, Avildsen said he thought 'boxing is just about the dumbest thing in the world, but this is a sensitive story'.

And needed sensitive performers to put it over. Most of the principal actors brought together for *Rocky* would stay together for much of the series. Some stayed the entire course.

Talia Shire, the dark-haired sister of Francis Ford Coppola, had the right gamine looks for Adrian. She was an experienced film actress, having débuted in 1963 with a small role in the Ray Milland horror movie *X*, known in Britain as *The Man with the*

X-Ray Eyes, going on to play in two of her brother's movies, *The Godfather* and *The Godfather Part II*, winning an Academy nomination for the latter as Best Supporting Actress.

Veteran actor Burgess Meredith had been around in films since the 1936 *Winterset*, and all but vanished from the screen between 1949 and 1961. At the age of fifty-three he made up for lost time, when he began appearing in a long list of features, including *The Day of the Locust*, for which he was Oscar nominated in 1974. As the gritty, snappy trainer Mickey, he would last through to *Rocky III*, during which he would die in Rocky's arms.

The actor needed for Apollo Creed had to match acting talents with the convincing physique of a prize fighter, and this role went to Carl Weathers, who had once played football with the Oakland Raiders but who also had a few acting credits to his name. As the tenacious Paulie, the studio hired the burly writer-actor Burt Young, with whom Stallone immediately felt an affinity: 'I think of Burt Young just as I do of myself,' he said in 1977, 'as a writer who acts ... (he's) a puzzle of a human being, a walking dichotomy.'

For his five month physical preparation for the movie, Stallone went on a non-carbohydrate diet, limiting himself to a steady intake of shellfish and shrimps, with over a hundred vitamin pills each day. His training, supervised by former fighter Jimmy Gambina, involved a daily five mile run along the beach, and regular work-outs at a Chatsworth gym. During this period he also worked with Avildsen, Gambina and Weathers on the choreography of the crucial boxing match at the end of the film, viewing vintage footage of boxers such as the 'Rock' himself, Ezzard Charles, Muhammad Ali and Sonny Liston.

'I had to teach myself to be a flat-footed steam engine who took ten punches to give one,' said Stallone.

By February 1976, the film was ready for production, and was in the can after only twenty-eight days. Avildsen had brought it in for $960,000.

Stallone's screenplay told the story of Rocky Balboa, a hopeless warm-hearted bum boxer who fights cheap matches in downtown joints for peanuts. He is sweet on shy, repressed Adrian (Shire), the dowdy girl who works in the local pet shop from where Rocky bought his pet turtles and goldfish. Rocky wins a fight against a second-rate opponent and walks unhappily home through the streets he understands so well, to his seedy apartment.

He stares very hard at a snapshot of himself as a young boy, then looks at his adult reflection, silently wondering what happened to the hopes and dreams he once had. Now, he works as a collector for the asthmatic loan-shark Gazzo (Joe Spinell), who has a soft spot for Rocky despite the fact that Rocky won't obey his instructions to break a debtor's thumb.

Returning to the gym where he has trained for years, Rocky discovers the proprietor Mickey (Meredith) has had his kit bagged up and has given Rocky's locker to another boxer. The abrasive, seventy-six-year old trainer tells Rocky he's all washed up as a fighter. Down-hearted, Rocky nevertheless persists in his tender courtship of Adrian, whose fat, heavy-drinking brother Paulie (Young) arranges for Rocky to call round on Thanksgiving and take Adrian out. Paulie warns that if she doesn't start living soon her body will dry out.

Meanwhile, the black heavyweight champion of the world, Apollo Creed (Weathers) is unable to find a suitable front-ranked opponent for his next fight, and has the idea of giving a chance to 'a snow white underdog' – a clever ploy in a land of opportunity. He settles on Rocky, 'The Italian Stallion', a southpaw from the streets, to catch the public imagination and, naturally, to ensure that on the night Creed wins a massive victory.

On Thanksgiving Day, Paulie, who is trying to lean on Rocky to get him a job with Gazzo, takes Rocky home, but Adrian locks herself in her room. Blindly, Paulie throws the turkey she has been cooking into the garden and tells her to get out of the house. Rocky is uncomfortable talking to the door of her room, but eventually Adrian emerges in a woolly hat and tightly buttoned winter coat. Rocky takes her to the skating-rink but an attendant explains the place is closed because of the holiday.

'Are you closed to the general public or are you just closed to everybody, do you know what I mean?' asks Rocky.

In a gentle and funny scene in which Adrian and Rocky totter over the ice, he confesses his father's advice to him as a child: that he had not been born with much of a brain so he had better make use of his body. Adrian tells Rocky her mother had said the opposite to her.

Rocky takes Adrian back to his apartment. At first she is

unwilling to go in, but Rocky persuades her and gently coaxes her to remove her hat and spectacles. They make love. Rocky accepts the challenge to fight Creed, and is almost immediately made to look stupid during a television interview. Touchingly, he tells Adrian this 'bothered' him.

Gazzo realizes that Rocky has never had any good luck, and gives him 500 bucks to help with his training.

But Rocky knows he has been chosen to play the fall guy and plans to train himself, until Mickey arrives at his apartment and offers to manage him. Mickey talks about his own far-off triumphs, and of the bad way he was treated.

'I want to make sure that all this shit that happened to me doesn't happen to you,' Mickey tells him, but Rocky, annoyed and frustrated, storms at him and rages about the stinking rooms he has to live in. A broken, rejected Mickey stumbles out in to the street. In one of the loveliest moments of the film, we see the figure of the old man making his way off in to the distance, and suddenly we see Rocky running after him. He stops Mickey and, still from far off, we see them talking together. Rocky has found his manager, and his best friend.

When he begins training, Rocky is out of condition. He is crippled by stitches when he tries to jump the steps of the Philadelphia Art Museum, but in the cold store of the slaughterhouse where Paulie works (and where, nervously, he asks Paulie who has killed all the animals) he sees Paulie slap a carcass, and catches on to this novel way of preparing for the fight.

Paulie, of course, is inquisitive about Rocky's relationship with Adrian, and Rocky explains that he has gaps and Adrian has gaps, which together they fill. A blossoming and articulate Adrian gives Rocky the bull mastiff Butkus to accompany him when out jogging. Frustrated Paulie, returning home drunk to find Rocky and Adrian together in the house, begins a violent quarrel with them, filled with anger at his futile existence. Adrian stands up to him, telling her brother that she has always looked after him, and proclaiming she is not the loser he thinks her. She decides to move in with Rocky.

As training begins in earnest, Mickey tells Rocky, 'You're gonna eat lightning and crap thunder,' and soon Rocky is getting into better shape. He sets off through the streets in the early morning and leaps, exalted, up the length of the Art Museum's steps, but returning to the sleeping Adrian he confesses 'I can't do it; I can't beat him ... I was nobody before ... It really don't matter if I lose this fight ... Nobody's ever gone the distance with Creed ... You see, when that bell rings and I'm still standin', I'm gonna know for the first time in my life, see, that I weren't just another bum from the neighbourhood.'

On the night of the contest, Rocky prays in his dressing-room and goes into the ring wearing a robe emblazoned with the name of a meat-firm (an advertising ploy by Paulie) while Adrian waits backstage. Creed enters in a razzle-dazzle of showmanship dressed as George Washington, but when the fight starts it is soon clear that things are not going as Creed has planned.

A staggering display of stamina lasts through to the fifteenth round, when Rocky tells Mickey to cut open his eye, which Creed has closed up. When the final bell rings, both men are left standing and though Creed is declared the winner, the crowd goes wild at Rocky's achievement. Frantically, Rocky calls for Adrian above the cheering crowd. She rushes through the audience into the ring and Rocky's arms.

'I love you,' she cries.

'I love you,' he tells her, and folds her to him.

When the film appeared, it quickly became one of those movies that reminded critics of a handful of other movies, often very old ones. Emmanuel Levy claimed that *Rocky* had worked up ideas used in the 1955 *Marty* and mixed them with the conventions of the sports-prizefighting genre, and in doing so 'paved the way to the making and acceptance of other conventional, old-fashioned movies, movies about ordinary families and ordinary folks'. Leslie Halliwell was another ready to point to *Marty* and back at *Rocky*, and found the latter wanting. In fact *Marty*, with its story of a no-luck, physically unattractive butcher (Ernest Borgnine) who finds love in the Bronx with a plain girl, had clear parallels with *Rocky* and many other love stories from *Beauty and the Beast* onwards. *Marty*, incidentally, also had a script by Paddy Chayefsky, whom Stallone would soon meet at a certain Awards ceremony.

Danny Peary has referred *Rocky* back to the 1956 *Somebody Up There Likes Me*, a biopic of Rocky Graziano, comparing the romance between Shire and Stallone to that of Paul Newman and Pier Angeli, and in director Robert Wise's lingering depiction of poverty and what it does to hope, there is another strand which can also be found in *Rocky* – or, more accurately, in any truthful film about boxing. Elsewhere many other films about boxing, from the 1931 *The Champ* onwards, have been invoked in comparison to *Rocky*.

But *Rocky* remains its own film, and if its homespun story has nothing very new to it and doesn't go easy on the sentiment, its strong sense of place, straightforward tale of human achievement, and superb performances, nevertheless pack a terrific punch.

The sense of place, indeed, is one of the film's strongest points, and Avildsen knows how to look at the streets, when to keep his distance, when to give us sudden glimpses of beauty (the elevated railway that cuts through the landscape, the cosy confines of the pet shop, the mystery of Philadelphia early morning, the spontaneous camaraderie of the street-corner singers, the stretch of waterfront, the smelly gym). He seems, too, to have given his players time enough and room to move through their scenes as if they were happening, not acted.

Stallone's script and performance, of course, are what hold the piece together, and Avildsen lets the sensitivity slowly show itself, while Rocky's highly individual word-pictures amuse and touch us. For the first few moments, the hero may strike us as dim, and he's certainly messed up, but his kindness, his poverty, his very own stylish coming to terms with understanding and language, soon tell another story.

Rocky knows these streets and these people. On the way into a bar he picks up an unconscious drunk, carries him in and sits him beside another drunk: 'Here's a friend for you,' says Rocky.

Ultimately the most affecting result of Stallone's performance is the realization that Rocky will always be honest, individual, unable to do more than look at things his own highly coloured way, expressing thoughts in a way that – far from being evidence of brain damage – strips his soul bare. In a film that is ostensibly about boxing, such exposure of the fuzzy edges of masculinity is a peculiarly dangerous ingredient, and it is one that Stallone would return to many times.

Rocky's other advantage was its superb supporting cast, though Shire could do little to ease Adrian's sudden Hans Christian Andersen transformation from ugly duckling to, if not quite a swan, a bird of finer feathers, and anyway the down-trodden Adrian was always going to be more interesting and amusing than the new sophisticated version. As a team, the actors work superbly together, and overall there is a marvellous air of extempore dialogue – a feeling that there was a script somewhere that has been used and put away – that gives the movie its own special freshness and pace as the story builds to the superbly choreographed fight and the overriding declaration of Rocky and Adrian's love, that crowns the movie.

In fact, this very final consummation of love, when Adrian rushes to Rocky at the end of the match, was an afterthought, for the first plan had been to end the film with Rocky the champion alone in the ring. The switch back to what we can believe is the most important thing in Rocky's life – Adrian – underpins the whole movie, heightening its impact and reminding us that this has been a love story that happens to have been about boxing.

The studios were slow to recognize the true potential of their property, which was a classic example of a sleeper. As Stallone remembered in 1981, 'They gave *Rocky* no promotion or anything. It was just a throw-away project, with standard music. But it was a real freak case, one of those things that just happen. People passed on word of mouth, then the studios did try to save it, the album went platinum, and so on.'

Tom Milne in the *Monthly Film Bulletin* could only glow with pleasure, finding the film 'brilliantly scripted ... brilliant performances all down the cast list ... moving and brilliantly funny ... the metamorphosing medium of Stallone's quite amazing dialogue, most of it delivered by himself in a non-stop stream of semi-articulate gibberish that gradually begins to communicate his own very personal grasp of essentials'. Milne went on to perceive 'the lyric poet struggling out from under the loquacious Rocky's dim but infinitely expressive grasp of language'.

Some of the praise was pretty faint. Vincent Canby in the *New York Times* considered it 'a sentimental little slum movie ... Mr Stallone's Rocky is less a performance than an impersonation ... it's a studied routine, not a character', while Pauline Kael for the *New Yorker* thought *Rocky* 'a threadbare patchwork of old-movie bits, yet its engaging and naïve elements are emotional ... what holds it together is innocence'.

As an actor, there could be little doubt that Stallone could no longer be ignored, with the *New York Daily News* cheering 'his mixture of boyish intensity, lusty sexuality, and cheerful innocence', a view echoed by *Newsweek*'s opinion that he was 'innocently sexy ... his acting is unaffected (and) he conveys deep vulnerability but without baroque psychological nuances'. Patrick Bergan dug deeper to suggest the movie might be positively harmful to society, describing it as 'another example of the American Dream as an opiate, lulling people away from responsibility and change into a Panglossian garden'.

Turning to Avildsen, Kael wrote that he 'slams through the picture like a poor man's Sidney Lumet', and suggested that 'a more painstaking director would have been too proud to shoot the mildewed ideas and would have tried to throw out as many as possible or to conceal the others – and would probably have wrecked the movie'.

They were canny words, for it was clear Avildsen had made *Rocky* the way he wanted to make it; as the opening credits announced, this was a John G. Avildsen film, not, as its creator and star argued to have it billed, a Sylvester Stallone film. If there was a combative air between the two men during the shooting of *Rocky*, it appears to have been merely professional, with neither losing his respect for the other. This did not mean there were no arguments, however.

Rumours leaked out that some of the disagreement had been pretty violent, that at one point Stallone had slapped Avildsen up against a door to push home an important point. Throughout the shoot, Stallone would also suggest how the other actors should approach their roles, never the best way to win a director's affection, and neither was Stallone happy about some of the editing of the fight sequences (and he would often criticize them in public) or the deliberately unclear ending Avildsen had given the movie. In Stallone's screenplay, Rocky should be seen to be the loser of the fight, but, in the last frenetic moments of the finished film, the fact that Creed has won the fight is deliberately obscured. It was the first of many endings to his films that Stallone would argue over.

From the tight-lipped cast, only Burt Young suggested that there might, here and there, have been a little friction.

'He was tough,' he said of Stallone, but from Avildsen there were no complaints.

'I have never found the hustler instinct in Sylvester,' he said later. 'During the entire experience of *Rocky* he was exceptionally enthusiastic, even naïve. He was terrific to work with – he had no pride of authorship. Everything was for the good of the project ... He faced everything with a smile on his face. At least that was when I worked with him. Before he was a star.'

That stardom would eventually mean Stallone being able to direct the sequel to *Rocky* on a rather more impressive budget than Avildsen had to juggle with, but the strictness of Avildsen's regime seemed almost an advantage, giving the movie its special feel. Economies, of course, had been paramount.

Not only had the actors been hired at reasonable (for Hollywood) rates, but Frank Stallone had been brought in as the timekeeper for the final match, Frank Stallone Jnr was the leader of the street singers and also contributed to the film's score, while Sylvester Stallone saved the producers some money by doing a few voice-overs. Using Butkus also cut down on dog trainer's fees, and went further to making *Rocky* a very family affair. It would have been even more so had the by now heavily pregnant Sasha's brief appearance in the movie not been left on the cutting-room floor, while Jacqueline had turned down the one line role her son had wanted her to play.

Avildsen's clever way with his resources meant the lack of extras was never felt on screen. Perhaps it is no coincidence that when Rocky and Adrian go to the rink it is deserted, and the final fight, taking place in a huge stadium, is managed with a handful of extras, skilful lighting and some good matching stock footage.

There was no doubt that, whatever the critics thought, the Academy of Motion Picture Arts and Sciences had been impressed when *Rocky* was labelled with ten nominations, including two for Stallone himself – one for Best Actor and one for Original Screenplay; the only other people who had ever been cited for both awards were Charlie Chaplin and Orson Welles. The other nominations were for Actress (Shire), Supporting Actor (two nominations, for Meredith and Young), Film Editing, Sound, Music (the song 'Gonna Fly Now'), Best Picture, and Direction.

On the night of the Awards ceremony Stallone sat and watched both his personal nominations lose out to *Network*, Paddy Chayefsky (the writer of *Marty*, sometimes singled out as *Rocky*'s progenitor) winning for his screenplay and, for the first time ever, the Academy had made a posthumous award, to Peter Finch for his starring role. There was some compensation when, at the end of the evening, *Rocky* was given the accolade of Best Picture, but Stallone could ill-disguise his disappointment. At the last moment his bow-tie had broken, and it had been an unkempt, rather surly looking Stallone that accepted the award from the night's Best Supporting Actress (again for *Network*) Beatrice Straight. Going to the altar of his profession with his shirt unbuttoned under his tuxedo looked suspiciously like cocking a snook at his hallowed elders. Whatever prizes *Rocky* had won, when it came down to it Stallone had won none, and the bitterness he felt spilled over into his interviews. Time would prove he had some justification for feeling miffed. Hadn't he written and starred in the film that would end up making over $55 million for the studio?

'The Oscar will never again mean what it would have meant this year. Not for me, and all the people who believed in me. Justice was not served ... I wanted a duplicate of that statue, the one for best picture. I wrote it, I acted in it, but they wouldn't give me one. They gave statues to the producer and director. That bothered me.'

Sasha, meanwhile, had probably been earning an Oscar of her own. The vindication of critics and box-office had proved beyond doubt she had been right to believe and support her man through the years of struggle. The change in fortunes meant the couple were able to move into more substantial, even ostentatious, accommodation: a four-bedroom Coldwater Canyon residence that had once belonged to the TV comic Ernie Kovacs. The Stallones' personal happiness was sealed when, in the Spring of 1976, Sasha gave birth to a son. The event, Stallone insisted, had been astrologically planned to give the child the best possible opportunities in life. The father, who had once written under the name of Q. Moonblood, decided the boy should be called Sage Moonblood.

Happiness, it seemed, was there to stay.

5 Whistling Past the Graveyard

The gains in wealth and prestige that followed the reception of *Rocky* were balanced by Stallone's tremendous sense of loss at the death of his agent and closest advisor Jane Oliver. Oliver, a highly respected Hollywood figure, had gone into hospital suffering from cancer during the promotional tour of *Rocky*, but the true seriousness of her condition had been kept from her protégé. He telephoned her husband one day and heard she had died. Now, his sadness at not winning his own Oscar for *Rocky* was compounded by his anger at her leaving him.

'I didn't even want the statue for myself. I wanted it for Jane Oliver. She was in the hospital and I wanted to take it to her ... Frigging cancer. She didn't tell me. She was my mentor, my psychiatrist, my mother, the most important friend in my life. Now that she's gone, I can't trust anybody anymore now. There's such a void that she's left. Now I can only trust people from the past.'

Stallone's awareness of such professional isolation at so early and crucial a stage in his career was a tragic underscoring that would surely but slowly have its effect on his life both on and off the film set. To plug the gap left by her death, he went to Jeff Wald, another experienced Hollywood agent whose style was noticeably more hard-headed and flamboyant than that of Jane Oliver.

One of Wald's first actions was to turn up on the set of his client's next film with his earnings from *Rocky* (thought to be about $1 million – he would subsequently earn a great deal more from the movie) in an armoured van. United Artists had been slow to part with the money, but Wald had wheedled it out of them and played it up to the hilt. He could work this sort of stunt with aplomb, but the alchemy that had apparently existed between Stallone and Oliver could not be repeated.

'She was the stabilizing force in my life,' said Stallone later. 'She was the subtle stroke. I've never been a very subtle person. So I went on a rampage when I thought I was infallible.'

Before the dust settled on *Rocky*, there was the problem of how to follow it. It was never going to be an easy decision.

With Hollywood's new recognition of Stallone as sole screenplay writer of *Rocky*, it might have been expected that his second major movie would also be one of his own invention, but instead Stallone seized on a script that had been sitting on Hollywood's shelves for several years, and nailed his reputation to a film based on the life of James Riddle Hoffa, the American warehouseman who rose to be President of the Teamsters' Union from 1958 to 1971 and who – after resisting various indictments for bribery and other corruption – was in 1967 given an eight-year prison sentence for tampering with a jury, and in 1969 a further five years for misuse of union funds. Released in 1971 by the pardon of Richard Nixon, Hoffa vanished in 1975, and it was never discovered whether he had simply disappeared or been murdered.

There were good reasons why Stallone should have been attracted to the making of *F.I.S.T.*. Playing a character from young man through to late middle-age demanded reserves of acting that hadn't been needed by Rocky, and the character was a ready-made American hero, even if there was more than a suggestion of anti-hero about him. And this was one of the first problems Stallone came up against in the original screenplay by Joe Eszterhas: how to play down the shadier sides of Hoffa, and play up those elements of the story that allowed another little guy to be part of the American Dream. Apart from this, Stallone thought Eszterhas's script was too long and unwieldy, but he was enthusiastic about the project.

The director was to be the Canadian Norman Jewison, who had graduated from television to such successes as *The Cincinnati Kid* (1965) and *The Russians are Coming, The Russians are Coming* (1966). More recently, he had proved less deft in the lumbering screen versions of two musicals, *Fiddler on the Roof* and *Jesus Christ Superstar*. Jewison had sent the screenplay of *F.I.S.T.* to Stallone who had telephoned back within twenty-four hours saying he would do the picture, providing he could tailor the lead to his own needs. Perhaps at the time none of the parties involved realized what trouble this would store up.

From the start, Eszterhas and Stallone were uneasy bedfellows, with Norman Jewison the uncomfortable referee. Jewison insisted that Stallone's script changes be done in his presence, and the actor set to work, looking forward to *F.I.S.T.* becoming 'a landmark film, the ultimate blue-collar movie', and doing his best to ignore rumours that Al Pacino and Jack Nicholson had previously turned down the picture.

Jewison was enthusiastic about this leading man, claiming he had managed to sign him before *Rocky* had been released, a point challenged by the unhappy Eszterhas. As Stallone worked to ensure that the character of Johnny Kovak (alias Hoffa) of the Federation of Interstate Truckers (alias Teamsters' Union) would turn up on screen as a leader who brought 'dignity to working men', the Hollywood bush telegraph was busy with its own simmering disapproval of its new wonder-boy.

The antagonism he was experiencing didn't always stop at words, as the public set about proving to the fledgling star. One girl shouted verbal abuse at him, but another socked him on the jaw. Stallone complained.

'I asked her why she'd done a thing like that. "Because you got what I want," she says. I'm not a person anymore. I'm someone to be challenged and taunted and stripped of my own identity. At last I understand about McQueen, Streisand and Newman ... how they became reclusive.'

His admirers' dissatisfaction with his seemingly aloof manner was aggravated by the very fact that, during the *Rocky* period, Stallone had gloried in the publicity, had gone out of his way to be up-front. He had views, and was not shy of expressing them. Some of these, while couched in vague terms, didn't fool his detractors, who thought they detected the sound of a five-minute wonder handing out tablets of Hollywood wisdom. When it came to his own contribution to cinema, he was also ready to suggest at least one reason for his success.

'There are not enough real men to go around today and the world is short of heroes,' he said. There were times, too, when he sounded dangerously like the self-appointed Messiah of the cinema. 'Any film that has heart, energy and humour is a definite winner,' he announced. 'The combination isn't new, it's not unique – it's just been forgotten.' The implication, of course, was that Stallone had been the one person in the industry to remember it. And, as well as all this, he was displeased at the constant comparisons to Brando, which Paul Newman had also suffered after his Rocky Graziano role in *Somebody Up There Likes Me*. Stallone, however, was having none of it:

'That's just because we both seem to slur words and we wear tee-shirts. Brando is deeper, more sombre and petulant. Anyway, I've got a sense of humour.'

He also had his views of Hollywood's star system, which he said he would keep outside. He wouldn't let it swallow him up, as it had so many before.

'The superstars have had it,' he said. 'Brando is just a joke. Three million dollars for three weeks' work is just stupid. I get insulted if people compare me with Brando.'

When in July 1982 Stallone was interviewed on British television, the critic Herbert Kretzmer looked on, remembering the unspoilt young man he had met at the time of the first *Rocky* film.

'Dressed to the nines, swallowed by the Hollywood system,' Kretzmer wrote, 'he was a far cry from the Hollywood visionary I had encountered when all his dreams were new.'

Anyway, a hero like Rocky was essentially of and for the people, who could get ugly when their boy-made-good didn't oblige by letting them near the flesh of the dream he had created. By June 1977, a sourness had touched Stallone's relationship with the strangers who wanted to be part of that story. There was a time, even, when it seemed his fans were turning into his enemies. 'I'm getting paranoid,' he said. 'As soon as they touch me, my hand balls up into a fist.'

If there is a suspicion, in the mere use of the word, that Stallone's new attitude to his paying customers smacked of Johnny Kovak's defiant use of the clenched fist, it may simply be that once again the division between Stallone's real life and that lived by the character he was playing, was blurred.

The locals brought in as extras when shooting for *F.I.S.T.* began in the state of Iowa, looked for a popular, accessible, friendly Rocky-like figure, the ordinary guy who had made it and been left unspoilt. Instead, they found an inaccessible, heavily guarded actor who sat in his dressing-room and only emerged into the crowd when necessary. Such exclusivity went against the image he had promulgated and asked his fans to take on trust, but Stallone maintained he needed isolation before facing the cameras if he was to give of his best. To many of the uninitiated, and to those who had heard Stallone declare himself to be an actor who didn't bother with any sort of 'method' acting, this seemed no less than precious affectation.

The fathers of Dubuque had even offered the ultimate accolade when, on his arrival, they presented him with the key to the city, but even this was uncomfortably received by Stallone, whose self-conscious inability to cope with the wonders of stardom made him appear awkward and unappreciative.

He also had a professional hill to climb, for there was certainly never any doubt that *F.I.S.T.* would be Stallone's first really serious film, in so much as it was dealing with a serious subject and was based on an important episode of American history.

It is in Cleveland, 1937, that Johnny Kovak, a warehouse labourer for Fleckner Foods, leads a revolt against the hard-line management's unjust treatment of its workers. Johnny, the son of Hungarian immigrants, and his best friend Abe Belkin (David Huffman), are dissatisfied with their lives. Johnny organizes some arm-wrestling in a drinking house, where Abe fancies waitress Molly. Johnny wins concessions from the management, but turning up for work the next day finds he and the men have lost their jobs. The local F.I.S.T. representative Mike Monahan (Richard Herd), who almost apologizes to Johnny that the union he works for is 'not much of one', offers Johnny a car and commission if he can persuade more men to sign on with the union. Abe works alongside him but the men are slow to come over.

Johnny uses the car to impress the spiky Lithuanian Anna (Melinda Dillon) who insists that rather than follow her about he should call on her bearing flowers and prepared to talk about the weather to her mother. The bosses of the Consolidated Trucking Company offer Johnny a handsome salary to work for, instead of against, them, but he refuses, and gets beaten up. Abe, on his way home from dating Molly, is also viciously attacked, and this makes Johnny more determined to screw the management. He organizes a strike.

'Damned Roosevelt,' says the chairman as he looks down at the scene. 'What this country needs is Douglas MacArthur.'

In a violent clash between strikers and employers, Monahan is killed, and Vince (Kevin Conway) a good friend of Johnny but also a racketeer, tells Johnny he is 'whistling past the graveyard'. At Monahan's funeral Johnny breaks down in tears and assures Vince that all he needs for the union to succeed is 'the push'. Abe protests that bringing people like Vince into the union will only mess it up.

The President of F.I.S.T., Max Graham (Peter Boyle), tries to stop Johnny's militant influence over the men, but Johnny intimidates him and sends him packing. Lying to the members that Graham has given him his wholehearted support, Johnny whips the men into a frenzy with a cry against injustice that rings bells rung by Rocky Balboa:

'You don't win a fight taking a punch. Nobody ever won a fight taking a punch. Do you see what it says?' he asks, pointing to the union's emblem emblazoned with its initials. 'This ain't a bunch of letters like any other union. It says FIST and that's what we are. A fist. One fist, one fist, one fist ...'

But increasingly Johnny's visionary politics are backed by the criminal tactics of Vince Doyle. After a bloody conflict, Consolidated concedes to the demands made by Johnny, but such success has to be paid for by the loss of Johnny's integrity. He visits a leading union figure Frank Vasko (Brian Dennehy) who is speaking out against union policies, and warns him that there can be 'no exceptions'. Doyle's men follow up Johnny's call by terrorizing his wife.

As the union grows in strength and numbers, Johnny opens another dubious relationship with the Mafia boss Babe Milano (Tony Lo Bianco) who wastes no time in offering bribes as favours: he offers Johnny and Anna, who are about to marry, a home.

Abe overhears this, confronts Johnny with it and tells him that he and Molly are leaving to live on the West Coast. Johnny cries as he holds Abe's face in his hands, telling him that this is where he belongs. To Johnny, Abe is like a brother – the only guy he can trust.

Many years later, the success of F.I.S.T. and Johnny's part in it, has been consolidated. Suspicious Senator Andrew Madison (Rod Steiger) of the Rackets Committee, asks Johnny how he always manages to get such good deals for his men. Johnny tells him anything can be got in America with a little push.

Abe reunites with Johnny and informs him that Graham is

Sylvester Stallone

swindling the union supporters. Convinced that Graham's dealings are crooked, Johnny puts the squeeze on him, and Graham resigns from the presidency of the union, leaving the position free for Johnny.

Meanwhile, Madison has been pursuing Johnny, and uncovered his associations with the leaders of organized crime. Johnny opposes a wildcat strike begun by Abe, still clinging to his old principles, and the strike turns into a savage confrontation. Madison persuades Abe to testify against Johnny, while the hoodlum bosses try to persuade Johnny to resign as President of F.I.S.T. – he refuses. Johnny visits Abe and warns him not to get involved in the investigation, otherwise his family might get hurt. Abe tells him that he simply wants everything cleaned up. Tearfully, Johnny tells him to do what he feels he must.

At the hearing, Madison tells Johnny that Abe has been murdered and implies that Johnny was responsible. Johnny storms out of the Senate, to be confronted by thousands of union members, their trucks blocking the streets, their hooters proclaiming their loyalty to their leader. That night, a depressed Johnny returns home, but Anna is missing. Johnny runs crying through the house and comes face to face with two gunmen.

'A fairly decent film,' said Stallone of *F.I.S.T.*, though in a more critical mood he later described it as 'just too heavy. It was like sitting down and eating a nine-course meal of warm cream'.

For Norman Jewison, there was a different view.

'There was this incredible sense of power in the film and some interesting visuals, but nobody came to see it because I don't think young people are interested in political movies; they're interested in *Star Wars* probably.'

Jewison's argument may not hold a great deal of water (political movies rise or fall, like any others, by their ability to hold their audiences), but there do seem to be a number of reasons why *F.I.S.T.* did not do well with its public, and the most obvious one, so far as Stallone was concerned, was unavoidable: *F.I.S.T.* wasn't *Rocky*, and Johnny Kovak wasn't Rocky Balboa.

Such a realization was compounded by the fact that Johnny was, at best, an equivocal hero, his morality sold out to the gangsters who could help him achieve his ambitions. Stallone clearly recognized the problem and was at pains from the first to ennoble the character, but this process was at complete odds with the basic drive of the story, which stresses Johnny's ruthlessness and ability to, while not quite condone the thuggery that surrounded him, at least turn a blind eye to it. Johnny, like Rocky, won through against all the odds, but Rocky comes out on top with his nose clean, Johnny doesn't.

Stallone went on to argue that 'Rocky is an idealist where Kovak is a realist', but this explanation doesn't make Kovak any sort of hero; it merely suggested, again, that in reality idealists like Kovak are perverted by real life forces, and deftly consigns Rocky's morality to a land of Never-Never. If Stallone really imagined that Kovak could in any way be made comparable to Rocky, he was misguided. His public certainly wasn't fooled for a moment.

Symptomatic of Stallone's general unease with the project was his attitude to the closing scene. He wanted a feeling of hopefulness and uplift rather than giving the audience a classic downer – the death of the hero. Jewison made three alternative endings to the movie: his own preference (Johnny being mowed down by the very people whose backs he had driven to success on), an ending where Johnny vanishes, and Stallone's preferred ending, a final shot of Johnny putting up a clenched fist at the Senate in a last act of defiance.

Jewison's ending was the only one which would, at least, round off the story and not leave a question mark over Johnny's fate, and it was the ending that found its way on to the final print. Jewison had ignored his star's entreaty that the film should close on 'a definite upper ... for him to die is for the American labour movement to die; my ending has a lot to do with the American way of life, which is always to bounce back after defeat'.

Post-production arguments did not only centre on the closing moments, however. Stallone was heard complaining about the choice of takes used for many of the scenes, claiming that Jewison had concentrated on the less exciting moments of his performance, leaving the best of Stallone on the cutting-room floor. Crucial scenes, explaining developments in Stallone's performance, had simply been missed out, including a confrontation between Stallone and Steiger in which Stallone had let out the cry 'of a dying bull'. Stallone said that moment put a harder edge on the picture, but Jewison cut it out anyway.

Linking moments in the movie, giving Stallone the chance to slowly deepen Johnny's voice, were also dropped, suggesting that Stallone had quite suddenly, in mid-film, dramatically darkened his voice to a coarse whisper. Confusingly, Stallone doesn't then manage to carry the change of timbre through to the end of the picture.

Whatever the truth, and whoever was responsible, it seemed unlikely that Jewison and Stallone would ever be able to work together again, as Stallone continued to point the finger of blame.

The fact that he and Eszterhas were credited as co-writers didn't, however, mean they were a happy pair. Eszterhas felt Stallone had stepped on his project, had taken it over and, frankly, spoilt it. At one point, the relationship between the two men became almost farcical, with Eszterhas offering to meet Stallone in the boxing-ring. The fact was that Eszterhas was one of the first of many casualties in Stallone films over the years. Happily, the pair shook hands again when the film premièred. When they read the reviews, they shook heads.

Stallone's involvement with *F.I.S.T.* was, he said, 'like giving the blueprints of a house to a construction team and not going back until it's built – and then you wind up saying, "My God, they've put the kitchen in the bedroom and the bedroom in the basement, and everything's wrong." Most of my efforts were butchered'.

Enough of a film was left to appreciate Stallone's fine performance, with admirable underplaying and clever pacing of most of his scenes. In the first half of the movie he exercises his gift for quirky romantic scenes with Anna, and a typically Stallone humour pervades the social interchange with Anna's mother. Parked on a sofa and clutching a tight bouquet of red roses, he ties himself in conversational knots about his preference for certain kinds of weather, finally admitting in desperation that he likes it both ways – he likes being hot and cold at the same time.

Throughout, Stallone manages a balance between Johnny's strong-armedness and his softer qualities, which are mostly exercised in his scenes with Abe. Here, as in the majority of Stallone films, it is in the male-to-male relationships that the character's emotions are stripped to the bone. Women may be a source of attraction, and can even be allowed to kick up a storm and demand marriage, but they do not stretch the emotional walls of most of Stallone's characters, and Johnny is no exception.

Nothing works as well in the second part of the film where the mood grows more unrelievedly sombre, apart from an amusing sequence when Madison questions the squirmingly guilty Vince. Stallone can do little with the older Johnny. Melinda Dillon starts out as a sparky adversary with a nicely caustic edge to her early scenes, but she gets soppier as her relationship with Johnny solidifies, even crying – like Annie in *Paradise Alley* – when Johnny gives her a present.

Second-billed Steiger does not catch fire as Madison, and it is left to Kevin Conway as the weasly Vince to stand out from the supporting cast. The real stars, apart from Stallone, were the production designer Richard MacDonald and photographer Laszlo Kovacs who contrived to give the film an authentic and beautifully depressed look. The factories, puddles, smoke and gloom of the period were ably melded together under Jewison's careful direction.

F.I.S.T. was long and rather confusing; it lacked a sporting theme, had a hero who wasn't really a hero and certainly wasn't much fun, and made a violent lurch in time in its middle from which it never really recovered, but the film was never quite the catastrophe Stallone's comments may sometimes have suggested. When, later, he said that making the film had been very unpleasant and not worth the seven months he had taken making it, such a devastating repudiation may have had more to do with the professional and personal problems he had to endure during production, than with the film itself.

It was certainly, as he said, a change from any of the movies he had made before.

'Most of the films I was in before *Rocky* were shot by Freaky Films Inc. from the back of a pickup truck with somebody looking out for the gendarmes,' he told Roger Ebert, and *F.I.S.T.* was 'the first sophisticated film I've ever done'.

But happy it wasn't, and the failure was happening alongside unhappy developments in his personal life: Sasha seemed remote; *Rocky* had to be eclipsed; an image had to be supported. Carping voices were constantly being raised against him, as when Rex Reed explained to his readers that 'Sylvester Stallone carries on his shoulder an ego the size of a forty-pound eggplant'.

'The most drastic change was my values,' said Stallone. 'I really became envious and coveted other people's success ... In doing all that, I got so far away from whatever it took, like talent, to do *Rocky* ... I felt I was really slipping down.'

6 The Worst Reviews Since Hitler

Before *F.I.S.T.* was exposed to a generally disinterested public, Stallone moved into offices at Universal to begin work on the novel of his next project, *Paradise Alley*, a re-working of his old 'Hell's Kitchen' idea, renamed because, according to its author, 'Paradise is a feminine word. Alley is a masculine word, and therefore you appeal to everyone.' However, when the novel appeared, published by Putnam, Universal's publishing arm, it appealed to very few of the critics. The *New York Times* announced that it showed 'no verbal imagination whatever', while *Newsweek* found fault with its 'too, too solid prose'; other reviews were equally dismissive. Even the publishers had resisted his style, which they had thought 'alien'. The post-*Rocky* Stallone was nevertheless ready to pontificate on his contribution to literature.

'*War and Peace* would make a great novelette if it was condensed, but it's tough to read,' he said. 'I want my books to be read within two or three hours – and the entire impact is there.'

The cover photograph for the novel showed Stallone, his head in his hands, seated at his typewriter, his questioningly intellectual eyes peering sadly through his fingers into middle space. In fact, *Paradise Alley*, dedicated to Sasha 'who takes away the rain', is a highly coloured, young man's novel, full of quirky vignettes, and written with an obviously adept technique that did not always lift the words off the page. To read the mannered prose is to enter a world of Damon Runyonesque characters seen through a T.S. Eliot-like gauze. The snappy dialogue and descriptions sometimes shift from prose to blank poetry, using a basically cinematic approach that had the author writing in quick, short blasts; fifty-four chapters in just 200 pages. Today, the novel can still strike the sympathetic reader as personal and interesting enough to make one wonder how Stallone would have shaped up if he had persisted as a novelist.

For the present, however, there was the fact of the critics' dismissal of his first novel. It was a blow to Stallone the writer, and an inauspicious omen for the film he had written and was just about to direct and star in. The Hollywood buzz was that the still-to-be previewed *F.I.S.T.* was far away from being a winner, and that the bumptious newcomer was on a rapidly downward trip.

The fate of *Paradise Alley* could not but assume an almost awesome importance to its creator, who concentrated his entire energies on it – after all, even more than *Rocky* had been, it was his entire responsibility, his own child, and the chance to prove himself a consummate cinema artist. No less, it was a golden opportunity for his detractors who looked for nothing good from this ultimate ego-trip. Damn it all, not content with writing it, directing it and starring in it, didn't the guy even bellow the opening song?

Before work on the production itself began, however, there was the niggling fact that the producers who had snapped up Stallone's *Hell's Kitchen* screenplay back in 1975 and seen it through to realization as *Paradise Alley* were none too pleased that *Rocky* had, in their view, stolen much of the content of their property: that Stallone had, in fact, pinched ideas from himself. Riding this particular storm, Stallone was able to make some deft alterations that deflated the artistic tension, substituting wrestling for the original script's boxing. The fact that many of these adjustments were mainly cosmetic suggested that producers Roach and Suppa did not in fact want to move too far away from a *Rocky*-type work. And their writer-director-star had his own very definite ideas. He wasn't prepared to back into corners as he had with *F.I.S.T.*.

'I think the day of the one-dimensional performer is drawing to an end,' he said. 'An important actor has to have the power to impose his ideas about the film on anyone connected with the film making process.'

From *Paradise Alley* onwards, he acted on this belief. When producers hired Stallone, they knew his influence would go far beyond the playing of a role. Now, he would be seen as a writer and director who also acted. It was only to be expected that he would bring all these talents to bear on any project he became involved in.

In preparation for the movie, Stallone made an intense mental and physical commitment to the job in hand, maintaining a diet composed mainly of fruits, nuts, juices and other easily digestible foods. At least there would be no gruelling physical training necessary for his own role, for although *Paradise Alley* had a wrestling theme (among its many themes), the screenplay did not involve him in any of the sporting action, though he does run in the beautifully shot roof-top chase that opens the picture.

Shooting of exterior scenes began in January 1978, mostly on West 80th Street (actually beyond the true Hell's Kitchen area), on the docks by the Hudson River and at other Brooklyn locations. By this time, Stallone had employed a bodyguard to protect him from the more unwelcome of his admirers, but this didn't prevent one woman from breaking through to him and jumping on his back.

There was bad publicity, too, when an article appeared criticizing his arrogant attitude to press photographers. Annoyed at what he read, Stallone banned photographers from the set. Even more silly were newspaper reports claiming that his ego was now so immense and his confidence so insecure that he only agreed to work with actors shorter than himself. These rumours could at least be denied with confidence – for starters, his co-star Lee Canalito was a towering 6ft 5ins – and Stallone turned aside to the business of creating his most important, most expensive, most personal film to date.

It seems no coincidence that the story of *Paradise Alley* takes place in 1946, the year of his own birth, in the Hell's Kitchen into which he had been born – he was going back to his own beginning. The three Carboni brothers, existing at the lower depths of life, are an unprosperous trio. Cosmo (Stallone) is a streetwise loudmouth, posing as a cripple to earn money from passers-by and wanting a way out and upwards; Lenny (Armand Assante) is the elder brother, an embittered hobbling war veteran, soured and scarred and working in a grim down-town mortuary; Victor (Canalito) is the baby brother, mild, sweet and strong, scratching a living delivering blocks of ice, and devoted to a little caged bird. Victor's simplicity is endearing; nothing pleases him more than to have Lenny do a pretty feeble impression of Charlie Chaplin's funny walk, and when Lenny isn't doing his Chaplin he broods and limps through life.

Cosmo has big ideas for getting successful, and persuades

Victor to arm-wrestle Franky The Thumper (Terry Funk), the most vicious member of Stitch's (Kevin Conway) gang of marvellously comic grotesques. Victor, urged on by Lenny's whispered entreaty to believe in himself and win, conquers Franky, and Cosmo claims the dead organ-grinder's pathetic chattering monkey from Stitch. The monkey, it turns out, will not even dance for Cosmo when he takes it on to the streets to make his fortune. Stitch sums Victor up by declaring, 'That guy's too stupid to be scared. He's a primitive.'

In fact, kindly Victor is in love with Susan Chow (Aimée Eccles) who is teaching him English grammar, and together they dream of an idyllic future on a Jersey houseboat – perhaps in eight years time Victor will be able to afford it. Cosmo fancies the red-headed sculptress Annie (Anne Archer) – once Lenny's girl – but for the past three years has been calling by to sleep with blonde Bunchie, whom Cosmo describes as a professional bed warmer. Lenny asks Annie to take him back and, in a moving scene, she refuses, but he walks her home, they kiss, and their relationship begins again. Cosmo looks through the window and sees them in bed together. The next day he confronts Annie, accusing her of betrayal, but Annie reminds him that theirs has always been a friendship, not a love. Bunchie consoles the depressed Cosmo and tells him that she, at least, loves him.

Meanwhile, Cosmo's determination to exploit his kid brother's fighting potential grows, and he persuades Victor to stand against the brutish black wrestler Big Glory (Frank Macrae), the champion of Paradise Alley. Victor wins. Later, he goes with Cosmo to visit Big Glory, a broken and pathetic figure living in the rat-infested basement of the alley. Undaunted by this meeting, Cosmo puts increasing pressure on Victor to wrestle for big money, but Victor is uncertain, while Lenny positively resists Cosmo's selfish exhortations.

At this point in the story, the brothers' attitudes undergo a tremendous change. The bottom falls out of the ice business and, in a beautifully made sequence, the exhausted, depressed Victor hurls a block of ice from the top of a long flight of stairs. His decision is made. To match this catharsis, Lenny now decides to handle the business side of Victor's new career while Cosmo, voicing serious doubts about the rightness of what he is doing to his mother's third son, is designated the trainer. Soon,

Victor is successfully thrashing opponent after opponent, while Lenny, now viciously acquisitive, even refuses to please him by doing his Charlie Chaplin.

Needing a gimmick, Victor goes in to the ring wearing a waistcoat of salami, and is known as Kid Salami. Cosmo tells Bunchie he will take her away soon, that she will no longer have to sell herself. Annie, hurt by Lenny's new greed and self-absorption, rejects him once more. At Christmas, still coming to terms with the sadnesses of life, Cosmo dresses as Santa Claus. He fights off muggers and goes to see Big Glory; together they go for a ride in a truck and Big Glory is happier than he has been for years. He warns Cosmo of the bleak future awaiting Victor and tells him he is going to drown himself. Making Cosmo promise he will not try to save him, Big Glory jumps off the quay, and Cosmo smiles, for Big Glory lands on a solid bed of garbage. The old wrestler smiles in appreciation of a last ironic joke, and jumps into the river to his death.

Now Cosmo frantically tries to turn Victor away from his vicious destiny, but Lenny plans one last great contest opposite Franky The Thumper, telling Victor that a win will mean he will be able to buy the houseboat in Jersey. An enlightened Cosmo tells Victor, 'Guys like us, we don't live on houseboats,' but Victor wagers the entire fortune his endeavours have accumulated – $9,000 – on winning the match.

Lenny snarls that if Victor loses this fight the brothers will be garbage again, but Victor, with an innate inner strength, tells his brother he has never been garbage. That night, during a tremendous thunderstorm, the ring awash with continuous rain, Victor wades into the most crucial of his confrontations and tells the repentant Cosmo he should be proud. Cosmo asks why he should feel proud? 'You started everything,' replies Victor.

The ferocious fight seems to finish with Victor being defeated, but he comes back at Franky and, like Rocky thirty years later, wins, while the vile Stitch is revealed as a cross-dresser, trying to explain away his stockings and suspenders. Victor tells Cosmo and Lenny he had meant to lose the fight on purpose because he liked it better when they were just brothers. They fall into each other's arms, happy and together again.

Excuses for the failure of a film come in all colours, and watching it today, *Paradise Alley* still offers up various suggestions for its poor box-office performance. The movie's major fault may have been simply that it wasn't *Rocky* all over again, and it wasn't modern, and Stallone wasn't its bare-chested hero. That responsibility fell to Lee Canalito, who provided what was clearly an amateur performance, an often remarkable resemblance to a young Brando, and a liquid softness of face and voice that gave the picture its only quota of charm – no mean feat from a heavyweight boxer from Houston whom Stallone had first noticed on television. Subsequently, when Canalito's acting career went nowhere, Stallone financed and promoted his boxing career, even moving him into his own home. 'He's like my brother,' said Stallone later. 'I want to prove that what I created in fantasy can be duplicated in reality.' It was a heavy responsibility for the young Houston hopeful.

Armand Assante, playing his first leading feature film role, was quite striking in the early scenes, and any character who arrives for work to find a body propped outside wearing a label with instructions to 'Bury Him Fast' deserves some sort of sympathy. However, with very little in the way of sub-text, Assante's Lenny (and, come to that, Stallone's Cosmo) could make little sense of the volte-face their characters suffered halfway through the film. Surprisingly, only Victor stays steady to his true self, even growing in wisdom and acceptance as he submits to the punishments of the ring.

In the gallery of male supporting roles Stallone splashed out with flavoursome characters that owed not a little to the America of Damon Runyon, including Joe Spinell (from *Rocky*) as the ghastly Burp, proprietor of Paradise Alley; but the film proved, as his screenplays would go on proving, that as a writer Stallone had much less success with the female characters, never allowing them to round out and extend. Bunchie is nothing more or less than the well worn tart with a heart of gold, with nothing interesting about her; she's put down in front of us and we're expected to feel sorry for her. Annie, so sensitive and charming and talented with a palette knife that it's a mystery why she's still knocking around Hell's Kitchen, is more adequately drawn, but even she seems mostly passive. The women in this world stand on the sidelines and wait patiently for a man to love them.

Of course, *Paradise Alley* tried to be several things. It was an obvious hark back to the grittier pictures of another day, those black and white hymns to the American spirit of the forties, and audiences couldn't help but get this message when Universal's modern logo was replaced by its black and white predecessor, the aeroplane circling the globe. At its core the film was just another episode of no-good bums making it through to success, but of almost central importance, overriding all else, was the style of the piece, and it was this very particular quality that may have discomfited audiences and critics alike.

Certainly, Stallone's basic approach to film making seemed incredibly consolidated, considering *Paradise Alley* had been the first film he had directed. To some ears, it sounded as if he was offering himself as the panacea to the cinema's ills.

'I think we'll have even more of a revival of good, old-fashioned movies,' he announced. 'There's a definite formula in reaching audiences: provide them with heroes and heroines who pull themselves up by the bootstraps and out of the depths of despair. You can just hear the audience saying, My God, that's the kind of person I want to be.'

But in the public's first brush with Stallone the film director, there was some uneasiness with the often jerky transition from scene to scene, the wordless close-ups of characters – Lenny glaring at the windows of the dance-hall, Annie quietly sculpting – that were simply offered as visual hints and snatched away, the almost inexplicable picking up and dropping of strands, the silly jokes, Victor's infantile singing to his bird, the sudden edgy atmospheres that spring up whenever someone mentions mothers. 'Let's leave mothers out of it' becomes almost a stock phrase of the brothers, and we are supposed to paint a picture of their own mother from this one seed.

Stallone himself grew to recognize what he considered the film's errors of judgement, later even going so far as to regret ever making the picture and taking its central role. In fact, he put much of the blame on poor Cosmo, describing him as 'really despicable. No redeeming qualities at all … instead of being the supplier of the energy, I was the foul spark plug, just sputtering'. Intelligent audiences will see that Cosmo was none of these things, and it's puzzling to know why Stallone so turned against his creation. In another act of desperation, he claimed that three astrologers had advised him against releasing the film in November. Unheeding, the distributors had gone ahead and the picture, zodiac doomed, had bombed.

Astrological intervention might also have helped United

Artists avoid the April unveiling of *F.I.S.T.*, which opened to reviews that ranged from disappointing to downright rude, and to very few of the paying public. By now, its star and co-author had pretty well distanced himself from the unhappy project, but the critical shafts could not be avoided.

Many of them went straight for the jugular: 'Big, bad and botched,' said David Ansen in *Newsweek*; 'a mess', said Rex Reed in the *Daily News*, going on to tell us that 'Stallone has turned a viable story of union corruption into a massive ego massage without the talent to back it up'.

There was some light coming through, however, including some kind words from *Variety* which praised Stallone's performance, as did the *New York Times*' Vincent Canby. Marsha McCreadie for *Films in Review* thought the film treated its theme with a 'late seventies gloss of camp ethnicity ... the proletarian feel doesn't always come through, despite some wonderful touches', while Gordon Gow in *Films and Filming* found it 'quite a creditable follow-up to his *Rocky* ... during the film's rather dull beginnings, I feared that he was putting so much emphasis on the character's ox-like persona as to diminish if not relinquish sympathy. But Johnny, like the movie, grows on one'.

The film had pretty well the opposite effect on Richard Coombs of *Monthly Film Bulletin*, who thought the film started well and fell apart halfway through, becoming 'virtually indistinguishable from one of the TV "bestseller" series'. As for the star of the piece, 'Stallone is also unable to do much with the store-dummy patriarch at this end of the film, though he manages to inject a surprising degree of life and verbal vigour into the earlier scenes ...'

As if all this professional trouble was not enough, his personal life was in crisis too: in March 1978, his wife filed divorce proceedings, claiming 'irreconcilable differences'.

In fact, the reasons for what was going wrong were probably as professional as they were personal. Sasha had made a brief visit to the *Paradise Alley* set early in the production and then returned home to California, leaving Stallone with all the pressures and temptations of the hot-house world of film making, and it wasn't very long before it became obvious he was having an affair with his blonde co-star Joyce Ingalls. He moved himself into the Sheraton Universal Hotel and did a lot of heavy partying, riding the crest of his new-found stardom. In nightclubs, on dance floors, he was identified by the *paparazzi* as the escort of various attractive girls.

Not unnaturally, Sasha went through the gamut of reactions, but used her enforced freedom to further explore the possibilities of a professional career in photography, filling in her other time with her son, scuba diving, and an active interest in feminism. She was certainly not interested in finding a replacement for Stallone; perhaps she felt that with time, her husband would come to his senses, would come home. He also made it clear to her that he didn't want her to see other men, even though he was in a relationship with Ingalls. Sasha had stood by him throughout the long years of struggling for any sort of recognition, and to see the first whiffs of success knock him off balance and desert her must have been a very bitter pill to swallow.

Even during this period, however, she and Stallone were seeing each other, and there remained an obvious fondness between them.

'He was home three or four days a week,' said Sasha. 'Our sex life was still passionate. He remained very involved as a father and a loving husband.'

Over the years Stallone has philosophized about his various dalliances. Looking back on the times when Sasha was left high and dry for another woman, he realized that he had been following his heart, not his mind.

'Outwardly it appears that I was the villain in all of this, but none of it was done out of maliciousness. When people say you're cheating, cheating has such a negative connotation ... And I gave in to the weakness, or should I say the strength, of the moment. I just felt I had to be true to my basic instincts, otherwise I was altering the animal. I had flaws, but I was an excellent husband. But leading the life I lead ... Temptation is presented in spades. It's there so much that one doesn't even consider it temptation, it becomes almost a ... rite of spring.'

The relationship with Ingalls carried on as Stallone and Sasha discussed their past, their future, and tried to come to terms with what had happened to them. The actual rift was to last four months before Sasha took him back – another event that, though highly personal, was played out in the glare of publicity, with Stallone putting himself up front as the wrongful party. He had worked hard at the reconciliation, which took place the night before *F.I.S.T.*'s official première. He apologized in public for the embarrassment he had caused his wife. Ingalls' reaction is not recorded.

Professionally, there was more distress ahead when *Paradise Alley* was released. Stallone summed up the notices by claiming 'they would actually ignite, they were so hot. They would say, "The egomaniac has made a film that warrants nothing but banishment from the archives of any cinema student" or "He's taken every bad habit since film began, since *Birth of a Nation*, and made it worse".'

In fact, the press had been hitting the film, and its star, long before its opening, but not quite everybody was prepared to bury it. Richard Coombs in *Monthly Film Bulletin* was a champion of sorts, noting that 'the most impressive aspect of Stallone's highly coloured direction is that, through the excess with which it renders the grotesqueness of poverty … it also renders the pain … That the style is so dependant on his own unique reserves of feeling and expression is probably responsible for the accusations of personal indulgence. But *Paradise Alley* is undeniably charged with more promise than the cynically manipulated package of *Rocky*'.

It would have been too much to expect all the critical reaction to be as sympathetic as this. David Denby writing in *New York* thought the film 'so synthetic you don't believe a minute of it', and Frank Rich in *Time* wrote that 'as an exercise in egomania, *Paradise Alley* almost puts Barbra Streisand's *A Star Is Born* to shame', though he did confess that the film showed 'an original comic voice struggling to get out'. In a more lengthy evaluation, Pauline Kael congratulated the monkey on giving the only touching and authoritative performance, but went on to insist that the film's leading man 'doesn't seem to know about restraint, or what can be accomplished by understatement. He writes, directs and acts in a form of Esperanto – a basic, reductive approach to human possibilities'. She had enough brickbats for Stallone in his three capacities. As a writer he was 'a primitive mining the mass media, without any apparent awareness of how stale his ideas are'; as a director he was responsible for 'tumescent film making'; as a performer 'after three starring roles Stallone's limitations as an actor have become very apparent'.

Stallone's own view of *Paradise Alley* is not far west of his critics. He prefers, he suggests, to watch the film with one eye closed.

'The first time I got behind a camera,' he has said, 'I was nervous, but I thought, God, there's the opportunity. I understand why it turned people off. I didn't approach it properly. I just lunged into it.' Looking back to it, however, it would be surprising if *Paradise Alley* – written and directed by, and starring, Sylvester Stallone – is not ultimately accepted as one of the most endearing and fascinating of his works.

7   Sequel

'I would like to do Rocky at age forty, when I'm forty, at age fifty when I'm fifty. Nobody has ever followed the same character through like that.'

These comments were made in 1977, and Stallone went on to say that *Rocky II* would be about the hero's conflict with his wife:

'She's still growing as a person and Rocky is back playing stickball ... They are growing apart.'

In fact, such a scenario didn't turn up in *Rocky II*, though this outline bore some resemblance to what was happening in Stallone's private life. Professionally, too, things didn't look good. *F.I.S.T.* and *Paradise Alley* had done poor business, but the follow-up to these disappointments wasn't conceived in desperation to revive a flagging career – it had been discussed at the time of the original *Rocky*, and John Avildsen had been asked to direct it. His ideas didn't match Stallone's, however. Avildsen wanted to open out the boxing theme, make Rocky more politically active, perhaps having him run for mayor of Philadelphia. United Artists delivered the project wholly into Stallone's hands, his three capacities as writer, director and star (as in *Paradise Alley*), proving that Hollywood now accepted him as a power base of cinematic activity – or someone who could make a very great deal of money for them.

Stallone built up his creative team, going for the best, if they met his mother's astrological approval.

'Of course I'd prefer to have people agree with me all the time,' he said during this period. 'I'd like them to wear buttons saying "yes". But that's no way to make a movie. So I just surround myself with people I'd like to strangle.'

There would be no hint of experimentation as there had been with *Paradise Alley*, where such touches had gone unappreciated. *Rocky II* closely followed the tracks set down by Avildsen's

Looking out on a career that Rex Reed called 'as mysterious as cot death'. To Stallone it sometimes seemed to have happened by accident: 'I fired a bullet into the ground and struck oil'.

The four Lords of Flatbush – Paul Mace, Stallone, Henry Winkler and Perry King – hoping for bigger contracts and better money.

Coping with the threat of marriage from Maria Smith in *The Lords of Flatbush*. Stallone's brilliant playing of Stanley in this cult classic remains one of his finest moments.

Stallone's creation, Rocky Balboa, before the Big Time, Rocky's impact on Hollywood and America was considerable, but Stallone was denied the personal Oscar he felt he deserved.

Rocky and the faithful Adrian: Stallone with Talia Shire in *Rocky II*. Theirs was a partnership that carried through five movies.

original treatment. It would be what the public expected and, while advancing Rocky's development, would in many ways be quite a literal revival of Avildsen's mood, though in at least one respect *Rocky II* was light years away from its predecessor. It had a budget eight times that of the original *Rocky*, and the studio, from the start, was putting its full weight behind it.

At a stroke, it was a chance to show that its star could also direct successfully, despite what audiences had thought of *Paradise Alley* – and Stallone grasped the nettle with a single-mindedness that spelled success for *Rocky II* and eventual disaster for Sasha. He sat down and wrote the screenplay in 29½ hours, then got to work on the various re-writes.

The physical preparation for *Rocky II* was even more gruelling than that for *Rocky*, for Stallone knew the final sequence – the re-match with Creed – had to top everything that the original had offered as the most important set-piece of the movie. The fight was the first part of *Rocky II* to be filmed when shooting commenced in October 1978, to allow ample time for Stallone to oversee its editing. As would often be the case with his work, the editing took much longer than the whole process of making the film, and Stallone had almost to be dragged out of the cutting-room.

His training came close to punishment, and he pushed himself much harder than ever before. Before shooting began, a too strenuous workout left him with a ripped pectoralis major which ultimately meant an operation and 156 stitches. 'The whole side of my chest was torn off,' he explained. 'I have a scar that goes all the way down my side like a zipper.' It was a price that had to be paid for a fight sequence that was, according to its creator, 'choreographed by the Marquis de Sade'. Throughout his career, Stallone would be justly proud of this extraordinary evidence of the suffering he had undergone in the cause of his career. Tim Pigott-Smith, who worked with him on the subsequent *Escape to Victory*, recalls Stallone exhibiting his injuries with great pride.

In the event, *Rocky II* proved to be a delightful reunion with its hero in a film which, though full of genuinely funny sequences, also enjoyed the expected wallow in sentimentality.

The film begins with the closing minutes of *Rocky*, and picks up the story immediately after the fight with Rocky and Apollo being taken to hospital. Apollo tells Rocky he will fight him again and beat him, but Rocky insists he is retired. Adrian is there to whisper the fact that she loves Rocky, and Paulie wastes no time in asking if Rocky can get him his old job as a collector for Gazzo. In the quiet of night, Rocky finds Apollo's room in the hospital and asks if the champion gave him his best.

Discharged, Rocky takes Adrian to the zoo and proposes to her. She accepts, and they marry. Now Rocky has every intention of earning a respectable living, and Gazzo asks him what he intends to do with the $37,000 he won from the fight.

'How about investing in Condominiums?' he asks.

'Condominiums? I never use them,' says Rocky, and begins celebrating married life by going on a spending spree. He buys a swank car but can't really drive, and – in a brilliantly funny scene – looks over a new house with Adrian, and decides to buy it:

'I like these bricks, they're very nicely done here, look very solid ... D'you know, these numbers almost add up to nine here. I like that, it's a good omen.'

Adrian becomes pregnant and Rocky tries to earn a crust by featuring in an after-shave commercial, but he can't read the idiot boards and is fired. Back at home, Rocky practises reading out loud to Adrian, in preparation for a good office job.

'Do you have a criminal record?' asks a prospective employer nervously.

'Nothin' worth braggin' about,' says Rocky, but the best he can get is a job cleaning up in the slaughterhouse. The work is demeaning and hard but Rocky is disappointed when he is laid off, and Adrian tells him she will go back to part-time work at the pet shop.

Mickey tells Rocky his boxing career is over, that his eye injury means he will never be able to fight again; if he got into the ring with the champion again Apollo would hurt him 'poimament'. Rocky fights back tears as he asks for a job at Mickey's gym; it is where he belongs.

But Apollo is haunted by the humiliation he suffered at Rocky's hands ('I won but I didn't beat him,' he explains) and is obsessed with getting Rocky back into the ring opposite him. At the gym Rocky is slopping out buckets of spit, but begins to respond when Apollo publicly taunts him. Mickey starts training Rocky for another challenge, but Rocky is out of condition. Mickey tells him he is no good, that he should go back to being a hopeless bum.

At the pet shop Adrian collapses and begins haemorrhaging, is taken to hospital and gives premature birth to a boy. She slips into a coma and Rocky devotedly stays by her side, reading aloud to her, crying at her bedside. Mickey joins him in the hospital chapel and together they pray. When she recovers, Rocky promises her that he will not go on with the fight if she does not wish it. Adrian tells him she only wants one thing – for him to win the fight.

Rocky throws himself into his training and runs through the streets, followed Pied Piper-like by the children of Philadelphia, who jump with him up the length of the Art Museum steps. On the night of the contest, Rocky leaves Adrian and Paulie at home, knocks his priest up and asks him to throw down a blessing. At the stadium, there is a brief tranquil moment as we see Rocky alone, praying, and Apollo, isolated in his dressing-room.

The fight is gladiatorial, with both men taking a terrible beating. Rocky's eye closes up but he refuses to let the fight be stopped. Finally, both men crash to the ground and it is only at the last count that Rocky staggers to his feet as Apollo slumps onto the floor; Rocky is the new champion. He lifts the belt high and tearfully tells the watching millions of his devoted wife. At home, she weeps softly and can only mumble, 'I love you'.

Rocky's expressiveness reached comic heights in the opening scenes, notably in his attempted breakthrough into commercials which (even if it recalled similar moments in *Singin' in the Rain* and the little known British drama *The Comedy Man*) had, in Rocky's self-conscious lopsidedness, its own piquancy. Then there was the delight of Rocky's spending spree and the hilarious house-buying scene, a glorious celebration of what the world might think his complete lack of taste, working with his brilliant selflessness. *Rocky II* also had far more energy and fun than the *Rocky* audiences had seen before, though his serious, more contemplative side is by no means dimmed.

And all this was cleverly set against the thrust of Creed's nagging lust for vengeance (superbly suggested in Weathers' obsessed performance). If the love scenes between Rocky and Adrian bordered on the embarrassing, with their adoration mostly expressed in whispered exchanges of 'I love you', they undeniably worked, underpinning the film's explosive finale.

All told, *Rocky II* was a canny re-working of many of the

original *Rocky* ideas with enough character expansion (at least for the hero – Paulie, Adrian and Mickey are less interesting here than in the first film) to make it stand as a major achievement in its own right. Though script, performance and direction were excellent, this time around there would be not even the hint of any Academy interest, and the critics – perhaps suffering from a surfeit of the superstar image Stallone had been thrusting at the press since the first *Rocky* – were not throwing their hats in the air either.

Rex Reed, who had loathed the original *Rocky*, surprisingly found its successor 'a sequel that soars', but the tone of the notices was elsewhere generally faint, though Julian Fox for *Films and Filming* raved about it as 'a stunning work in every sense of the word', marking Stallone as 'one of the great originals'. John Pym was more guarded in the *Monthly Film Bulletin*, admitting that 'up to a point it is hard not to admire the audacity with which Sylvester Stallone, here acting as his own director, has so faithfully reconstituted the plot and ingredients of the first *Rocky*'. This latest *Rocky*, Pym suggested, 'perceives, however dimly, that he can actually live off his image'.

Muhammad Ali was particularly interested to see *Rocky II*, starring, as he put it, Apollo Creed as Muhammad Ali, but found much to criticize in the boxing sequences. He claimed Stallone didn't have the right moves for a boxer, that no fighter would have tolerated a screaming trainer like Mickey, that the only chickens found near boxers were served with vegetables, that weight-lifting was the worst thing a boxer could do, that no referee would have allowed a fight to go on with one of the fighter's eyes so obviously closed up. Having got rid of the technical niceties, Ali went on to give his own explanation of the Rocky myth, and the reason why Creed could not remain champion:

'For the black man to come out superior would be against America's teachings. I have been so great in boxing they had to create an image like Rocky, a white image on the screen, to counteract my image in the ring. America has to have its white images, no matter where it gets them. Jesus, Wonder Woman, Tarzan and Rocky.'

Throughout the making of *Rocky II*, Sasha was pregnant, and a son, Seargeoh, was born in May 1979. But in what should have been a together time for the couple, the pressures of Stallone's image, and his wholehearted commitment to his professional life, were once more throwing shadows across his marriage. Since his involvement with *Rocky* (writer and star) he had gone through *F.I.S.T.* (co-author and star), *Paradise Alley* (writer, director and star), and now *Rocky II* (writer, director and star). In such a high-flying existence, the studio became his real home; the role of husband seemed petty and restricting. It seemed that, like Oscar Wilde, he could resist everything except temptation, and in June 1979, after finishing *Rocky II*, he walked out on Sasha for the second time, into the arms of another blonde. The fact that he had also left a baby son at home didn't paint too good a picture in the press.

Susan Anton was a 29-year-old Southern Californian who had once been runner-up in the Miss America Beauty contest, and was now pursuing a mild career in films, having just completed her first movie, *Goldengirl*, in which her fresh healthy looks were put to use in the role of an athletic heroine. She was out on the road publicizing the film when Stallone was on the road selling *Rocky II*, and they ran into one another. Only a few weeks after the meeting, Stallone had walked out on Sasha and the newly born baby, and Anton had left her husband-manager of seven years, Jack Stein, to set up home together in a substantial beach house in Malibu, set in three and a half acres of land – a place Anton described as her 'slice of heaven'.

What was more, Anton talked to the press about marrying her lover and having a family with him. Once again, Sasha's resilience was called into play, and the banner of forbearance still fluttered.

'I figured it was the same old story,' she has said, 'helping a man to get to the top, then he wanted other things. I was a victim of the success syndrome.'

But Stallone was his own victim, too. His usual problems of living a normal life in the world outside were considerably heightened by the position he had got himself in, underscored by an unsympathetic showing in the press, and he and Anton spent most of their time together in the enclave of their home, though Stallone did take time out to appear in *The Muppet Show* where no doubt he was the cynosure of Miss Piggy's sexual fantasies. In the autumn of 1979 Sasha would again petition for a divorce that didn't happen, for by March 1980 the affair was over. Anton left the arena with the tantalizing comment that her companion had been 'terrific in bed – physically', and went on to find a partner in Dudley Moore, while Stallone and Sasha later referred to the episode as having been almost necessary, a way for the star to work through his emotional problems.

'We met on April Fool's Day and we parted on April Fool's Day,' said Stallone of Anton. 'We were very foolish. Those nine months gratified my vanity but I never found the gates of Oz.'

1980 had other surprises in store for his admirers, when he admitted to having lived previous lives. One of his earlier existences had been as a boxer who had been killed around 1930, and at some time, Stallone claimed, he had roamed the earth as a wolf. There was plenty of evidence to support this, until he explained that he was talking about the four-legged kind. He also had recollections of losing his head in the French Revolution, supported by the fact that 'whenever I see a guillotine, I get a strange feeling of serenity'.

There was still plenty to worry about in his present existence, however, not the least of which was the film he moved on to after *Rocky II*. And having restored his box office clout after the débâcles of *F.I.S.T.* and *Paradise Alley*, he went on to pick two films that would come as near as anything to finishing his career, two films that rivalled each other in awfulness. The first – for which he left Susan Anton in Malibu and made for New York – was for Universal, and had a working title of *Attack*, later to reach the screen as *Nighthawks*.

The picture should have been a rest cure for Stallone, who was only required to star in it, and a rest cure was probably what he most needed at this point in his life. *Nighthawks* didn't need him as director (Gary Nelson was in charge) or writer (David Shaber adapting his own story), merely requiring him to concentrate on his being the first-billed star of the movie. But, as might now be almost expected of any project in which Stallone was involved, things didn't quite work out that way, and *Nighthawks* would wind up among the several films which held unpleasant memories for him, and some not very pleasant ones for the other people involved.

Producer Martin H. Poll, whose previous credits included such disparate movies as *The Lion in Winter* and *The Man who Loved Cat Dancing*, appreciated his star, calling him 'co-operative, supportive and a hard worker with great humour. I think there's a range of his talent that hasn't been reached yet'.

Unfortunately, Poll's affection didn't extend to Gary Nelson, a director who had distinguished himself with several excellent TV movies, and who got shown the door. Poll replaced him with Bruce Malmuth, but there was a brief interregnum between Nelson's departure and Malmuth's arrival when the production had no director, and it looked as if shooting would have to stop.

Rather than let this happen, Stallone stepped in as director for a day, and the Directors' Guild passed a vote of thanks on his action by fining the production $50,000. By his readiness to help out, the troubled star had again given the press more ready-made proof of his arrogance and disregard for the organized morals of his industry.

This wasn't the only problem to crop up during production; another major hiccup concerned the use of the crucial cable-car which had been commandeered by the production much to the annoyance of the residents of Roosevelt Island who needed the car to get across to Manhattan. A priest headed a protest that tried to get a court injunction to suspend filming, and Stallone stepped in, taking it on himself to play arbiter between the production and the people, in an effort to win the people's support and facilitate filming. However, the residents were not altogether happy to be approached by a man who had set himself up, through the existence of Rocky, as the little man's champion. Feathers were ruffled, but the studio stepped in with an offer to use the cable-car only at agreed off-peak periods, and topped this gesture with a gift of $20,000 for a new youth centre on the island. The residents were happier, and the studio had got away with it pretty cheaply. As for Stallone, perhaps he had tried to take advantage of his public standing to effect a reconciliation in the matter, and had not been altogether successful.

Meanwhile, the plot of *Nighthawks* unfolded before the cameras. Despite his heavy beard and moustache, Deke Da Silva (Stallone), a New York City decoy cop ('the gung-ho Lone Ranger of the Street Crime Unit') poses as a woman to ensnare muggers, but finds himself and his buddy Matthew Fox (Billy Dee Williams) pulled off the streets to join the Anti-Terrorist Action Command, a special force that fights international terrorism. The arch-criminal behind a series of worldwide bombings is the ruthless Wulfgar (Rutger Hauer), but Da Silva is reluctant to adopt the shoot-to-kill attitudes insisted on by the assignment's boss Hartman (Nigel Davenport).

'You're training us to be nothing but assassins, and the only difference between him and us will be the badge ... I didn't join the force to kill people,' says Da Silva.

Hartman tells him the only way to combat violence is with greater violence, offering advice that one John Rambo would pick up on in future years. Hartman reminds Da Silva that his wife Irene (a negligible role for Lindsay Wagner) has already left him for his 'cop on the beat mentality', and points out that in Vietnam Da Silva distinguished himself with fifty-two registered kills.

The chase for Wulfgar eventually boils down to a personal vendetta between the terrorist and Da Silva, his resolve strengthened when Fox is injured, and consolidated when Wulfgar's accomplice Shakka (Persis Khambatta) murders Hartman. Wulfgar hijacks a cable-car, and Da Silva is winched aboard to rescue the baby of the woman Wulfgar has assassinated. Holding the passengers to ransom, Wulfgar's demands transport and escape arrangements, but the bus in which he makes his getaway crashes into the river. Wulfgar's body is not found. We see Wulfgar returning to Irene's home. He gets into the house and approaches her, ready to stab her in the back. She turns, and we see it is Da Silva masquerading as his wife. He shoots Wulfgar dead.

There was nothing very interesting about *Nighthawks*, lumbered as it was with its silly plot. With much more than a nine o'clock shadow, Da Silva seemed a little hirsute to be dancing down the streets dressed as a woman – the most short-sighted mugger might have been expected to notice this. And besides being implausible, the people were not in the least interesting, with Da Silva's domestic problems dragged in to give his character more depth. The audience's feelings, however, were not engaged. Indeed, *Nighthawks* was remarkable only for one or two things – it was the only film in which Stallone wore a beard and, more tellingly, it was the first movie he made as a major star in which violence was a crucial ingredient (if you accept that *Rocky*'s violence is merely incidental or, looking at it another way, merely sport).

When, after a delay that suggested the studio wasn't altogether happy with it, it reached the screen, *Nighthawks* was largely regarded as the undistinguished little action adventure it was. Its villain, the up-and-coming Dutch blond actor Rutger

Hauer, stole what little praise was forthcoming, but for him the movie had proved a sad affair, and he left no doubt as to why this was so:

'I had to fight on that film all the time, fighting to preserve my character. I was really fighting with Stallone, to keep what was in the script because he saw it as some competitive thing and he always wanted to ruin my part. I have never been so aware, so awake as on that film.'

Any student of Stallone's career can well imagine him holding his hands up in horror at what had happened in *Nighthawks*. The bad guy had been allowed to become more interesting than the good guy, and when that good guy was played by Sylvester Stallone, the grossness of the injustice was clear. Identified forever with the image of the all-conquering Rocky, Stallone had so turned his back on the losers he had played around with in the scripts he had churned out in his Hemingwayesque tiro period, that a revival of such attitudes had to be resisted.

Some of the problems were quite basic. He complained that Hauer was simply getting too much screen time, and that the whole film was biased in favour of the villain. This might have sounded petulant, but Poll succumbed to the suggestion to the extent of preparing a second edited version of the film which was tried out alongside the original version on preview audiences. The bad news for Stallone was that they preferred the version where Hauer was more prominently in the picture, and the Stallone-biased version was ditched. The displeased star criticized the film's moral imbalance, but, at the last moment, nobody had listened.

Billy Dee Williams, who had described Stallone as 'a perfectionist, quite brilliant', admitted that the star had expressed 'strong ideas that weren't always accepted on the set'.

Nighthawks suggested once again that, outside of *Rocky*, Stallone might not find a ready audience, but the final version 'was not the movie I set out to make. They re-cut it and made it a formula film. It was originally a movie with a whole underground of subsidiary characters that they just eliminated. It turned into a standard cop-chase film, which was better off not being made at all'.

8   Eye of the Tiger

Shortly after completing *Nighthawks*, Stallone flew to Budapest to begin work on his next movie, *Escape to Victory*, or – as it was called in America – *Victory*. It must have seemed like a good idea at the time. It had an international cast (more starry than anything Stallone had done before), a sporting theme (football) melded into a war adventure, and a truly great director. There seemed no foreseeable way it could fail.

'This film is the first chance I've had in a long time to just act and relax without any responsibilities,' said Stallone.

It was to be directed by the 74-year-old John Huston, just recovered from a serious illness, whose outstanding contribution to cinema had included such classics as *The Maltese Falcon* (his first effort, which he had also scripted, in 1941), *Key Largo, The African Queen* and, in 1972, *Fat City*, a film where boxing had been exposed as the sad, degrading thing it had never seemed in *Rocky*. It would be the first time Stallone had worked with so distinguished a director, and the extraordinary line-up of the film's players, headed by Michael Caine and Max Von Sydow, was another incentive, as well as the inclusion of a whole team of real international footballers including the Brazilian Pelé, the Argentinian Osvaldo Ardiles and British Bobby Moore.

Despite the personal troubles Stallone was going through at the time, he gave himself over to the physical preparation for playing the brawny athlete who gets to play goalie in one of the most unusual sporting events ever held. He shaved off the *Nighthawks* image and slimmed down for the movie via 300 daily sit-ups, weight-lifting and rope-skipping, and by the time filming began he looked in peak form; not that the scenes on the playing-field came easily to him.

'I liked everything about soccer, except the pain,' he said, referring to a broken finger, water on the knee, three cracked ribs and various other minor injuries that he sustained during the shoot.

To avoid such troubles, the original idea had been to have a real-life goalkeeper disguised as Stallone and standing in for him during the crucial game scenes, but Stallone insisted on the part being all his own work. He set about adding football to the list of sports he had conquered for his Rocky followers.

The original script, not surprisingly, had him as a superhuman saviour, a not unlikely extension of his Rocky persona which the scriptwriters probably thought might be a bankable idea. True to form, however, Stallone insisted on having his say apropos the shooting script, and saw an opportunity to bring off a perfectly Rockyesque miracle to close the picture. During the final moments of the film Stallone suggested his character should leave the net, run upfield and score the equalizing goal. Bobby Moore tactfully pointed out to Huston that such a thing was, to put it mildly, a little unlikely. As it turned out, it would at least have been in tune with the rest of the movie. Maurice Roeves, playing in *Escape to Victory* a facsimile of the role played by James Garner in *The Great Escape*, suggested that the outcome of the crucial football match should hinge on a dubious penalty given to the Germans by a biased referee. Huston accepted the idea, and the scene was shot.

Roeves recalled to me that 'just as the penalty kicker is running back to kick the ball, Sly, in his wonderful manner, comes out of the goal mouth, walks right up to the kicker and gives him the Muhammad Ali glare, which worked terrifically. It was very funny, very clever. Sad to say, I didn't receive my assistant director's credit'.

The twelve-week schedule was made more difficult by the depressing effect Budapest had on Stallone. The production had gone to Hungary to keep the slated budget of $15 million down, for facilities, locations and – crucial in a movie that demanded thousands of spectators for the final sequence – extras, came cheap, but the oppressiveness of the regime and the dull greyness of the people's lives were anathema to Stallone, who probably felt a dose of *Rocky* heroism would work wonders for them.

Not that he saw much of Hungary. During gaps in the schedule he got out of the country as much as possible. Roeves remembers one Friday afternoon when Stallone was in a great hurry to get to Paris, and left Daniel Massey to play a scene with his stand-in (a role helpfully filled by Roeves himself). When the star returned from his weekend trip he had, says Roeves, 'a huge grin on his face'. Though Stallone got on well with Caine – the two men, after all, had not dissimilar histories – Stallone wasn't the great social bear some of the company had imagined. Caine enjoyed eating with the company at some riotous evenings in a local restaurant, but Stallone stayed away.

'He's archetypal Hollywood rags to riches,' Daniel Massey told me, 'and his story of how Rocky came to pass is one for the history books. I came to like him, but the initial impact is of a very guarded, rather chippy and, in some ways, insecure person, clinging wherever he can to status.'

Another fellow actor on the movie, Michael Cochrane, found Stallone sympathetic and genuinely considerate, describing him to me as 'a good actor who looked you in the eye and got on with it – no messing. And helpful. He "knew" the camera from both sides, suggested I might turn this way or that to favour me rather than him. Pretty unusual! Thoroughly professional and thoroughly pleasant to all'.

Huston seemed just as approving, making a point of announcing to the press that he had found his star to be 'as modest as one could hope for. He couldn't be more disciplined'. The truth was rather different. Huston got on famously with Caine and Pelé (whom Roeves describes as 'a great human being') but couldn't begin to warm to Stallone. Huston didn't even bother to direct, or even watch over, some of Stallone's scenes, leaving them in the hands of his assistant, Tom Shaw. It was an unmistakably dismissive gesture from one of Hollywood's legendary directors, who obviously didn't rank Stallone with some of the greats he had worked with in the past. But Stallone, at least in the early stages, remained disciplined, just as Huston had said, and discipline was clearly needed if anyone on *Escape to Victory* (a recklessly optimistic title) was to get through it.

At a press conference, Huston was asked why he made movies. 'For two reasons,' he answered. 'Either because I like them, or for money.' 'Why are you making this one?' the reporter asked. There was a pause before Huston replied, 'For both reasons.'

The story of *Escape to Victory* was fanciful and derivative. At a

German POW camp, Major Von Steiner (Von Sydow), a Nazi who in 1938 played football for Germany, sees some British prisoners playing the game under the leadership of Colby (Caine), and asks Colby if he would like to head a POW team against a German team. Colby tells him he won't agree if it's confined to officers: he wants a decent team, he wants the lads. But Steiner's homely, good-natured idea is taken up by Nazi HQ, which organizes a huge match in Paris as a propaganda exercise at which, of course, the prisoners will be defeated. The camp's escape committee want their players to make an escape with the assistance of the French Resistance. Hatch (Stallone), whom Colby grudgingly takes on as a trainer ('I just wanna be around the guys,' Hatch cries), is to be the contact who will set up arrangements for the escape.

Hatch breaks out, meets the Resistance, develops a hopeless and brief affection for a pretty freedom fighter, and then has to get recaptured by the Germans so that he is returned to the camp where he can pass information back to the team. Colby persuades Steiner that Hatch is needed as goalie (not surprisingly, as Colby has deliberately broken the real goalkeeper's arm), and the team travel to Paris where, by half-time, they are heading for a tremendous defeat at the hands of the enemy. The escape has been planned for half-time, but the sturdy players, with true patriotic grit, insist on going back and giving the Germans hell until the end of the game, at which time they made a speedy exit to their dressing-rooms and freedom.

If this sounded faintly like Julie Andrews and the Von Trapps escaping in *The Sound of Music*, Bill Conti's music sounded all too much like the score of *The Great Escape*, and had a whistling theme that was heavily reminiscent of another perky war-film score.

Stallone, in fact, was the best thing in the film, despite wearing probably the most restricting pair of shorts ever seen on any footballer. His entire wardrobe, looking as if it had been borrowed from Cosmo in *Paradise Alley*, seemed rather superior wartime issue, beautifully laundered. One anonymous member of the cast, when the star's spotlessly clean vest worn in the tunnel scene was pointed out, smiled and said, 'That's Stallone, I'm afraid. He just couldn't bear to be seen in a grubby vest.'

But he did manage a few typically Stallone touches with one

or two lines that sounded suspiciously like his own, though he wasn't credited with having written any dialogue. In the changing-rooms, he chatters on about 'any little inconveniences like anal bleeding, tuberculosis, growing tumours. I'm just trying to get a little team spirit going here, right guys?'

Tim Pigott-Smith, another of the distinguished British actors playing opposite Stallone in the movie, feels that 'at the beginning, Sly was very friendly and incredibly committed. He really threw himself into it and was really working hard. He took the job very, very seriously. Up to a point, I thought Sly was almost taking Huston's place and getting in there, trying to motivate the thing in a very strong way'.

That commitment wasn't reflected by the production team, and during the last few weeks of filming Stallone was heavily involved in the writing of the next *Rocky* movie. Nobody seemed able to focus interest on the job in hand. One day Max Von Sydow was asked to give two directly opposing interpretations of his performance to two cameras at the same time; the superb professional, he did the two things alternately, and never turned a hair. Meanwhile, Tim Pigott-Smith looked on as Stallone's interest waned.

'Sly got disillusioned, and his attitude changed. He started arriving late on the set in the mornings, and behaving unprofessionally – I think, encouraged by his management team. They advised him badly, and to some extent encouraged him to behave badly. And you wouldn't get that from Michael or Max. No way. I felt Sly let himself down by beginning to transfer his interest to something he was completely committed to.'

Sometimes the star's behaviour could seem quite petty. In probably the most effective scene of the movie, Stallone had a dialogue with Clive Merrison, who gave a wittily observed performance and was well served by Huston working at his very best. It was at times like this that Stallone pulled rank. He simply wouldn't speak to Merrison, but addressed all his comments to him via the director. In such ways, Stallone removed himself from the movie.

Escape to Victory was naturally handicapped by having actors who couldn't play football and footballers who couldn't act, even after Caine's cheery advice to them to 'just fucking say the lines'. And it abounded in laughable stereotypes: a nasty Nazi wearing an eye-patch; a nicer Nazi (Von Sydow) at first as inscrutable as Emperor Ming but then realizing that the rules of fair play had been sacrificed to the glory of Hitler, and an escape committee of English types, dressed up in cardigans and moustaches, that provided its own parody. 'I don't think London is going to take very kindly to this,' says Daniel Massey, doing a marvellous Noël Coward impression as the committee's supremo, Waldron.

Ultimately, the picture got the thumbs-down from Stallone for whom it 'wasn't worth the time and sweat that went into it, because it never started to live up to the way it was conceived'.

At least the critics agreed with him. Tom Milne in the *Monthly Film Bulletin* dismissed it as 'ludicrous beyond belief' and suggested that 'even readers of the *Boys' Own Paper* might have blenched', while in *Films and Filming* Adrian Turner thought that 'where Huston seems content with providing a harmless romp, the script seems determined to invest the narrative with layers of political significance and allegory ... the script simply scores a succession of own goals'. And Turner went on to be the wag who praised the fact that 'the film and the match don't go into extra time'.

In her book on films and the Holocaust, *Indelible Shadows*, Annette Insdorf had a less flippant condemnation of the film.

'(The film) presents an ultimately pernicious illusion about Nazis, their prisoners, and the bravery of the average Frenchman,' she wrote, going on to suggest that 'the benign Nazi – in a film that contains no contrasting image of a German soldier – is a distortion.' *Escape to Victory*, she concluded, was 'closer to Rocky Plays Ball with the Nazis than to a realistic assessment of the relationship between the SS and captured Allies'.

The best thing about the Hungary episode was the reconciliation with Sasha that began when he telephoned her and begged her to fly out to him, sure that they could make their marriage work again. Personally, he was at his lowest ebb.

'I felt that it was over,' he said. 'I was finished. This was it. This film would probably be my last. I just didn't care anymore. The fame game had gotten me. I was lost.'

For Sasha, all hope had not been abandoned.

'There is a deep love between us,' she said, 'that goes beyond living together. Sly never humiliated me. Perhaps he was a humiliation to himself. I have no desire to get even with him.'

Sasha's astrologer (who hadn't been called Jacqueline) had earlier told Sasha she would meet the man of her dreams on her birthday, 17 July, and when the day came, she found herself in Budapest with her estranged husband. He told her he wanted to get back to the people he had loved and trusted before success had changed him, while she, in a speech that sounded something like what Adrian would be telling Rocky in a few months' time, brought him, at least temporarily, out of his darkness.

'You've got to stop acting for other people,' she insisted, 'or just for money. Or for me. You've got to do it for yourself. Otherwise, you're going to hate yourself for the rest of your life.' Now, it seemed as if Stallone was listening to her warnings. She was gratified that he agreed to come back to her. He was coming home. That home was a French style country house in Pacific Palisades, guarded by a battery of security cameras and kept away from the world outside by high walls. Whatever their marriage would be, it would mostly be conducted within the enclave of this little fortress.

When filming closed on *Escape to Victory*, Roeves tried to get Stallone to play Benedick in his proposed Los Angeles stage production of Shakespeare's *Much Ado About Nothing*. Roeves had developed an admiration for Stallone, and thought, if Stallone would trust to his direction, that he would bring a great deal to the role. Stallone seemed interested, but this fascinating challenge wasn't taken up because Stallone couldn't fit the play into his schedule. There is little doubt, however, that in playing Benedick, Stallone would have been putting his reputation as an actor very much on the line, even if only in the relative privacy of a Los Angeles theatre.

Meanwhile, the need to revive Rocky and re-energize his particular American Dream was arising almost naturally, and it is not difficult to see how. The desolation and depression he had seen in Hungary had made him realize, again, how important a triumphant streak of heroism was; his coming together again with Sasha had been a crucial stepping-stone. As he said, 'After *Rocky II*, I wanted to finish the trilogy, but I didn't have a valid story … until it happened to me. I said, my God, this really is a godsend.'

Another factor helped clear the way for Stallone at this

Rocky at home in the ring. In the *Rocky* films the bum boxer lived out the story of Stallone's own life.

Stallone surrounded by *Rocky* memorabilia. The *Rocky* industry was colossal, but its very success often undermined Stallone's other projects.

Directing *Rocky III*. Making the film, Stallone admitted 'your movie set becomes your reality and your real life is the fantasy'.

Despite the thoughtful gaze, Stallone spent years trying to convince cinema-goers he was not as slow as Rocky.

period: religion. His secretary introduced him to Bernice Osman of the Church of the New World Unity who, according to her new disciple, gave off 'a lot of positive energy. She's a magical person'. Even on touching her hand, he felt a strange sense of power coming from her. The prayers in the cult's 'bible', written by Bernice's husband Alan, were a constant source of consolation and inspiration to Stallone, who buried himself in its edicts.

'I accept the responsibility to be in divine love at all times,' was only one of the beliefs the Church of the New World Unity supported him in.

The way to *Rocky III* was now clear, the latest parable of the life of Sylvester Stallone, the bum from nowhere who had climbed and won and lost his way again, seemed unable to hold on to what he had, and then regained it through the twin magics of a woman's love and self-determination. If it wasn't a very subtle mirroring of real life, it was potent, and when the screenplay was done, Stallone began to prepare for Rocky's third screen call.

Under the guidance of trainer Ray Nataro, Stallone now wanted – far more than in either of the earlier Rocky stories – to reach the physical standard of a true boxer. Once again, diet and a strict training regime ruled him.

Ten raw egg whites a day and a quarter slice of burned toast (burned so that it contained no water) and no dinner – this was the intake he restricted his body to. He then expected it to go eighteen rounds of sparring, a two-mile run, two hours of lifting weights, and another run in the evening. By the time *Rocky III* was ready for production, he had worked himself to an incredible 29½-inch waist and 47-inch chest. He had reduced his body fat level to 4½ per cent; the average American carries 15 to 20 per cent. As had happened before, however, he pushed himself too far. During a swimming practice he collapsed in the pool and had to be given oxygen. But the pace didn't let up.

'On *Rocky III* I'd be up at six, work all day, do the boxing, eat my dinner while watching dailies till ten, then go and work out until eleven-thirty, finally going to bed at twelve … Your movie set becomes your reality and your real life is the fantasy. It's an unreal existence.'

For *Rocky III*, Apollo is retired, which meant a new opponent, and one that would eclipse anything pussycat Apollo had ever been. Stallone's original hope was to have the new adversary, Clubber Lang, played by a real fighter, which would have been a meaningful compliment to the star's physical prowess. But after auditioning Joe Frazier and heavyweight contender Ernie Shavers and facing their formidable punches, Stallone decided against it.

The part was eventually landed by a sort of performer calling himself 'Mr T' – real name Lawrence Tero – who had been a distinguished bouncer and had also acted as bodyguard to Diana Ross and to Ali himself. With his brilliant black physique, long feathered ear-rings, brutal Mohawk hairstyle, and jabbing tongue, he was a ready-made character whom even Stallone couldn't have begun to invent. Though his acting was pretty basic, Mr T played Ali even more than Weathers had played Ali, and there was a vicious side to Lang's character that Apollo's had never come close to. Mr T would go on to find television fame as the jewel-encrusted member of *The A-Team*.

When Stallone first worked on the script of the new movie he decided that, this being the last part of what he saw as a trilogy, Rocky should die at the end of the picture. On the way home, he puts his head on Adrian's shoulder and, tired but victorious, dies. The studio, however, didn't like it, or the idea that they might have to re-incarnate him if there was a fourth Rocky, and anyway – as Stallone himself realized – it would have been the ultimate downer. Less drastic events were mapped out for the hero.

Fireworks spell out Rocky's name in celebration of his winning the world championship from Apollo Creed, and he begins a series of title defences, vanquishing every opponent as Mickey and Adrian cheer him on. In the crowd, we see the up-and-coming black challenger Clubber Lang ('Mr T') who wants to fight Rocky, but Rocky is busy enjoying the rich life, sharply suited and gliding effortlessly through commercials for credit-cards when he isn't embracing Adrian, flowers in her hair. Paulie is still drinking and complaining about how unjust life has been to him. Mickey, more wizened and tired looking than before, has moved into the palatial Balboa residence.

Rocky takes on a charity fight but is horrified to see his opponent, the massive blond wrestler Thunderlips (Hulk Hogan), 'The Ultimate Object of Desire'. Mickey tells Rocky nobody would do so much for charity; Rocky tells him Bob

Hope would. Thunderlips goes berserk and almost slaughters his opponent, but Rocky comes back at him and the match is declared a draw. The wrestler happily poses with Rocky, Adrian and Rocky Jnr. for a friendly Polaroid.

When Rocky unveils a statue of himself on the steps of the Philadelphia Art Museum, he is close to tears as he announces his retirement from the ring. Lang comes out of the crowd to challenge Rocky to a title defence before quitting, claiming that all the matches he has played since winning the championship have been nothing but set-ups. Rocky is fired to take up the challenge, but Mickey refuses to have anything to do with it, and stalks back to the house where he packs his bags. Rocky follows, and Mickey tells him that Lang is a real threat. And Mickey tells him more: that the worst thing has happened to Rocky that could happen to any fighter – he has become civilized. He tells him that all his opponents have been hand-picked, easy-to-lick fighters chosen by Mickey who has been keeping his protégé healthy and winning. Rocky, close to tears, explains that he can't retire knowing what he knows, that he needs the one last fight against Lang, that he needs Mickey to train him. Mickey agrees, but Rocky's training is little more than a publicity circus, while Lang's fierce no-nonsense preparation for the bout ensures he is on killing form.

On the night of the match Mickey collapses when Lang pushes him to one side in the dressing-room. Rocky wants to cancel the fight but Mickey snaps at Rocky to get out and 'do it'. Adrian stays backstage to nurse Mickey, and a doctor is called.

In the second round Lang flattens Rocky and wrests the championship from him. The battered Rocky staggers back to Mickey and, wanting the old man to die happy, tells him that he has won the match.

'I love you, kid. I love you,' whispers Mickey, and dies. Rocky falls, wracked with sobbing, on to his body. After the funeral, he wanders through his old haunts and, defeated and demoralized, goes back to Mickey's gym where Apollo is waiting for him with an offer to become his trainer and promoter.

'You had that eye of the tiger, that edge,' Apollo tells him, 'and the way to get it back is to go back to the beginning.'

Rocky starts training in the broken-down gym where Apollo started, but he is sluggish and tired and finally Apollo tells him his days as a fighter are over. Rocky admits to his fears when

Adrian steps in to deliver a pep-talk by the sea. She tells him he must do it for himself alone and that if he loses he will be losing 'with no excuses, no fear'. The impact on Rocky is dramatic; he trains like a champion and, after a race along the beach with Apollo, the two cavort triumphantly in each other's arms among the splashing waves.

Lang promises to demolish Rocky, but Rocky defeats him and recaptures the world championship. Apollo claims the favour he has earlier asked of Rocky – a friendly, private sparring match.

'In *Rocky III*,' said Stallone in 1982, 'I learned two things. Don't beat people over the head with the drama if you already have a strong theme, and time your punches like a fighter. That way one's enough, just like in the ring.'

If box-office performance was the yardstick by which this recipe for success was measured, the lesson had been well learned. The returns fell over themselves to break records. *Rocky III* grossed a new record of $16 million in its first four days showing in the US, for though *Superman II* had taken more, it had run in 4,558 more theatres than *Rocky III*. After *E.T.*, it became the highest grosser of 1982, turning in an extraordinary performance for a sequel, far outstripping both *Rocky* and *Rocky II*. By the end of the year it had returned over $66 million to the studio.

There was no doubt that audiences were still fascinated in Rocky's life, as if his fictional existence was being lived out, along the years, in parallel to their own. The fact that the movie now showed signs of working to a formula didn't seem to matter, for the formula worked. Rocky triumphs in the first few moments of film (a carry-over of the previous film's finale), Rocky stumbles, doubts, fails, cries, Adrian and a strong male friend revive his beliefs, Rocky does a training montage, Rocky wins.

Perhaps in a subliminal way the public looked to Stallone to strip his own life bare in the guise of Rocky, and to a large extent this had been Stallone's intention throughout the series. Rocky got rich, got easy, got blasé, just as Stallone had, though the actor's marital problems – not a minor matter in the star's life – were not transferred over to the screen version (a philandering Rocky would surely have risked losing his audience's sympathy). In *Rocky III*, our street hero looks suspiciously like a smoothie and – worse – his marvellous waywardness with language seems almost to have deserted him in a script that has none of the wit of *Rocky II*.

There was also a sense of sheer violence in the new movie that took the story down roads it had not travelled before. Even before meeting Lang, we recognize Thunderlips as a killer simply out to inflict pain. There is no development of character, so that the violent aspect of the character is all we have to hold on to. And though Apollo is not exactly multi-dimensional, he does engage our sympathy (even when fighting Rocky) in a way Lang never could. Lang is uncouth, hideously aggressive and with no hint of fun. Rocky's enemies are here revealed to be really bad meat, and perhaps Rocky's own character suffers because of it.

Adrian's doubts about the fight game certainly seem to have been overcome, for we see her as cheer-leader at the ringside, even accompanied by her little son, come to watch Daddy being battered. Neither does her new-found wealth seem to have helped her; her attitude to the servants is shown to be superior, and she and Rocky seem only to care about each other and their own little world. The quite interesting loan shark Gazzo, so well played by Joe Spinell in the first two *Rocky* epics, has vanished, but Paulie remains as objectionable as ever. For the rest, the street corner kids and their beautifully harmonized impro-visations have gone, the elevated railway no longer runs, the pet shop is perhaps under new management and is not seen, Mickey has even left his grim apartment to sit among the gilded emptiness of the Balboa mansion. This Rocky, in fact, is corrupted, and the new awareness that he has much to lose pervades the film. Under such circumstances, even Rocky becomes perhaps less lovable.

When filming was over, the division between its fantasy and the real world blurred again. It occurred to Stallone and the production team that it would be a worthwhile gesture if the statue used in the film were presented to the Philadelphia Art Museum, to stand at the top of the steps that had come to epitomize Rocky's triumph over physical and spiritual poverty. The sculptor, A. Thomas Schomberg, had spent months building the 8½-foot bronze representation of Philadelphia's street hero for a fee of $60,000. As he unveiled it, an emotional Stallone said, 'You can break that statue into a million pieces and you'd find a piece of it in every Philadelphian ... It belongs to you.'

A bemused museum board didn't quite know how to react to this munificent present, but finally decided to give it back to their benefactor. The statue sat in Stallone's back yard until a stalwart gang of supporters persuaded the city fathers to take the statue to a sports stadium, The Spectrum, well known for its many boxing matches. In a spirit of good will, the museum agreed to place the statue at the top of their steps for a few weeks before it found its final resting-place.

A similar reserve to that of the museum's keepers was found among the critics when *Rocky III* showed up in May 1982.

Tom Milne, a great admirer of the original *Rocky*, now felt it was time for his hero to take the final count. The *New Yorker* looked back to the original *Rocky*, which it thought had been 'primitive in a relatively innocent way. (*Rocky III*) is primitive too, but it's also shrewd and empty and inept'.

Danny Peary found it 'lacks the cohesion of his earlier efforts', and in *Films and Filming* Derek Elley gave his recipe for Stallone's latest movie: 'Press a button – out comes the script; season with blood, tears and sweat; lay Conti's music tracks over several montage sequences; light the blue touch paper and retire laughing.'

. In the *New Musical Express* however, Richard Cook was unstinting in his welcome: 'Cinema is many things to me,' he wrote, 'but if any film this year has made me want to stand up and cheer, head and heart bursting, it is *Rocky III* ... Stallone renews film's ability to transcend: Rocky's jousting is ecstatic in its suspension of disbelief.'

During the 1982 promotion tour for the film, Stallone visited Glasgow and offered a glowing vision – perhaps influenced by the teachings of Mrs Osman – of what his audiences might expect from him in the future.

'I want to do something now for the younger generation,' he said, 'something spiritual. I'm not out to preach religion, but there does have to be something that separates us from other animals. I think they call it soul, and I'm going to try to portray on the screen what I find out.'

The spirituality of Stallone's next contribution to cinema was not, however, always clear to his critics. Whatever the qualities of the character Stallone was about to introduce into the

American consciousness, saintliness was almost certainly not one of them. At least, Jacqueline's famous son seemed still to nurse quite modest ideas about his own capabilities. 'My problem,' he said, 'is that my ambitions far exceed my abilities. That's a real bummer. So if I have a mind to do Hamlet, I then have to resign myself to doing it in the shower.'

But it wasn't always easy to feel sorry for his predicament. There had been a chance offered by Maurice Roeves to show the world that Stallone could even tackle Shakespeare, but he had passed it up. Instead, he introduced a new character into his repertoire, a character that would have a devastating effect on his career and fortune. Eventually, Stallone would look upon the character as little more than the modern equivalent of an Elizabethan dumb-show. Without knowing it, he was again starting out on a road that he would have to travel down many times.

9   Enter Rambo

With the tremendous success of *Rocky III* behind him, Stallone was again riding the rainbow after the dips of *Nighthawks* and *Escape to Victory*, and about to set out on another phase of his career with the portrayal of a new character that would have an extraordinary effect on the American consciousness, outstripping anything *Rocky* had ever achieved. The character would give Stallone a place not only in histories of the cinema but in histories of the United States. That character was John Rambo.

Warner Bros had bought the rights of David Morrell's novel after its publication in 1972, and a script had been prepared but never used, until Mario Kassar and Andrew Vajna came along. Under the auspices of Carolco Services, they were experienced at selling the films of independent producers to the international market, and had built up an excellent understanding of the sort of product ideal for these customers. It seemed a natural progression for them to set up a production of their own, and they picked up on Morrell's novel, recognizing its potential as a superb vehicle for Stallone. He agreed to star for a fee of $3.5 million, providing he had script control. Ted Kotcheff, the Canadian director of *Life at the Top* and *The Apprenticeship of Danny Kravitz* (and a famed television play, *Edna the Inebriate Woman*), was brought in as director.

At first, Stallone had doubts about the popularity of the film's theme.

'I had thought the subject matter was out of vogue,' he said. 'The way I saw it, people didn't want to remember the war. But the picture went beyond the war, got into morality and man's dignity and civil rights.'

Hollywood's treatment of the Vietnam horror said as much about the motherland's sensitive social adjustments to the conflict as about Hollywood's film makers. John Wayne was one of the first to break silence on the subject with the 1968 *The Green Berets*, in which John Rambo himself might well have been one of the extras. Wayne's cut-and-dried enmity of the Viet Cong struck a ready chord with audiences back home. In *First Blood*, of course, Rambo is not really required to give us his views on the Viet Cong – here, he is only concerned about the enemies he has found after leaving the war behind. In subsequent movies, Rambo would see things very much through the eyes of a John Wayne, but in *First Blood* the outright patriotism of the central character was distinctly muted.

From the start, Stallone took the portrayal of Rambo seriously. He wanted to understand the particular plight of the Vietnam veteran, the hero (if not always conquering) returning home to a society that preferred to forget the devastating blow the Vietnam War had dealt to America's confidence. What *First Blood* would do would be to reawaken the difficult truths about America's own lost generation. Rambo would stand to remind the people of things they would rather have forgotten.

Filming of *First Blood* began in November 1981 in and around Hope, British Columbia, and the Golden Ears Park, in one of the worst winters the area had experienced for years. Freezing rain and snow made the shoot even more difficult than it was already bound to be. For Stallone, the physical demands were as extreme as anything he had endured for *Rocky*, and here he was also dealing with timed explosions and stunts that most other actors would have taken one look at and handed over to a stunt man.

In fact, Stallone did use a stunt man to make Rambo's hair-raising jump into a canyon; Stallone was then filmed making a mere 4-foot drop into the branches of a tree, but he landed badly, and the short journey left him with four broken ribs. His co-star Brian Dennehy cracked three ribs in a scene in which he fell through a skylight, and cut his hand against Stallone's 15-inch hunting knife, part of Rambo's crucial survival armoury. A mistimed explosion left Stallone with a burned hand, and the scene where Rambo knocks a passing motorcyclist off his machine and drives off on it, left him with a cracked vertebra and a pulled back muscle.

These were not the only troubles *First Blood* had to get through, however. The extraordinary arsenal of weapons used in the film was carefully guarded, but thieves managed to walk off with $50,000 worth of them. Professional gun runners were suspected. The other blow the production had to recover from was the loss of Stallone's co-star, Kirk Douglas.

Douglas had been among Stallone's favourite stars – after all, Stallone's screen persona owed not a little to the sort of figure Douglas himself had cut for the silver shadows – and, in a career that had not been distinguished by the number of big Hollywood names he had worked with, Stallone had looked forward to a promising pairing. But, after only a few days shooting, it was clear all was not well between the two men.

Stallone's far-reaching influence over the whole project was probably to blame again, for Douglas had apparently believed he would be allowed some script control, certainly over his own scenes; this conflicted with Stallone's understanding. And when it came to the final scene, the great emotional outburst that Rambo pours out on his old commander, there was a problem about whose scene it would be. Kotcheff had also previously agreed to go along with Douglas's insistence that Trautman would kill Rambo in the final moments, in line with the hero's fate in Morrell's novel. As this would in effect have proved that Rambo's behaviour had been wrong throughout (and deserving of execution), this ending was hardly likely to find favour with Stallone or the producers. Apart from any more aesthetic consideration, it would have ruled out any sequel. It became clear to Douglas that Kotcheff and the producers would go with Stallone's viewpoint, and a disappointed and not surprisingly rather miffed Douglas withdrew from the picture. His place was taken by a competent character actor, Richard Crenna, who would stay with Stallone throughout the Rambo series.

The screenplay of *First Blood* developed very much along the lines of Morrell's novel. John Rambo, a solitary wanderer across America, goes to look up a buddy from the Vietnam War, but the friend has died of cancer brought on by Agent Orange. Now, Rambo is the only survivor of the unit he fought with. He walks into a town rather inappropriately called Hope, and is picked up by the sheriff Teasle (Brian Dennehy) who tells him they don't want people like him in the town. Teasle drives him over the bridge and points him out of town, but Rambo turns around and walks straight back over the bridge.

Teasle arrests Rambo, 'just another smartarse drifter', for

vagrancy, and takes him back to the police station where the masochistic Galt (Jack Starrett) roughs him up. The prisoner won't have his fingerprints taken. He is hosed down and the police are puzzled at the horrific scars that cover his body. Throughout these processes, Rambo is haunted by the treatment he received as a prisoner of the Viet Cong, incarcerated in a pit in the ground. When the police prepare to shave him, the sight of the razor is the trigger to his violent attack on his warders.

Fighting his way out into the street, Rambo pushes a passing motorcyclist off his machine and escapes into the wooded hills above the town. Tracker dogs are brought in to find him. Galt rides a helicopter which tracks Rambo to the edge of a ravine. Galt shoots to kill Rambo, but Rambo jumps into the ravine, where the branches of a tree break his fall. Galt forces the pilot to follow Rambo down into the gorge, for he is intent on killing him. Rambo throws a stone at the helicopter screen which smashes. The pilot loses control and Galt falls to his death.

Rambo offers to give himself up to Teasle, but his trigger-happy men keep firing at their escaped prey. Teasle learns that Rambo is a Green Beret, a war hero with the Congressional Medal of Honour. 'Those Green Berets, they're real bad asses,' says one of the men, but Teasle, angered at the death of Galt, is now more determined to catch Rambo. The dogs close in on their quarry, but Rambo has set traps of sharpened spikes, and the dogs are impaled on them. The men understand this is no ordinary police chase.

'We ain't huntin' him,' says a greenhorn policeman, 'he's huntin' us.'

Teasle's men are ingeniously trapped by Rambo's jungle warfare techniques, suffering hideous injuries. Teasle himself is caught and Rambo warns that he will give Teasle a war he won't believe. Colonel Trautman (Crenna), Rambo's commander from the Vietnam War, arrives to tell Teasle he is dealing with no ordinary man. Trautman, not God, made Rambo, and he has come to rescue Teasle from him. Rambo has been trained to survive the most cruel conditions, to kill by attrition, to ignore pain, to withstand all weathers, to eat things that would make a billy-goat puke. Trautman tries to persuade Teasle to drop his pursuit, but Teasle says he has his duty to do. Trautman tells Teasle he can't win against Rambo.

But Trautman tries to talk Rambo out of it, when he speaks to him by radio. Rambo tells him that he is the last of his boys, that all the others have died. Trautman reminds Rambo that he is his friend, and Rambo explains that he had only wanted something to eat; they, not him, had drawn first blood. Part-time reinforcements are brought in to join the hunt, and the police think Rambo is killed when they blow up the entrance to an old mine. But Rambo has escaped into the workings and makes his way through the flooded, rat infested tunnels until he emerges into daylight again. Stealing an army convoy truck, Rambo drives back to Teasle's town for a final showdown. He blows up the gas station and starts exploding the rest of the town, while Teasle's personal mission to get him reaches its apex. Teasle crashes through a skylight and Rambo seems about to kill him when Trautman tells him his mission is over.

Rambo breaks down as he tries, in a naturalistic, somewhat garbled style, to explain his feelings to Trautman. It had never been Rambo's war, but one in which others had got him involved. Rambo had done his best to win the war, but the government had lost it. When he had come home, he had been reviled and spat at by his fellow countrymen who had no idea of what it had all been about. He cries as he tells Trautman of a friend who had died in his arms, his body shot to pieces, his legs blown off. Trautman listens, deeply affected, as Rambo sobs. He folds him to his breast and gently comforts him. Rambo is taken into police custody. Teasle is taken away by ambulance, and will, no doubt, survive.

Despite Rambo's tremendous emotional outburst in the closing moments of the film, far outstripping any similar explosions in his earlier movies, it is difficult to accept Rambo's impassioned soliloquy as an adequate reason, or even excuse, for the devastation he has wreaked. Audiences could be left with the sense that Stallone had piled violence on violence, thrill on thrill, and hoped to vindicate the outrages by Rambo's utter collapse. The horrors Rambo had unleashed thus became the responsibility of the Vietnam War, the local police, and the whole of American society that simply hadn't been able to understand its war heroes. This sort of justifying coda would be tagged on to the end of *Rambo: First Blood Part II*, and *Rambo III*. Rambo's garbled diatribe in *First Blood*, muddled as it is, does at least go some little way to showing why Rambo's mind had flipped; the later Rambo scripts were less fussy about feeling they had to give their hero good enough reasons for his almost ritual slaughtering.

As for *First Blood*'s screenplay, it lay the heart of Morrell's superbly written story bare, and lost most of the novel's shading. Morrell's book is bloody, violent adventure, but it is much besides. Stallone's treatment of the material turned out a bloody, violent adventure, and little besides. The difference is particularly noticeable, for example, in the representation of Teasle. In the novel Teasle is a far more complex, rather sad, figure than Stallone's screenplay begins to suggest. Morrell carefully builds the relationship between the dog-handler and Teasle, telling us much about Teasle's inadequacy.

All this is lost in the film. Dennehy's performance is so skilful that he does manage to make Teasle almost a likeable character, but one can hardly understand his devotion to such sadistic brutes as Galt, while the rest of the police force as shown in the film seem to have strayed out of a pastiche of backyard America by way of Li'l Abner.

The overlay of religiosity in the film can hardly be missed. Rambo's first scene (Stallone at his acting best) has him walking through the misleadingly gentle countryside until he is betrayed, by the often intangible forces that belay him, and ends up in prison. Rambo is then persecuted, not only as Rambo was persecuted in Vietnam, but as Christ was tormented. When Rambo appears in the closing moments of the film, Trautman stands to one side and gazes up at him, and we are left with the impression that Rambo has now quite metamorphosed into an absolute Christ figure. For most of the film, Rambo's actions may also be seen as god-like, if only because he survives against all odds. But if a god, he is a vengeful one.

Trautman, too, does not escape the hints of religious opulence. We first see him silhouetted mysteriously against the light, an image to recall the more memorable appearance of Conrad Veidt as the Christ-like figure in *The Passing of the Third Floor Back*. Trautman is certainly some sort of saviour, either of Teasle or Rambo. Crenna's often rather light approach to the role doesn't rub this in, however, and any superhuman aura seems to fade quite away in the final scene, where his lip trembles dangerously as he listens to his boy's cries. The Green Berets are thus revealed as human, susceptible to all emotions, misunderstood, and Trautman has been allowed to forgive Rambo on behalf of society.

Here, as elsewhere, the psychology at work behind *First Blood* is revealed as being acute, as the film manoeuvres itself into an almost unarguable position of strength. Such deft handling of its material is not always appreciated at a first viewing. What, after all, is its viewpoint? It criticizes the American government, for its actual running of the war ('somebody wouldn't let us win', says Rambo), for its use of Agent Orange, and, after the killing was done, for its treatment of the redundant soldiers. The military, of course, shares some of the responsibility. The American people, too, have played a part in all this, and are also responsible for what Rambo has become.

But having levelled the blame, Rambo, never less than a superbly trained soldier with that unquestioning patriotism that strikes the right sort of chord with all right-thinking Americans, does what any right-minded self-respecting American would do in the same circumstances; he fights to get out of the corner. Rocky, in a milder way, had done the same thing. There may be a case for seeing Rambo as merely a militarist regeneration of Rocky, but such a perception of Rambo is difficult to sustain.

The portrayal of Rambo may, however, be so limited as to cloud our understanding of him. Of John Rambo the person, we know nothing. We learn nothing of his interests, his loves, his hates, what sort of food he likes, what sort of friends he likes. And this is a completely male world (that would change with *First Blood*'s sequel) where Rambo seems not to need a woman, where he never seems to think about one.

Sometimes Stallone would make sweeping statements about the Vietnam conflict, statements that might well have coloured his approach to playing Rambo, and his understanding of the tragic débâcle the war had become.

'Five per cent of that war was fought against Communism,' he said, 'and ninety-five per cent to line the pockets of the big chemical industries.' Much the same sort of accusations had been made in the screenplay of *No Place to Hide*. But the final print of *First Blood* didn't let Rambo come out with any allegations of that sort, only a simplistic pleading for the misunderstood war hero. 'What I want,' said Stallone, 'is to get across his alienation and his wanting to get back into the mainstream of society ... I have dialogue just at the beginning and end. The rest of the time I speak with my body.'

When *First Blood* opened in the United States during October 1982, following an advertising campaign that itself had cost a staggering five million dollars, it took more than twenty million dollars in its first seventeen days.

David McGillivray in *Films and Filming* recognized 'an expertly constructed survival adventure with a fresh and persuasive angle to its social comment' and 'the precise, unstereotyped drawing of the characters'. David Quinlan thought 'it gives its audience what they want in the form of continual, violent, fluid and well-staged action, with a hero it's easy to identify with ... A pity he still has delusions of acting grandeur: with a more straightforward, power-house finish, this could have been, and still nearly is, the action film of the year'. For sheer physical effort on Stallone's part, it probably had been. 'It was the toughest film I was ever involved in,' said Stallone after the shoot had finished. 'Of course I say that with every film I do. So films must either be getting tougher to make or I'm getting softer.'

Stallone's performance may have reminded audiences of primeval values, but off the film set he was still eager to make it clear he was not a walking meatloaf. In July 1982, having emerged from *First Blood*, he talked to Lewis Grossberger of *Rolling Stone* who found that Stallone 'likes big words and literary preferences. He wants you to know that he reads, and he tosses Faulkner, Frost, Dos Passos, James T. Farrell and Edgar Allan Poe into the conversation. It's as though he needs to intercept your presumption of imbecility with a barrage of high-powered verbiage'.

Stallone might have added Tennessee Williams to his list, especially as, in 1981, it seemed certain he would be playing the Marlon Brando role of Stanley Kowalski in *A Streetcar Named Desire* for a cable TV production. By December, however, Stallone had decided to pull out, a decision no doubt influenced by the fact that he would certainly have been compared to Brando, a comparison he was not ready to invite. An interesting project, one that would certainly have tested Stallone's acting talents, was shelved. There was some suggestion, however, that the role worried him.

Other projects also fell through. Stallone had agreed to star in producer Robert Evans' $20 million film *The Cotton Club*, a colourful extravaganza about the famous Harlem nightclub of the twenties and thirties, in a deal that had him paid two million dollars for his performance as well as taking twenty-five per cent of the money saved if the production came in under budget. After agreeing, however, Stallone made it clear through his manager Jerry Weintraub that he wanted changes made, and there were attempts to displace Evans as producer. Three weeks after signing, Stallone withdrew, drawing a bitter response from Evans who wrote to inform Stallone that his behaviour had been 'repugnant, ill-mannered and self-destructive'. Evans went on to wave his one-time star goodbye as he told him, 'I hope Mr Weintraub will find you that magic property that will elevate you to be a bona fide star without having to wear boxing gloves.'

The Cotton Club was eventually directed by Francis Coppola and scripted by *The Godfather*'s Mario Puzo, with Richard Gere stepping into the leading role. The critic Brian Case said of Gere that he 'phones in his performance from the wardrobe department'. If nothing else, there was some consolation for Stallone in the fact that sometimes the critics sharpened their knives for actors other than himself.

10   Fairy-Tales with Music

Perhaps it was surprising that at any stage of his career Stallone should want to do for the musical film what he had done for the good old-fashioned action movie. When it happened, it can have come as no surprise that many of the old autobiographical strands were back in evidence, that the spirit of Rocky himself overshadowed the projects, and that Stallone would want to exercise as much personal control as he could over his bold venture into a genre that was quite foreign to him.

In fact, it was in 1982 that he first agreed on a major musical film which was the first of two musical outings that cut a decidedly distinctive wedge out of his career. In the first of these he would be dealing with a sequel, and there was nothing particularly concerning about this – his box-office pull with the *Rocky* series had made him a king of sequels – except that in this instance he was involved with a follow-up to an original success with which he had no connection whatever. True, the hero of *Saturday Night Fever* had a photograph of Rocky and Adrian on the wall of his apartment, which was some sort of culture acknowledgement to Stallone and the legend he had created, but Stallone had in no other way contributed to the 1977 John Travolta super-hit. He was now charged with bringing in the next episode in the life of the sassy disco dancer Tony Manero: *Staying Alive*. The Bee Gees, who had written the score for *Saturday Night Fever*, would be brought back to write much of the music for the sequel, but this time round a good deal of the score came from Frank Stallone, much to the publicized annoyance of the British pop-group.

Stallone looked forward to working with Travolta, pointing out that 'he's had his problems, I've had my problems, but I think together we can override that ... I'm glad he's going back to this material. But it's no more of the disco and Brooklyn. It's more lonely, solitary. It's about the birth of a young artist'.

John Badham had directed *Saturday Night Fever* and was asked to take on the sequel, 'but I said no, I did that already. And I really don't want to be trying to go home again. I thought it was a smart idea to get Stallone involved – (he and Travolta) do make a cute couple'.

Just how involved the new director was to get was ultimately to give his critics more sticks to beat him with. As well as directing the picture, Stallone co-produced and co-wrote, with all the highly personal colouring this would give the storyline and characterization, as well as signing on his brother to write three of the songs, and – a final irritation to a few – even making a brief non-speaking appearance in the picture himself, brushing up against Travolta in a street scene, and glowering back at the camera. The castigators saw it as evidence that the old ego was still working well, and that it even extended to stealing Hitchcock's quirky little trade mark. What everybody saw was the way that the original concept of the film had undergone telling and not always very subtle changes, metamorphosing from a Travolta vehicle into a Stallone vehicle.

Long before filming commenced on 4 January 1983, this process had begun in earnest. Initially, Stallone's attention was focused on the script which had been prepared by Norman Wexler, the screenwriter for *Saturday Night Fever*. His plans for the sequel again teamed Travolta as Tony Manero with his supple girlfriend from the original film, Karen Lynn Gorney, who had now become his agent and guided him from disco to jazz orientated dance. Stallone's version threw all this out, introducing two new female roles – one the homespun girl-around-the-corner willing to wait up with the hero's slippers, and the other the glamorous, tempting and essentially hard-hearted go-getter – which would mean the hero having to make a moral and physical decision. Which girl would he decide on? The parallels between this on-screen dilemma and the one being faced by Stallone off-screen often seemed uncomfortably close, but this was not the only area of the film to fall under the new director's shadow.

Everywhere, the film showed traces of the philosophies of Rocky and his creator, accurately mirroring Stallone's own experiences as a struggling young actor. Tony Manero's apartment is almost uncomfortably reminiscent of Rocky's own hideaway, and of those endured for a time by Stallone himself. Tony showers with his clothes on, just as Stallone himself had done in the less palmy days. Agents reject him, and his career seems to wash up on him, just as Stallone's career had sometimes seemed about to before that critical Wepner-Ali confrontation. And, like Rocky and Stallone before him, Tony eventually learns that success is there to be achieved, and that the best way to enjoy it is to try to keep as close as possible to his emotional roots – with the girl waiting up with slippers.

These signs of Stallone's influence were almost invisible beside the obvious device that he used to make over the character of Tony Manero (and consequently of the actor playing him) in the image of Rocky Balboa-cum-Sylvester Stallone. It might almost have seemed like a replay of his interest in the boxing co-star of *Paradise Alley*, Lee Canalito. Stallone had become his guardian and saviour, wanting to prove he could create in reality what his films had created in fantasy, and with Travolta he seemed determined to repeat the exercise. He set about rebuilding his star.

There was at least a valid starting point for his decision, for Travolta was not in peak condition when he signed on to make the movie. Out of shape, he carried about twenty pounds surplus weight, hadn't worked out in over a year, and had last been seen dancing on screen in the 1978 *Grease*. Stallone wanted to bring out Tony's 'fire and urgency ... he's a street animal who has this generic sense of survival' and, four months before shooting began, he switched his leading man on to a rigorous diet and strenuous six-day week training schedule, working him up to fourteen hours a day, trimming and building muscle.

Only five weeks into the punishing programme, the physical benefits of the new regime were becoming obvious, and Travolta happily persisted, even later going on to write a book, *Staying Fit*, celebrating the advantages of peak fitness and body happiness. Throughout this time, the friendship between the two men deepened.

'If John keeps it up I'll have to fight him in *Rocky IV*,' said Stallone, while Travolta, who had recently been impressed by the adrenalin pumping quality of *Rocky III*, looked on his director as 'a throwback to the old days of making stars look good ... He gave me everything he may have ever wanted a director to give him – support, energy, real direction.'

Such pre-production activity promised well, as did the film's promotion. 'Five years later and the Fever is still burning,' declared the posters, trying to kick up a storm of anticipation. And if Stallone's personal astrologer could be relied on, the various personalities behind and in front of the cameras would come up with a winner of a movie – for everybody on the production had been vetted. If the stars did not smile down on even the most talented, they were not hired.

The story that eventually reached the screen picked up on Tony Manero's uphill struggle to become a professional dancer, five years after audiences last saw him. He teaches at dance class, earns food-money as a waiter and gets hustled for sex by hungry girls, makes a profession of being turned away by agents and has an on-off sleeping arrangement with faithful chorus girl Jackie (Cynthia Rhodes). He perks up when he is instantly attracted to the principal dancer Laura (Finola Hughes) and gets to sleep with her. Jackie stands patiently by as Laura cruelly drops him, and eventually Tony and Jackie get into the *corps de ballet* of a new Broadway dance show – leading lady, Laura – during rehearsals of which the director barks out the film's message to the assembled dancers. He tells them the show, 'Satan's Alley', is a journey through Hell ending with a triumphant ascent into Heaven, 'and you might think it's simple but if it's gonna work you've gotta bust your asses'. This well-worn sentiment only served to remind audiences of Warner Baxter's more memorable outburst fifty years before in *42nd Street*, for only by a whisker had Tony's director avoided telling him he was 'going out a youngster, but you've got to come back a star'.

Ambitious Tony means to do just that, and helps push the originally cast leading male dancer out of the show, himself taking on the principal role opposite Laura. On the opening night, he makes a huge success of it, and a fool of Laura, to the delight of his mother and the revivified Jackie. Like Rocky and his creator, Tony has fought his way to the top of the heap.

In the event, it was only really possible to say two positive words about *Staying Alive*: John Travolta. Badham had been right in saying he was 'a terrific actor – very sensitive and very bright ... He understood that character in tremendous depth'. Travolta was the *raison d'être* for the picture, his toothy, welcoming sexuality suggesting he had once been a fully paid up

Lord of Flatbush; he gave the picture all the drive it had, and managed to carry away good feelings about the whole experience.

'I loved *Staying Alive*,' he said later. 'I was so happy and excited to get in shape that I didn't care about the consequences ... the most important thing (to me) was my dancing. For Sly it was my body. His directorial point of view was that he wanted to see this fat boy get into great shape and then feature it as a highlight of the film. I think it ended up 50-50.'

Elsewhere in the cast, Cynthia Rhodes was a capable if uninteresting Jackie, and Finola Hughes as Laura showed little inclination to act. Only in the brief scenes featuring Julie Bovasso (the sole survivor, apart from Travolta, from the original *Saturday Night Fever* company) as Mrs Manero, did humour threaten to break in. There was no hope of a joke from Steve Inwood as the all-seeing, all-understanding Broadway director who might, on a foggy night, have been mistaken for Stallone himself. Perhaps this was wishful thinking on the studio's part, for Paramount had originally tried to persuade Stallone to play this role as well as direct the film, but it didn't happen, and Inwood was left to suggest the familiar Rocky-like entreaties to effort and achievement.

Ironically, as it turned out, *Staying Alive* itself had involved a tremendous effort and achieved very little. Viewed overall, the script seemed to lack resource at all turns, the casting was questionable, and the direction – making much of brief gobbets of action and dialogue, a technique used to rather better effect in *Paradise Alley* – seemed to pull any potentially good scenes apart.

Also, the show-within-the-show, 'Satan's Alley', was the silliest of spectacles that surely would have opened on Broadway on a Thursday night and closed on the Saturday. All the dance sequences were badly patched together, undermining the very momentum that should have been the bedrock of the film, and there was not even enough dancing from Travolta himself. His best moment came at the very end of the film, when he announced his intention to go out on the sidewalk and 'strut'.

All in all, *Staying Alive* had proved a great disappointment to everyone caught up in it, and not least to Stallone. Costing $18 million (Stallone's fee as director was $1 million) with a further $12 million spent on distribution and promotion, the picture returned a creditable $65 million to Paramount's coffers, but this was little compensation for the critical panning that awaited it on its release in July 1983.

The tenor of the reviews was sometimes depressingly familiar. Tony Crawley in *Photoplay* declared it to be '*Rocky IV* with Bee Gees music, and what's so wrong about that?', but Pauline Kael in the *New Yorker* was much more dismissive. 'Stallone doesn't bother much with character, scenes or dialogue. He just puts the newly muscle-plated Travolta in front of the camera, covers him with what looks like oil slick, and goes for the whambams.' Neither was Stallone pleased by the way his brother's musical contribution to the film had been criticized or, at best, ignored.

Staying Alive's condemnatory notices sounded even more authoritative when lined up against Norman Wexler's own critique of what Stallone had done to his original screenplay; the co-author now found the work 'vacuous, impoverished, crass and crude'. Nick Roddick's *Monthly Film Bulletin* assessment was that the film was 'by turns exhilarating and absurd' and considered it had been directed 'with glorious crudity', a view echoed by *Films and Filming*'s Ronald Bergan.

To him, Stallone was 'a director in tune with his audience and certainly not interested in the views of jaded critics over twenty-one ... *Staying Alive* is a ninety-minute pop video disc. It should not be shown in cinemas with seats ... Although the numbers never build satisfactorily, the choreography and the music have a sameness, and the use of slow-motion and strobe lighting doesn't help, Travolta communicates the delight he has in his own vibrant, energetic dancing'.

And it seemed no better to Tom Hutchinson in *Photoplay* who thought that 'Stallone's way with a story is of the meanest. Basically, it's only a slight anecdote to be told in a few minutes and to stretch it out convincingly takes far more dramatic pull-together than we have here – a confused, mawkish mess'.

Still on the musical kick, there was talk of Stallone starring in Paramount's musical film about the life of the short-lived pop-singer Jim Morrison, but nothing came of the idea until it was picked up many years later by director Oliver Stone who cast Val Kilmer as Morrison in *The Doors*. Stallone was reported by the press as planning a movie about the British criminal

Francis Farmer, but nothing more was heard of it. There was also a possibility that Stallone and Travolta would team up for a *Godfather III*, which eventually turned up with Al Pacino and Andy Garcia. Around this period, there was a suggestion that Stallone was to play the seedy club-singer opposite Woody Allen in Allen's *Broadway Danny Rose*, but what would have been a fascinating change in career direction for Stallone never happened. Meanwhile, a screenplay written by Stallone, *Pals*, loosely based on the story of Brando, didn't get off the ground. His script for *The Bodyguard* had no better luck.

It worked out that for his next project Stallone would go to Twentieth Century Fox for the Country and Western spree *Rhinestone*, to be directed by an old colleague, Don Zimmerman, making his directorial début after establishing a reputation as a film editor. Once again, Stallone brought script control into his contract, contributing to the screenplay of Phil Alden Robinson, and carrying on a personal tradition he had begun on *The Lords of Flatbush*, whose credits had first acknowledged his 'additional dialogue'. More importantly, *Rhinestone* would be his first out-and-out comedy role, with room enough for some romantic sequences, and his first attempt at singing on screen. It was also the first time he had ever played opposite, and on equal terms, with a genuine female star.

From his earliest films, his leading ladies had played mostly peripheral and essentially subsidiary roles (think of Jerry's girlfriend in *No Place to Hide*, or the assorted girls of *Paradise Alley*) or been non-existent: *Escape to Victory* and *First Blood* hadn't exactly helped to reduce the number of out-of-work actresses. Even though Talia Shire had broken through into the public's consciousness as Adrian in the *Rocky* series, her role in the epic is of secondary importance, never allowing her to emerge as a star performer in the way Stallone is perceived. With *Rhinestone*, this was not the case, for at last Stallone (fee $5 million) drew a fair match in his new co-star Dolly Parton (fee $4 million). To date, he hasn't made another attempt to pitch himself against a female performer of equal charisma.

Perhaps actress was quite the wrong word for Parton, the wasp-waisted, hour-glass-figured Blue Grass singer whose brief flirtation with Hollywood had brought huge dividends to the studios. In 1980 *Nine to Five*, her second film, had been a girls' outing with Jane Fonda and Lily Tomlin, and a big box-office hit, after which she had played the madam of *The Best Little Whorehouse in Texas*, a tame 1982 reworking of a dull Broadway musical, in which she was teamed with Burt Reynolds. If unquestionable maleness was the requisite for her male co-star, Stallone seemed the best available choice, and for him it was another major change of gear after his last two acting roles in *Rambo* and *Rocky III*.

But whatever hopes held high when filming began in Los Angeles and Memphis during October 1983, the outcome was to prove yet another bad disappointment, for as a singing cowboy Stallone did very little for the majority of critics, many of whom pointed out that the film's central theme, the transition of a no-talent city hick to outstanding Country and Western sensation, was undermined by the fact that Stallone's singing was as bad at the end of the film as it had been at the beginning. He had been nervous even at the prospect of trying to sing in a film with the super and natural professional playing opposite him, and early filming was hampered by Stallone's psychosomatic laryngitis that, with Parton's encouragement, had to be worked through. Throughout their time together the two kept a good working relationship, from which Stallone was to benefit spiritually as well as professionally.

'I grew up a little,' he said of his partnership with Parton, acknowledging that she had brought him closer to the understanding that 'acceptance is what happiness and peace of mind are all about'.

For the film itself, however, he was to have little fondness in the years ahead. The good feelings were soured quite early into the project when Zimmerman not only failed to keep shooting up to schedule but was criticized for the laboured pace that showed up in the rushes. Fox brought in Bob Clark, whose reputation was based on such commercial successes as the 1981 *Porky*'s (he had even done a sequel, *Porky's II: The Next Day* in 1983), and whose style at least seemed sympathetic to *Rhinestone*'s preoccupation with heavy sexual jokiness. Zimmerman's dismissal was nevertheless a personal sadness to Stallone, who certainly was not a complete stranger to the troubled politics of the studio floor and changing personnel.

His original belief in the project was based on the possibilities of contrasting his urban character against Parton's rural persona, but 'it didn't work; it just laid there. They would have to hide the sharp objects. I'd sit there and watch the dailies and say, we are dying'. So dispirited did he become with the film that when the studio urged him to take an active part in its promotion, he protested that it was 'like giving away free rides on the *Titanic* ... I'm telling you, it won't float'.

Turning against so warm-hearted and well-meaning a film as *Rhinestone* seemed almost unnecessarily cruel, as if its star was vindicating the negative reaction of his fans, who probably went expecting one kind of movie and found another. For the perceptive, there was considerable pleasure to be had from Phil Alden Robinson's transplanting of the Pygmalion story to Tennessee hillbilly country, in a screenplay that claimed to be based on the Larry Weiss song 'Rhinestone Cowboy'.

The Rhinestone was the Country and Western club owned by the obnoxious Freddie Ugo (Ron Leibman), fondly known by his girls as 'The Sultan of Sleaze'. He paws his singing star Jake (Parton), who tells him that there are two kinds of people in the world and he is not one of them. She wants to be free of the three years left on her contract, but he won't let her go. Amateur Night at the club falls apart when an atrocious new discovery of Freddie's flops (and gives Robinson the chance to write quite a funny Country and Western pastiche lyric). Jake bets Freddie that if it was left to her she could create a Country singer out of any man she came across ('no lepers, no dead people'), and he accepts the wager. If within two weeks such a protégé can get through one number at the Rhinestone, Freddie agrees to tear up her contract, but if she fails to work the miracle he will add another five years to the contract, and get to sleep with her.

At that moment a taxi-cab driven (in the manner of Rocky) by Nick Martinelli (Stallone) crashes to a halt at her feet. Nick's relationship with Jake doesn't begin too promisingly, and he loses his job and his taxi. She calls him a 'horny toad' and he calls her a 'hillbilly bimbo', but Jake explains the bet to him and he takes her to his home, above his father's funeral parlour, to show off his musical talents on his organ.

'It'd best be havin' music comin' out of it,' she warns him.

He does a frenetic version of 'Tutti-Frutti' without realizing a funeral is in progress below. Invited to lunch with his traditional Italian parents, Jake announces she is taking him to Tennessee, where she and her gentle father Noah (Richard Farnsworth) give the unwilling Nick a thorough grounding in country ways. A ghastly ex-fiancé of Jake's, Barnett (Tim Thomerson), becomes Nick's sworn but ineffective enemy, and cannot prevent the blooming love between the two protagonists.

With the beginnings of success as a singer, Nick returns home to an extravagantly Italian welcome party, but has a glorious bust-up with Jake when, Eliza Doolittle-like, he asks her what will happen when the experiment is over? She, Professor Higgins-like, appears to wash her hands of him and, in front of his relatives, lets slip that she has agreed to sleep with Freddie if the wager is lost.

Nick's opening night at the Rhinestone arrives, and Freddie has filled the club with expert hecklers. Jake goes to Freddie and asks him to call the wager off. Discovering where she is, Nick effects a Lone Ranger rescue, riding across town on a white horse to free Jake from Freddie's clutches. Returning with Jake to face his challenge at the Rhinestone, Nick's act takes a sharp nose-dive and he seems to die on his feet, but he raunches up his number, works the punters into a frenzy and wins them – and Jake – over. Together, they feel easy about discussing each other in public. Nick tells Jake she's a walking violation. She tells him she can see his pulse through his pants. Like everything that had gone before in the film, this is mere harmless fun, and if most of the wit was pretty obvious it nevertheless had a homey charm about it that generally carried the day. The songs were pleasant if not especially memorable, and the stars were buttressed by really excellent and well-observed performances by the supporting actors. But ultimately, of course, it was down to the leading players.

Parton, happily bursting out of a series of brilliantly engineered frocks, brought a fresh quality to the film that was always appealing, and the chemistry between her and her leading man was by no means negligible. She didn't appear to be artistically stretched beyond what came naturally to her, and it is almost impossible to imagine how the film would have turned out if Stallone had been obliged to carry it all by himself, or if Parton's role had been taken by a more actressy star.

There are moments in the film when Stallone seems almost painfully self-conscious, and he takes many of the comedy scenes by the scruff of the neck, playing them up to the top and then some. But if his singing is clearly amateur, this is completely in line with the character he is playing, and it's very doubtful if the studio's one-time intention to dub his singing voice with that of a more fluent professional would have improved the finished product. So far as he was concerned most of the blame for the picture failing was left with the script. 'I should've written it myself,' he said later.

Phil Robinson, *Rhinestone*'s original author, may not have agreed with this, but blamed the studio, not Stallone, for the changes his material had undergone before reaching the screen.

'If you take a non-housebroken puppy,' said Robinson, 'and put him in a nice house and he makes a mess on the floor, you don't blame the puppy. He's only doing what comes naturally.'

In a well measured notice for the *Monthly Film Bulletin* Tom Milne said that though it was 'too likeable to be described as a bad film, *Rhinestone* is nevertheless not very good, largely because it settles so readily for the obvious ... Stallone does his share of the singing surprisingly well. The script ... has a sharp line in repartee which surely betrays the Stallone touch'.

But the flirtation with musicals was over. Since *Staying Alive* Stallone has not directed a film in which he has not appeared. Since *Rhinestone* nothing has been heard of Stallone the singer. His audiences had not shown much interest in his involvement with these departures from the adventures that had made his name. Again, he would turn to the inescapable Rambo and Rocky.

11 Again, with a Vengeance

When the sequel to *First Blood* eventually appeared, it was as if the first movie had been no more than a playful cartoon. When Rambo came back, it was with a vengeance, with more violence, more killing, and – from the critics – an outcry against the superhuman soldier-machine that paraded across the screen as the self-appointed all-purpose vigilante of America. Against a background of vilification and accusations of moral turpitude, Stallone played out one of the greatest successes of his career. This film would prove not only that Rambo had an enduring place in the affections and political psyche of the American people (and, even more strongly, the peoples of Europe), but that Sylvester Stallone had succeeded in consolidating a reputation that had once seemed based on the creation of Rocky Balboa alone. Nothing else he had presented to the public – either as star, writer or director – had matched that. But with the re-introduction of the anti-hero of *First Blood*, there is a case for arguing that only a consummate actor (and writer) could have brought off so stunning a cinematic coup; the bringing to life of two such disparate characters as Rocky and Rambo.

There can be little doubt, too, that with *Rambo: First Blood Part II*, the way Stallone and Rambo were perceived by the public underwent a dramatic change. Critics began, far more than had been the case with *First Blood*, to hold up their hands at what they called the pornography of violence. Violence, of course, had never been far away from a Stallone film, but now, for many, it seemed the focus of his work, almost its only reason for existing.

The director, George Pan Cosmatos, who by his own admission had a talent for directing 'slick American pictures with a European sensitivity', had a cast that included Richard Crenna encoring his role of Trautman, Charles Napier as officialdom's baddie, and Steven Berkoff as the brilliantly sadistic Russian villain. It seemed that here America and Russia were equally untrustworthy in Rambo's eyes, America's treachery to its heroes being the more painful because its heroes had so strong a love of their country. Whereas *First Blood* had explored the extreme difficulties of Rambo being eligible for re-entry into society, the sequel assumes that so far as civilized society is concerned Rambo will always be an outsider. It seems to be one of the indecencies of that society to only make use of this particularly faithful citizen when dirty work, and killing, is to be done. Society, and the government, have washed their hands of what they have turned into a mercenary.

Rambo, who still has five years' sentence to work out, is doing hard labour in the prison quarry when Trautman visits with a proposal that will temporarily reinstate Rambo in the Forces, and may even mean a Presidential pardon. The mission: to establish if there are any American prisoners of war still detained in Vietnam. Rambo has a few doubts, but agrees, and asks Trautman if, this time, they will win the war.

Rambo is flown out to meet Colonel Murdock (Charles Napier) in charge of the technologically sophisticated operation. Murdock is impressed by Rambo's Vietnam record and, with pride, tells Rambo of his own. He explains that there are 2,500 servicemen missing in Vietnam; the government needs proof that they are being held by the Viet Cong. Rambo is to go to a known prison camp and take photographs of what he sees, but on no account to engage in any action. Trautman instructs Rambo to let technology do most of the work, and to forget the old Vietnam, which is dead.

'I'm alive,' says Rambo. 'It's still alive, ain't it?'

Equipped with weaponry, Rambo is dropped into Vietnam, where he has thirty-six hours to achieve his mission and reach the extraction point. His guide is the pretty Co Bao (Julie Nickson) who takes him downriver by boat. Rambo tells her of his return to America after the Vietnam War, only to find that there was another war, against returning soldiers, being fought at home. Nevertheless, Co's dream is to go to America.

They reach the camp, and Rambo, against all orders, gets inside, and discovers American soldiers suffering appalling privations in vermin-infested cells. He rescues a prisoner and escapes to the boat, but the owner has betrayed them, and they are ambushed by the Russians. They break free and make it to the extraction point, but when Murdock learns Rambo has an MIA (Missing In Action) with him, he aborts the mission and instructs the rescuing helicopter to fly off, leaving Rambo a prisoner of the Viet Cong.

Trautman furiously accuses Murdock of setting Rambo up, but Murdock tells him the fact is that there are American soldiers in Vietnam who cannot be allowed to get out.

Rambo is chained up in a pit of pig-manure, but is pulled out to face the sadistic Russian commander Podovsky (Steven Berkoff), who tells Rambo to radio his headquarters to say he has been captured and condemned for espionage, and that no such criminal aggression should be attempted in the future. Co gets into the camp. After torture, Rambo agrees to speak to base, and asks for Murdock. He tells Murdock he is coming to get him, and, with Co, escapes from the camp, intending to travel to Thailand and then on to America. Co asks if she can go with him. He agrees to take her, and they kiss, but at that moment Co is gunned down. Rambo cries as she dies in his arms. He takes her lucky necklace and wears it.

Trautman wants to rescue Rambo but Murdock tells him he is under arrest. Now, Rambo goes on a killing rampage to get himself out of Vietnam. He liberates some MIAs and blows Podovsky to pieces. Arriving at base with the escapees, Rambo shoots up Murdock's control room. Finally, he corners Murdock and seems about to despatch him with his knife but, instead, he tells the terrified Murdock to go back and free the rest of the men.

Trautman tells Rambo his achievement will mean a second Medal of Honour, but Rambo is unconcerned.

'I want what they want,' he explains tearfully, looking towards the MIAs, 'and every other guy who came over here and spilled his guts and gave everything he had, once for his country to love us as much as we love it.'

Budgeted at $30 million, shooting on *Rambo* began in September 1984, but two months before flying out to Mexico (standing in for Vietnam) Stallone muscled up his body under the supervision of the twice-titled Mr Olympia, Franco Columbu, working out on a programme that left him with a 50-inch chest. Physically, his presence on screen would be remarkable. In tune with the sequel's relationship with *First*

Blood, Stallone seemed more sinewy, more muscular, more unbeatable. If Rambo was to progress, perhaps it was through the excellence of the body that this could be achieved. As time would tell, the almost superhuman, almost unnatural, and to some almost laughable bodily proportions he would display in *Rambo III* would seem to take Rambo's physical supremacy, and Stallone's own stamina, to the brink of impossibility.

Meanwhile, there was punishment enough in the making of *Rambo: First Blood Part II*. The inhospitality of the location quickly revealed itself. Appalling weather lashed down on the area around Acapulco, destroying the specially constructed bridge and causing damages that cost the production some $200,000. Such minor problems faded, however, beside the real tragedy of the shoot, when a special effects technician, Cliff Wenger Jnr, was killed.

It was supposed to be a happy moment. To celebrate a successfully accomplished effect, Wenger, who was newly married, stepped out on to the top of the waterfall to have a celebratory photograph taken by a colleague. He lost his footing, fell into the ravine and was swept to his death. The incident had a deep effect on Stallone. When the battered body was brought up, he had it taken into a tent and sent all the others in the production team away. Alone with the body, Stallone washed and tended it, not wanting Wenger's wife to see the very worst that had happened to her husband. Such behaviour would never have been expected of any star, and gave the lie to those who looked on Stallone as boorish, animalistic, brutal. Such behaviour showed him to be deeply sensitive. The film was dedicated to the memory of Cliff Wenger.

If justification was needed to deflect the barrage of criticism that greeted Rambo's second outing, Stallone was ready, even if his defence of the film sounded like a defence of its commercialism as much as of its morality.

'In the past I've devoted months of my life to making movies and then had every reviewer make spaghetti out of my ego. It's not worth it. If this is the sort of film they want to see, well and good. American audiences have waited a long time to display their patriotism.'

American audiences displayed their patriotism vociferously across the country. As Rambo wiped out the enemy, they rose to their feet screaming, 'Kill! Kill!' One of the film's undoubted successes was in sparking a dormant need for such fervour at a crucial time, and in inducing an alarmingly widespread mass hysteria. 'No man, no law, no war can stop him,' proclaimed the posters, evincing a point of view that was sure to have a special potency for *Rambo*'s target audience of teenage males. Now, it was enough for Rambo to be his own jury, judge and executioner. 'Rambo – a symbol of the American spirit', the hoardings announced.

In 1985, Rambo-mania appeared to be sweeping the world. Sometimes it seemed that, if the news was bad, Rambo was somehow to blame. In Australia, Rambo look-alikes began terrifying holidaymakers and killing animals. In the US and elsewhere, sales of guns and vicious knives increased dramatically, sold sometimes to hunters and sportsmen, but often to those with less legitimate needs. In Beirut, *Rambo* proved the most successful movie of all time, and was a particular favourite with soldiers who watched it to pass the time between bouts of real warfare.

In June 1985, after the release of American hostages held by Lebanese terrorists, Ronald Reagan did his bit to elevate Rambo to legendary status.

'Boy, I saw *Rambo* last night,' he said. 'I know what to do the next time this happens.'

Stallone's own political views, for example on the hostage crisis, showed him to be a Hawk rather than a Dove, for he felt 'someone would have to atone. There has to be a consistent and forceful reaction from the American government, punitively'.

The public's attitude didn't seem out of tune with this. When *Rambo* opened May 1985 in 2,074 cinemas across the US, it earned $32.5 million after only six days, a figure that had been surpassed only by receipts for *Return of the Jedi* (1983) and *Indiana Jones and the Temple of Doom* (1984). After two weeks, *Rambo* had earned $57 million, by late June $100 million. By September a figure of $150 million was reported in the press, confirming that *Rambo* had far outstripped the success of *First Blood*: 37 per cent of those who saw *Rambo* went back to see it a second time and 22 per cent of these returnees sat through it a third time.

'With *Rambo*,' said Marvin Antonowsky, who was responsible for marketing the movie, 'you're dealing with the emotional

Preparing to talk about the weather in *F.I.S.T.* – the star gave a strong performance but the movie didn't do anything for his career.

Meeting his fans during the making of *F.I.S.T.*, but soon admirers would be kept at arm's length, and gossips would speak of a star so conceited that he had his name baked into his cookies.

The Carboni brothers of *Paradise Alley*: Stallone with Armand Assante and Lee Canalito (in foreground). In many ways the film is Stallone's most formidable cinematic achievement, underrated by critics at the time of its original release.

With his first wife, Sasha, and John Travolta, at a showing of *Staying Alive*. The film's critical reception was about to wipe the smile off their faces.

Two of the raunchiest young stars in Hollywood, Stallone and Travolta, at the time of *Staying Alive*.

climate in this country. Audiences cheer when Stallone says that this time he hopes we'll win the Vietnam War. If the picture had come out two years ago, nothing like this would have happened.'

For Stallone, of course, there was always the hope that *Rambo* would have an effect on American, and governmental, thinking.

'We have to pressure our own government and the one in Vietnam. The war isn't over for the men trapped there ... and I like to have something positive come out of my movies.'

Nothing much had, so far as the critics were concerned. The *New Yorker* thought it was 'narcissistic jingoism', the *Wall Street Journal* 'hare-brained'. *Films and Filming* thought it 'exploitative, right wing and relentlessly awful'. Nigel Floyd for *Monthly Film Bulletin* discovered 'much to dislike about the film's dubious glorification of the technology of death; but as these sometimes confused undercurrents suggest, its right wing ideology is a good deal more complex and unsettling than it is likely to be given credit for'.

Such complexities, it is almost certainly true, were largely lost on its audiences, exposed to a chain of violence that gathered momentum as the film progressed. The positive things about the picture seemed unquestionable: that might was indeed right; that cultural, ideological, and personal truths counted for nothing under a canopy of war; that all means were allowable towards a patriotic end. Any doubts that Rambo might have about living in such a society (and, as we can see from his darkly thoughtful brooding at the start of the film, he obviously has them) are quickly put aside once his mind is made up to do what must, it seems, be done. That he is the only person with such doubts makes him more of a hero, and indeed may be the most potent reason for his legendary strengths, which may lie deeper in Rambo's personality than berating critics have realized.

Rambo's single-mindedness does at least here allow a female companion to enjoy a very muted romance with him, even if she is gunned down immediately after the first kiss; nothing seems to go right for this guy in the personal sphere. Though the girl is resourceful and daring, we find that her real heart's desire is to go to America and settle down with a big man just like Rambo, and in this willingness to subjugate everything to the goodies of Western civilization, the fervently macho feel of the film asserts itself all the more strongly, seeming – as with so many other Stallone movies – to present a negation of feminism.

The gentler qualities that might be associated with feminity are here reserved for Rambo, who again resorts to the well-tried Stallone technique of an on-screen emotional collapse. Rambo seems about to cry at the death of Co, though the camera turns tactfully away, but his deep disturbance really only explodes at the close of the film, when he sobs out his last, extenuating, speech between clenched teeth. But here, even more than in *First Blood*, Rambo's awkward burst of moralizing seems merely tacked on and utterly superficial to anything that has gone before, presumably in the last-minute hope of sending the audience away convinced it has been watching something with some kind of message. If in any doubt of it, audiences making their way out of the theatre heard Frank Stallone's voice hymning his own lyric, over the closing credits, of 'Peace in our Life', reminding them that 'the strength of our country belongs to us all'.

By the time *Rambo* was into production, it was already clear that Stallone's life with Sasha, so long threatened by the demands of professional life and his relationships with other women, was over, and, in late November 1984, for the third time, Sasha sued for divorce. This time, there would be no going back.

The reasons for the final split, putting aside the very public humiliations Sasha had suffered over Joyce Ingalls and Susan Anton, were many and complex, though they seemed sometimes obvious and superficial. In the early days of his post-*Rocky* success, Stallone had invited the attention of the press, willingly stepped into the spotlight, gone out to meet fans and friends, enjoying with Sasha the fruits of what together they had achieved. But the days of hitting the disco had grown far less; now, he wasn't much of a party-goer and still Sasha loved to socialize.

There had been another, traumatic family problem, which Stallone would only publicly reveal in an interview in June 1985. At the age of three, Seargeoh had been diagnosed as being autistic. The shock to Stallone and Sasha of discovering the son they had once believed to be normal and well advanced for his age was suffering from a condition that cruelly isolated him from them, was intense. The child was locked into his own world. When his father kissed him, Seargeoh wiped the kiss away with his hand. It was a painful experience for a father who, in his own childhood, had longed for affection that had not been forthcoming. He had always found communication difficult as a child; now, his son was denied it.

'I went out in the backyard,' said Stallone, 'and I cursed God. I said, "Why did this happen?" I thought I had paid dues in my life and thought I had tried to accomplish things in society.' For a time, Stallone was concerned with a theory that autism might be induced through a shock during pregnancy – after all, he had walked out on Sasha while she was carrying Seargeoh – but doctors assured him this was not the case. Together, Stallone and Sasha began a research fund for autism, raising considerable amounts of money.

For Stallone, it seemed that Seargeoh's autism had also strained his marriage greatly, and that though Sasha and he had worked together to bring Seargeoh into the family circle and, on a broader scale, to heighten public awareness of the condition, Sasha's preoccupation with his condition had further weakened her preoccupation with her husband. There was little hope that Sasha could have turned to Jacqueline for understanding. The mere fact that Sasha had early on in her own career given up her own hopes in order to support her husband was one that Jacqueline always overlooked. Sasha, even if she had considered it, could not look to Jacqueline for support. Her own parents, too, seemed remote from her marriage relationship. Her husband had spoken to her parents a couple of times on the telephone, but they had never met up. A remote benefactor, Stallone had bought a house for them to live in. He had got to know one of Sasha's brothers rather better, and had helped him go through college. But Sasha was truly isolated, with only her two sons as the family she could turn to, and one of them was locked into his own tight, uncommunicating, unsympathetic world.

Finally, however, there probably would have been no benefit from closer family support for Sasha; the heart of her relationship with Stallone was burned out. Stallone knew the end of the marriage had come when he arrived home one day and heard only echoes through the house. He had been locked out. Sasha denied this, saying she simply had packed her clothes and taken the children and left.

With Sasha gone, the restraint that Stallone had felt and fought against over the years was at once removed. It was a time when a man might have taken the opportunity to stand back and look around him, to take a holiday from his emotions. Instead, Stallone quickly became involved in a relationship that was to ensnare him utterly. It was a love that would envelop him completely, and end by crippling him. The hell he would go through would have to be got through alone, but it was lived out in the blaze of newspaper headlines, cheap accusations, snide suggestions. Perhaps Stallone's meeting with his own particular Nemesis might have passed off as a mere fling if the steadying influence of Sasha had still been around, but Sasha was gone, and he was wide open to the most devastating sorrow, anger and embarrassment of his life.

12 Brigitte

The little girl of eleven who had watched spellbound as Rocky Balboa grabbed the chance of his life and stood up to Apollo Creed in the first film of the series, had grown up to be a model with ambitions to be an actress. Her name was Brigitte Nielsen.

Brigitte had not been a beautiful child. She was tall and scrawny, wore braces on her teeth until she was sixteen, and wasn't particularly popular with her siblings. Her middle-class home life had been comfortable, with a librarian mother and a father who was an engineer. She would always feel she owed a debt to her father, who 'has kept my feet on the ground in a business where it's easy to fly and in the process lose both control over your life and your happiness'.

For a time, after leaving school, she had worked in a bakery for a pittance, but she blossomed. One version of her life has her, at age sixteen, taking a second-class ticket to Paris and landing unannounced on the doorstep of a leading model agency at five o'clock in the morning. Another version insists it all began when she was seventeen, and was spotted in Denmark by the photographer Marianne Diers, who gave her an introduction to one of Copenhagen's leading model agencies. In fact, it hardly matters how Brigitte's first lucky break came about; it was always going to happen. Once Brigitte had achieved, she warmed to it, and would very seldom in later years be denied anything she wanted. The face that looked out from the first magazines she graced already had determination, and the steely eyes betrayed the knowledge that she would succeed. The photographs showed a young woman of great sexual beauty, with amazingly long legs and cropped hair.

She was launched on a successful modelling career by the time she was seventeen, in demand for sessions in London, Paris, Rome and Milan, where she soon made her home as the live-in partner of Lucca Rossi, a leading agent. In 1982, she met and moved in with the Copenhagen-based songwriter Kaspar Winding, by whom she was soon pregnant. A son, Julian, was born. She had originally wanted to call the boy Sylvester, but her husband would not agree to it. She had then been discovered all over again, this time as a film star, by the film producer Dino De Laurentiis. She had been signed against international competition for a sort of sequel to *Conan the Destroyer* with Arnold Schwarzenegger. It was called *Red Sonja*, in which *Time Out* remembered her as playing 'some prehistoric bint'. Derek Elley in *Films and Filming* said she 'makes Schwarzenegger look like a sensitive actor'. This notice would possibly have upset Brigitte, who had announced that to her 'acting is very similar to modelling, and I found it easy to make the transition'.

She also, according to Wendy Leigh's biography *Arnold*, wasted no time when she arrived on the *Red Sonja* set in Rome in September 1984, in making a play for Schwarzeneger, and for a time the pair enjoyed a close relationship, but it was one that the Austrian body-builder-turned-movie-star soon tired of. There were those who suspected that, eager to be rid of Brigitte, Schwarzenegger had engineered her introduction to Stallone, confident she would be eager to begin a relationship with him, and that Stallone would be powerless in the face of her assault. As it happened, she did, and he was, but whether this was really a machination of Schwarzenegger remains questionable, and certainly seems a little unsubtle.

Since the early days of her crush on Stallone, Brigitte had written to her heart-throb. The letters had never been posted. Later, Stallone checked with her parents and they confirmed their daughter had been besotted with him since girlhood. In December 1984, her attitude had changed somewhat. She became more determined than ever to meet her hero: she mailed her letters to him.

Mail from adoring female admirers was nothing unusual for any Hollywood star of his kind, and often such persistent attention-seeking marks out the sender as a fanatic, to be avoided at all costs. But one day in New York Stallone opened one of the letters and read there about the girl of eleven who had grown up to be Brigitte Nielsen and wanted to meet him. Hadn't she told her parents all those years ago that their meeting would be something very special?

He tore up the letter, but that evening when he got back from a lunch appointment she had sent over another, with her modelling composite. It was raining outside, and he couldn't find a cab, but he ran down the street to her apartment, two blocks away. She opened the door to him, her hair flaming:

'I'm only going to stay fifteen minutes,' he said, 'but maybe I can stretch it into four hours.'

At first there were awkward silences between them, but these passed away and a remarkable friendship developed. She became the most important part of Stallone's world. And it had been she who had swept him off his feet, rather than he who had swept Brigitte off hers.

'She has heart, humour, beauty, athletic prowess, maternal instincts,' said Stallone. 'She's very family orientated. And she's classically true to her man – I mean, really dedicated to the maintaining and prolonging of this relationship. There's a permanency about it. I have not gone out or nothing. It's the same individual – and wonderfully so – for ten months.'

The heady optimism of such romance would bear the bitterest fruit in a very short time, and even at the first news of Stallone's new love the press was ready to kick out, as much at Brigitte as at her lover. If she had such fine maternal instincts, they suggested, why had she left her baby son with her husband in Denmark in order to pursue her own career? Stallone was at pains to point out that in that country no child could be taken away from its parent if he was a Danish citizen, though the official line seemed to be that custody was awarded to the parent thought most fit to look after the child. In an effort to keep a relationship going with her baby son, Brigitte would sometimes fly back home to see him. There was talk of Stallone offering over a million dollars to Winding if he would relinquish the child. He didn't. Brigitte explained her quandary:

'I'm not a bad mother who abandons her kids. I'm European and it is not as big a deal. So much was going on in my life. I'm heartbroken that I missed (Julian's) first steps … On the phone it tears me apart. He is just learning to say "Mamma".'

But Stallone kept on singing his love song. She was a home-bird who would as soon sit at home with her lover and watch television as go to a nightclub. Money didn't interest her.

'I've never seen anyone that extraordinarily beautiful put all the trappings of wealth in a drawer and go for all the trappings of love,' he said.

By February 1985 Brigitte had moved in with Stallone. A month later she was cast as the second female lead in *Rocky IV*.

By the time the film opened in America in November 1985, the likelihood of it providing another box-office bonanza was unassailable. Between them, the first three *Rocky* films had brought in over $300 million. As each film was followed by its sequel, the cost to the studio of the star-writer (and, after the first *Rocky*, director), and the cost of the production, rose sharply.

Rocky had cost under a million dollars, with Stallone receiving a basic union payment for his acting role plus ten per cent of the profits. His fee for *Rocky II* was $2 million, and the production cost $7,500,000. For *Rocky III* he had been paid $5 million, with the production cost of $15 million. By *Rocky IV*, the cost of both star and production had grown even more alarmingly. Stallone would receive $15 million plus two per cent of the profits. Production costs had rocketed to $30 million.

Of course, it was not only the budget of *Rocky IV* that outstripped its predecessors. Dramatically and physically, the movie would have to eclipse everything that had gone before. Rocky's adversary – the Russian boxer Ivan Drago – would have to make Apollo Creed, Thunderlips and Clubber Lang look like soft toys. The role went to the young Swedish athlete Dolph Lundgren, who at six feet six inches towered over his co-star. Lundgren had twice been the European kickboxing champion, but had acting ambitions. His physique was awesome, and his striking blond looks gave Drago a marvellously attractive and dangerous edge. For he would be no ordinary opponent. And, perhaps with John Rambo looking over his shoulder, Stallone in *Rocky IV* would fuse the various elements into a story that, far more than *First Blood*, would stand as a beacon of virtuous Americanism in a bad world.

Peeling away any layers of subtlety, the story would be presented as the most basic and eternal contest that has ever faced Man – the contest between Good and Evil – Good America and Evil Russia, the American Eagle that gets into the boxing ring by dint of struggle and grit determination, and the Russian Bear bolstered by political force, medical chicanery, anabolic steroids and technological intervention. *Rocky IV* would have its opponents in opposite corners that reflected the incipient warfare between the USA and the Soviet Union. The allegorical quality of this episode in the life of Rocky Balboa was not to be sketched in lightly. It would prove Rocky's greatest triumph to offer up his well-rehearsed philosophy for personal fulfilment and to have it taken up by America's enemy.

Even the trailer of the movie suggested the brilliant effect the movie might have on audiences (at least in the US). The stunning image of Stallone and Lundgren flashed on the screen and a voice warned the cinemagoers to 'Get ready for World War Three'. In the States, this promise alone was enough to work theatre audiences into a frenzy of anticipation; they rose to their feet shouting, 'USA! USA!'

It seemed that Rocky did not have to travel the ordered steps of democracy in order to become an unelected but universally acclaimed politician, who spoke what was truly in the hearts of his people. In fact, by the time of *Rocky IV*, Rocky was acting as a sort of surrogate President of the United States, and according to many people making a better job of it than the real article. If the message was blunt and obvious and, for many tastes, crass, it was also achieved with a knowing skilfulness that showed Stallone could still make over the old Rocky formula to brilliant effect.

By the time filming on *Rocky IV* stopped in July 1985 the physical demands on Stallone had taken their toll. Before production began he had spent five months in intensive training. When shooting the Siberian winter training scenes (in Wyoming) he strained himself pulling a sledge weighing over 1,000 pounds of rock. Later, he had taken so many hard punches from Lundgren, in scenes where the previous carefully choreographed moves had been abandoned for a more free style, that he collapsed and was taken to hospital where doctors told him he had no more than a bleeding heart muscle. Lundgren's convincing boxing had also pushed his diaphragm into his heart, but the suffering had to be worthy of the film's theme. Much to the irritation of the nursing staff, Brigitte refused to leave Stallone's hospital room, even sleeping there, and refusing to let Jacqueline anywhere near her son.

'*Rocky IV*,' Stallone promised, 'will be like a throw-back to the days when warring tribes would each select a champion and the two men would fight instead of the armies.'

The film began, of course, with the last moments of *Rocky III* carried over. They had made a limp ending to that film and made a limp beginning to the new one. When the new saga catches up with Rocky, we see him enjoying the comfortable lifestyle he has earned for himself, Adrian and Paulie. Paulie is just as boorish as ever, even when Rocky buys a flirtatious female robot as a birthday present for him.

But the placidity of their lives is interrupted when the superhuman Russian Ivan Drago (Dolph Lundgren) comes to America as an 'ambassador of goodwill', seeking an exhibition match with Rocky. Drago has been trained to an extraordinary pitch by technological wizardry and Soviet ingenuity; whatever he hits he destroys. His wife Ludmilla (Nielsen) explains at a press conference that, just like America's own hero Popeye, Drago has eaten his spinach every day. Apollo, who has been retired five years from the ring, decides he has to fight Drago, against the advice of both Rocky and Adrian, who asks if Apollo hasn't taken enough punishment in his life? Rocky suggests that the real fight would not be between Drago and Apollo, but a fight within Apollo himself. He and Apollo are changing, turning into 'regular people'. At a news conference announcing the bout between Apollo and Drago feelings boil over: 'This is us against them,' says Apollo meaningfully.

On the night of the bout, Apollo enters the ring to an orgy of patriotic flag-waving as a singer extols the joys of 'Living in America'. Drago's reception is violently hostile, and there can be no doubt now that the fight has come to be seen as a confrontation between the two superpowers.

Apollo, in his best razzle-dazzle style, tells the crowd it's showtime, but Drago knocks him out with a battery of vicious blows. Drago coolly accepts that his opponent may die at his hands. Apollo dies.

Rocky knows what he has to do, and accepts the challenge to fight Drago, for no fee, on 25 December in Russia. At the press conference, Drago's manager claims Drago has been intimidated and subject to American propaganda vilifying him, propaganda to support the antagonistic and violent American government. Paulie – on behalf of what he describes as the unsilent majority – springs to his country's defence, shouting back that America doesn't forcibly keep its people behind a wall.

Adrian tells Rocky that Drago will kill him, but Rocky is

haunted by the memory of Apollo, and in a montage from the earlier films remembers times along the way in his climb to success. Rocky bids a loving farewell to Adrian and his son and leaves America.

Siberia is the harsh environment he has chosen as his training ground. There is an unwelcoming reception, secret police guards, a wooden hut to live in and a distinct shortage of gymnasium facilities. He saws wood, helps pull carts out of the snow as puzzled peasants look on, acts as a husky and pulls sledges. Drago, on the other hand, is awarded every sophisticated assistance in his training. But Rocky has the resolve to beat him. Apollo's trainer tells Rocky that Apollo had been a son to him, and now he looks to Rocky to make sure Apollo did not die for nothing.

Returning to the hut one day, Rocky finds Adrian waiting for him.

'I missed you,' she explains.

'I missed you,' he confirms.

Adrian's presence gives an added boost to Rocky's mission, and – in a montage familiar and essential to all *Rocky* films – his fitness peaks, reaching its apotheosis when he runs up a snow-tipped mountain (the Soviet equivalent of the steps of the Philadelphia Art Museum) and, on reaching the top, gives the world the clenched fists of triumph. He is ready for Drago. On the night of the fight, Paulie weeps as he lets Rocky know how much he appreciates him.

'If I could just unzip myself and step out and be someone else, I'd wanna be you. You're all heart, Rock … Now bust this guy's teeth out.'

Rocky enters the vast stadium to a crowd emanating pure hatred. President Gorbachev and the Politburo gaze on from above. Drago enters to a display of well-marshalled mass hysteria, fireworks crashing, choral singing, while huge images of the boxer against the hammer and sickle reveal themselves to the worshipping audience. The two men face one another, a true David and Goliath, Drago towering above Rocky. Drago tells Rocky he means to break him.

In the early stages of the contest, this prophecy seems about to be fulfilled when Rocky fights back. The fighters' perception of one another changes. Rocky comes to realize that Drago is not a machine, but a man. Drago comes to realize that Rocky is

not only a man, but a machine. In the VIP box Gorbachev and
his party begin to look uncomfortable at the way the match is
going. For the crowd, too, there are changes. They suddenly
chant 'Rocky'. 'Russia is pro-Rocky,' declares the startled
commentator as the population works itself into an orgiastic
frenzy in support of their new hero.

Drago's manager harangues him to win for his country, but
Drago pushes him away, saying he means to win for himself
alone. In the fifteenth and final round (the same distance
Wepner had gone with Ali, the same distance Rocky had gone
with Apollo) their contest becomes a street fight as, exhausted
and bleeding, they slog it out to the end. Finally, Rocky knocks
Drago to the floor and is declared the winner. He is wrapped in
an American flag, grabs the microphone and makes his views
known to the spellbound spectators.

'In here there were two guys killing each other, but I guess
that's better than twenty million. What I'm tryin' to say is, that if
I can change and you can change, everybody can change.'

The crowd, having had all this carefully translated to them,
goes wild. Even sporting Gorbachev gets to his feet and
applauds, giving the Politburo a nasty look suggesting that it too
gets to its feet. Rocky sends a Christmas greeting to his son, and
tells him he loves him. Back home, his son squiggles in front of
the television and whispers 'I love you', as Rocky wraps Adrian
into the flag with him.

In *Films and Filming* Ronald Bergan considered Stallone
hadn't bothered with a characterization, and found the film 'so
macho that most of the kissing and hugging is done between
men, as when Rocky and Apollo are seen romping in the surf in
flashback'. Bergan went on to suggest that as a director Stallone
had been influenced by 'the great Italian director Asti
Spumante'. Shaun Usher in the *Daily Mail* dismissed it as
'ludicrous rubbish'; for Leslie Halliwell it was 'the pits'. Danny
Peary shot it down as 'phony baloney' and 'the worst, most
embarrassing film of the series'.

The shadow of Rambo, the intense jingoism, the mindless
flag-waving, are only some of the elements that set *Rocky IV*
apart from other films in the series. Much, of course, is as
before. The general trend of the film sees Stallone pulling the
formula out again. Rocky's smooth life is upset by an event, here
the death of Apollo. Apollo's defeat at the hands of Drago had

been Rocky's defeat also, and America's defeat. Rocky has to go back in and win again, clinging on to his old values whether at Apollo's funeral (by now Stallone's characters were frequent visitors to funerals, as in *F.I.S.T.*, *Rocky III* and *Over the Top*), or breathing sweet nothings in Adrian's ear in a bedroom scene that is almost a carbon copy of a scene in *Rocky III*.

At such moments the sentimentality is so heavy-handed that the manipulative intelligence behind the artifice is all too apparent. At Apollo's funeral, the camera even pans along the wreaths in slow motion. As for the Rocky-Adrian relationship, this seems limited to the repetition of a few short phrases bordering on inanity. They appear to have nothing of interest or substance to say to each other.

And what has happened to Rocky himself? *Rocky IV* has lost all the wit, the linguistic eccentricity of the earlier films. The few lumbering attempts at humour we see here are feeble and only serve to underline the smug, infantile pleasures enjoyed in the Balboa household. Rocky is not funny, he is not even fun. Very early on, we realize this film is meant to be very serious, and that Rocky will be rather serious throughout it. Sadly, he has even learned to drive properly. He has conformed, he has grown, he has altered.

This is all very well, but the matured Rocky has nothing distinguished about him. The remarkable, off-beat dialogue of the younger Rocky is vanished, and it is puzzling to know why Stallone, as a writer, did not realize the paucity of the character Rocky had now become. His talk and his views are here utterly commonplace. Adrian and Paulie have become mere ciphers. The formulaic feel to the movie extends, also, to the music, with two general moods. For scenes depicting love, doubt and remembrance there is tinkling, hesitant piano music, for all others driving, ambitious, up-tempo stuff. And the score for *Rocky IV* is noticeably more aggressive than for any others of the series, though it has a curiously dated feel to it.

Brigitte, freed from the sorcery of *Red Sonja*, dealt capably enough with a role that didn't exploit her body in the way her next film with Stallone would. Some of the production team noted how she carried it off with supreme confidence, and didn't take kindly to her boyfriend's suggestions. There were those, too, who saw how her extraordinarily blonde and arrogant sensuousness matched that of Dolph Lundgren who, in different circumstances, might himself have fallen victim to Brigitte's charm. As it turned out, any interest the film has centres on Drago, an almost non-speaking role that Lundgren fills admirably. Apart from being physically superb, he suggests a purely animal intelligence that comes off the screen surprisingly well. And by the end of the film, he threatens to be a more interesting character than Rocky himself, when he repudiates his manager's criticisms and becomes his own man. By a curious and perhaps unintentional stroke of genius on Stallone's part, at the end of the fight Rocky and Drago seem, in effect, to be on the same side.

The *détente* between Russia and America would very soon make *Rocky IV* a dinosaur, while other films that depicted Russia as America's enemy would not be so affected. *Rocky IV* had been so serious in its intent and so heavy-handed in its execution that it could not stand as a mere adventure movie; it would easily have qualified as an official product of a propaganda department, for when Stallone wasn't busy pulling emotional strings he was pulling political strings. The superb audacity with which he contrived to turn the screw in the final conflict between Drago and Rocky showed a deft understanding of audience psychology.

And there was a masterstroke in casting a Gorbachev lookalike (though Gorbachev is never mentioned) to give the final seal of approval to Rocky, and therefore America. Gorbachev becomes an admirer of Rocky, is absorbed into the myth, and his blessing suggests that friendships can yet be forged between the superpowers. This could be seen as a sharp piece of forecasting by Stallone, or as a stroke of the most amazing cheek. It is only a wonder that, in the closing shots of the film, Rocky does not wrap Drago close to him under the American flag instead of, as the tradition of any *Rocky* film dictates, hugging Adrian.

The summer of 1985 was a time when Stallone was hardly ever off the front pages of some newspaper, somewhere. Rambo-mania was sweeping the world, breaking all box-office records in America, playing in the Far East to packed audiences, and about to open in Britain, where voices were raised against it. The British Safety Council tried to have *Rambo* banned from British cinemas, claiming the film was nothing but 'mindless violence' and 'sadistic in the extreme'. That summer, too,

Playboy published photographs of a rather callow-looking young actor called Sylvester Stallone. They were stills from the forgotten porn movie *A Party at Kitty and Studs*, and he was naked.

In July, *Village Voice* published an article telling its readers Stallone had ducked the draft for the Vietnam War, a claim he vociferously denied.

'The strongest feelings a man has,' he said, 'are for his religion, his loved ones, and his country. If you don't have men willing to die for their country you don't have a country.'

All this paled besides the press attention that was to come. At the end of September 1985 the divorce settlement between Stallone and Sasha was announced. She would keep their Beverly Hills home and he was to make her a payment of $12 million (£8,500,000). She would have custody of the children, to whom he would have unlimited access. He would also pay their education and medical bills. In effect, the settlement meant he had lost half of his wealth to Sasha. It was a lesson he learned well enough to make sure Brigitte would eventually sign a pre-marriage undertaking not to sue for half of his fortune should they ever divorce. Not that such a thing seemed remotely likely to him. A Cartier watch he had presented Brigitte with was inscribed with the promise 'I'll love you till the end of time'. Now, Stallone looked forward to the time when he and Brigitte would be husband and wife, making films together, having children together. By some clever stroke, might it even have been possible for Brigitte to come back in the next *Rocky* episode as one of the regular team? It was a decision he wouldn't have to worry about, though there were all sorts of other considerations when it came to looking to Rocky's future.

'If I were to go into *Rocky V*,' said Stallone, 'I think he would have to go into politics, which seems to be the natural extension.'

But in *Rocky IV*, many felt Rocky had already conquered that one. Hadn't he brought East and West together by the most simplistic, most direct, confrontation between man and man? He had levelled politics, removed the need for anything approaching diplomacy, by plucking up his American Dream and translating it into Russian. What could have been simpler?

13   O.T.T.

Stallone married Brigitte on 15 December 1985 in a private ceremony at the home of Irwin Winkler. The groom arrived in good time for the service in an open-topped 1930 Rolls Royce. He wore black tails and a white tie. The bride had designed her gown of clinging white silk trimmed with white fur encrusted with pearls and heart-shaped crystals. One observer said she looked as if she had been spooned into it. The groom was thirty-nine, the bride twenty-two. As the bride walked in, the heads that turned included John Travolta and Donna Summer.

The bride's mother had flown from Denmark to be there, but the groom's mother was not present, nor his half-sister. There were rumours that Stallone had forbidden Jacqueline's presence, but perhaps after the remarks she had been heard making in the press about her new daughter-in-law, it would have seemed a little odd to find her throwing confetti. Jacqueline had squared up to Brigitte in a pre-nuptial slanging match that matched anything Rocky had ever done.

'Let me tell you something, you big pig,' she said to Brigitte. 'If you ever hurt my kid in any way, I'll personally smash you.'

Her opinions were wide open to the press. She hadn't cared for Sasha and she didn't care for Brigitte.

'I don't like the broad. I know perfectly well she just wants his money and not him. It will be the shortest marriage in history and a very costly romance.'

The ghost of Sasha had perhaps finally been exorcized. At last she had faded from the picture, consigned to the past, Rocky's struggle, the homely terrors of Hell's Kitchen, the lures of home and hearth, the years of his sons. By December, as her ex-husband married his new wife, a little of the fog began to clear for her.

'I'm a dreamer,' said Sasha, 'and I always hoped that in the

Stallone's other immortal – John Rambo. A few perceptive critics recognized Rambo as little more than Rocky at war.

Images of violence that went round the world with Rambo, and which contradicted the intelligence and vulnerability at the heart of his creator.

Peace at last. With Richard Crenna at the close of *Rambo III*, made at a time of great personal unhappiness for Stallone.

Still coming up with the action in *Lock Up*, but the movie looked like a desperate attempt to reassert all the old Stallone characteristics at a time when the public's interest was moving on.

With son Sage playing Rocky Jnr in *Rocky V*. Some critics were eager to suggest that Sage gave a better performance than his father. At last, Stallone promised this would be the final outing for Rocky.

end he'd turn out like Rocky. That's why I hung in there so long, always hoping.'

The actual act of marrying Brigitte was one he would look back on as if he had watched it from afar. When it came to the exchange of vows, he might well have recalled that other marriage, when he had felt faint and sat through the ceremony, when the bride had worn a pretty, modest dress she had made herself. There was never any fear of Brigitte's costume being home-made. In later years, he remembered a sense of foreboding at the moment when he slipped the ring on Brigitte's finger. He turned, he said, into Elmer Fludd, mumbling out 'Wid dis ring I dee wed'. It proved the potency of his old shyness, self-consciousness, and insecurity could still function. Perhaps his temporary loss of authority at that second was understandable. The wedding, after all, was very much Brigitte's achievement.

But his image seemed to be giving Stallone as much trouble as ever, even at the season of goodwill. At the beginning of December, he had been awarded the coveted Sour Apple prize by the Hollywood Women's Press Club in recognition of being the year's most inaccessible and least noteworthy star.

And Jacqueline fuelled the fires with more comments. Her son's new marriage would last 'about as long as a cheap face-lift'. In her mother-in-law's eyes, Brigitte was a gold-digger who would marry her son and leave him as soon as possible with a massive divorce settlement. Her son deserved something better, and she supported her argument by offering a potted history of her new daughter-in-law.

'She left home and lived on the streets, pounding the pavement. Who asked her to? ... She wants to be a big actress, and she has no talent. She spends a fortune on clothes ... I didn't raise my son to go off and marry someone like her.'

Bodyguards were posted to keep the public, and possibly Jacqueline, out. There had been threats to Stallone's life, which was another good reason to have a quiet wedding. Sources close to the couple said a big affair had been out of the question because they didn't wish to hurt Sasha's feelings. After the service, the party of over a hundred guests sat down to dinner and danced to a medley of songs made famous by the Righteous Brothers.

After a one-day honeymoon at a local hotel, the couple

reported on the set of their next film at 5 am the following morning. The movie was clearly intended to be a showcase for Brigitte as much as for Stallone.

It had taken Stallone just sixteen hours to produce the first ninety-page draft of this picture, based loosely on the British thriller writer Paula Gosling's novel *Running Duck* (published in America as *Fair Game*). In this case, however, the short labour and quick delivery did not result in one of his better efforts. It resulted in *Cobra*, and necessitated another change of image for its star. The blue jeans, black sweat-shirt, black gloves, shades and match-chewing mouth signalled another incarnation of male aggressiveness, his belt decorated with grenades, his fists clutching a gun.

Sinister, shadowed figures crossing axes above their heads in some cultish ritual gave the opening moments of the film a pulsing momentum, as if some great Götterdämmerung was imminent. The atmosphere is immediately squashed when a crazed gunman starts killing shoppers at a San Francisco supermarket. Even the disapproving Detective Monte (Andrew Robinson) agrees reluctantly that there is only one thing to do: call the Cobra, otherwise Cobretti, the most single-minded cop on the zombie squad, and a specialist who does the dirty jobs nobody else wants. The gunman justifies his actions by telling Cobretti that this is part of the morality of the 'new world', but Cobretti – ever ready to be judge, jury and executioner – kills him anyway. 'You're a disease and I'm the cure,' he tells the gunman before despatching him. A meddling reporter asks Cobretti if he used unnecessary deadly force on the gunman.

Meanwhile, Cobra's more conventional police colleagues have no resources against a series of serial killings in the city perpetrated by the Night Slasher (Brian Thompson) and gleefully assisted by Nancy Stalk (Lee Garlington) who also happens to be a policewoman assigned to Cobretti. His superiors give Cobra *carte blanche* to get the killers however he can and, once he finds them, to 'do what you do best'. When glamorous model Ingrid (Nielsen) witnesses the Night Slasher slicing a victim in the street, she becomes a target.

Stalk is worried that Ingrid will spoil the 'new world' and kill the dream she shares with the Slasher. Stalk whispers her doubts into the Slasher's ear in a brief scene that perfectly suggests their perverted sensuality.

From here on, the plot concentrates on the Slasher's obsession with killing Ingrid, pursuing her with a fanatical single-mindedness that colours several urgent sequences. Cobretti moves Ingrid to a safe house where a mild flirtation happens, in which neither seem to take much interest. The next morning, hordes of motor-cycle villains arrive, alerted by Stalk, to finish off Ingrid and Cobretti; Cobretti answers by wiping out the whole militia. Only the final confrontation in a foundry between the Slasher and Cobretti remains, allowing the Slasher one last chance to state his case. He tells Cobretti that the old world will never be rid of people like the Slasher. They will govern the new world; they will be the future.

'No, you're history,' replies Cobra, and, after a brutal fight, he hitches the trapped beast on to a giant hook that carries him into his own private furnace. A city at peace again has cause to be grateful to Cobretti, and when the conservative Monte shakes hands with him, Cobretti replies by good-naturedly smacking him in the face and strolling over to where Ingrid is waiting by his motorcycle.

'Ready Marion,' she tells him. 'Catchy name, isn't it?' he smirks, and together they ride off in to the credits.

The director, George P. Cosmatos, who had earlier had more luck with *Rambo: First Blood Part II*, announced hopefully that *Cobra* was 'not like any other movie. It's kind of a new genre for today ... a film noir of the eighties. I'm doing the films of the forties and the fifties in a flashy, stylish way'. There were certainly a few scenes filled with night shadows, and some hazy and natural ground mist, but the noir-ness was largely superficial. Cosmatos also sounded defensive about his leading lady who, he felt, 'really represents the audience in the film ... She's a natural. She is not studied, like some actresses today'.

The critic Ric Burns sounded less confident about the new Mrs Stallone. 'Gita's (*sic*) been implacably sitting in on Stallone's epics for some time now, and there's something irritatingly nonchalant about their rapport as she watches him go through his violent paces. She's not exactly the Madame Defarge of moving pictures, but then those aren't knitting needles she's got there either.'

The pronounced emphasis on the film's weaponry wore down the edges of the story, with Cobretti's armoury including a Jati sub-machine gun and a .45 auto Colt pistol, its ivory handle engraved with the head of a king cobra. More menacing by far was the savage killing gadget of the Night Slasher, part Swiss Army knife and part growth of multiple cutting edges; he salivates as he contemplates it and its capabilities. The other notable hardware was Cobretti's car, a 1950 Mercury coupé (registration AWSOM 50) with a chopped top and nitrous oxide system to enable immediate speed boost for the inevitable car chase sequence. In truth, the car had as much character as anything else in the cast.

Cobretti should have been of central interest, but the screenplay seems intent on making him in the image of Rambo, though Cobretti's war is not in any direct way political, but aimed at the most sick of humankind. Cobra, according to Stallone, is 'so right-wing, so committed to walking up to a psycho and dealing with him on his own psycho level' – in other words, the commitment is to the Old Testament policy: violence for violence, horror for horror, death for death. The end result is that Cobretti comes across as little more than a walking munitions factory.

This extreme response to social malaise consumes Cobretti so thoroughly that we have only the most grudging insights into what the real man may be like, though the film does allow a brief glimpse of his bleak home life. He is clearly bored. A television churns out Christmas inanities. He slices up a pizza with a bad looking knife. Cobretti does at least have a friendship with his sidekick, the junk-eating Gonzales, allowing Stallone some in-house dietary banter, but Reni Santoni is given no opportunity to create much impact, though he does give away Cobretti's greatest secret – his Christian name, Marion. This – a macho cop with a girl's name – is the film's best joke, and the only one.

Nielsen's leggy talent is at its best seen posing at a modelling session. Elsewhere, she has little to do but look very frightened quite often, which she does convincingly enough, but the role itself as written by Stallone was not negligible. After leaving Stallone, Brigitte would sometimes complain that her first film roles had exploited her body and left audiences with the impression that this was what she was, mostly, all about. Such ungrateful comments ignored the fact that her characters in both *Rocky IV* and *Cobra* were potentially interesting, and had been a gift from her husband.

By far the strongest impression in *Cobra* is made by Brian Thompson, whose extraordinarily vulpine quality gives the Night Slasher a compelling distinction not found anywhere else in the cast, suggesting that if the entire confrontation of the picture had been merely between the Slasher and Cobretti, a more incisive and coherent film would have resulted. Taking a lesson from *Rambo*, the quantity of bodies seems to have taken a high priority. As it is, the army of faceless nasties coming at Cobretti from all directions undermines the tightness, and the focus of the piece is lost. And what exactly is the poisonous cult to which the Slasher belongs? Is he its leader? Such questions are not answered, allowing the story to fizzle out.

Warner Bros decided to open cold without press reviews or any advance screenings in America, where *Cobra* hit 2,100 theatres on 22 May 1986, taking $15,500,000 in its first week, and thereafter managing a healthy profile in the top grossers, but the critical reaction in the States, and in Britain where the film opened in August 1986 was almost totally unenthusiastic, and often percipient.

Ric Burns in *Time Out* observed that, like Rocky and Rambo, Cobra seemed 'to view speech as a suspiciously sophisticated, possibly un-American evolutionary development. Go much further down the food chain and you begin to encounter resistance to standing erect, and opposite thumbs'. Anne Bilson's *Monthly Film Bulletin* notice found 'a glorification of ... the use of violence to combat violence ... Cobretti is presented as a supermensch, a killing machine only a few stops short of Rambo'. One critic was moved to write that sitting through the love scenes between Stallone and Nielsen was 'like waiting for pandas to mate'.

One of the questions that now engaged the two stars of *Cobra* was how Brigitte would follow her starring role. Stallone had made it known that she would be ideal as the eighties' equivalent of Marlene Dietrich in a re-make of *The Blue Angel* with Rutger Hauer, though whether Mr Hauer would have been very happy about working nearby his old sparring partner of *Nighthawks* is a moot point. As there was no suitable role for Brigitte in Stallone's next film, she moved on to being a colourful villainess in *Beverly Hills Cop II*, starring Eddie Murphy and directed by the British Tony Scott. These were two names that would reverberate in the next few months. And though Brigitte herself did not find her way into *Over the Top*, Stallone found a small role in the film for her secretary, Kelly Sahnger, who also worked on *Beverly Hills Cop II* as Brigitte's double. In the months ahead Stallone's bodyguard Bobby Martini would claim that Brigitte had helped Kelly in other ways.

Earlier that year, the shadow of Rambo had cast itself again over Stallone. In February the sweetness of being proclaimed Man Of The Year by the Harvard University's Hasty Pudding Theatre in Massachusetts had been tempered by the protests that accompanied the prize. Vietnam veterans and Asians were among the hundred or so people who gathered outside the theatre before Stallone arrived. At the press conference, three men were arrested after suggesting the citation should have been for the Nazi of the Year. On a happier note, Stallone took the pudding pot prize of long tradition but was also given a brassière fashioned from army camouflage material, with golden grenades for tassels.

The American Golden Raspberry Awards also featured Stallone's name – all too prominently, and didn't neglect those nearest and dearest to him, either. He all but swept the board. He was named as Worst Actor, Worst Director, and held responsible for Worst Screenplay and Worst Film of 1985 (*Rambo*). Brigitte came a little behind with her Worst Actress award for *Red Sonja*, and her Worst Supporting Actress for *Rocky IV*. Making it a real family affair, brother Frank was remembered for his 'Peace in our Life', and was named as Worst Songwriter.

Stallone looked for an improvement with his next movie, and a change of style. *Over the Top* would be directed by the Israeli Menahem Golan, whose reputation as a film maker was built on his relationship with his cousin Yoram Globus. Together, they had founded the Cannon film empire, based on their first venture, the Golan-Globus production company, but their outpourings had not been renowned for their artistic or commercial success. They hoped for better with their new star, whose track record was not exactly negligible. In fact, Golan's last picture, *The Delta Force*, a Chuck Norris adventure, could almost have been fashioned as a tribute to Stallone, or at least to John Rambo. Not that Golan considered Norris in the way he considered Stallone. He sounded prepared for what was in store when shooting began.

'He knows the camera like nobody else,' said Golan of his new star. 'He knows every lens, every angle. He knows how it will look on the screen. He's not just a man who stands in front of the camera and acts.'

Officially, Stallone was also co-writer of the new film with Stirling Silliphant, but the control he was able to exercise over the movie didn't mean he was altogether happy with the idea of it. At one stage, he threatened to withdraw, and there was talk of *Miami Vice* star Don Johnson taking over. But whatever his critics might think, the title, *Over the Top*, didn't refer to his image or his acting or his extravagant private life, but employed a term used in arm-wrestling. The film would surely do for arm-wrestling what Rocky had done for boxing. There was even a political dimension to it, according to Stallone who was given instruction in the finer points of the sport by the real-life US champion, Marvin Cohen.

'It's really a celebration of virility,' said Stallone. 'You know what I mean? Of manhood. But it's different from a lot of sports. Because no one really gets hurt. And anyone can afford it. It's a very democratic sport – as opposed to a Republican sport. What you have to have are the arms, not the money.'

Of course, any involvement in a sport raised the inevitable question of Stallone's status. To win or not to win was the question that taunted the director and his star as production began. For Stallone's character to win the arm-wrestling world championship might seem unlikely and obvious; for him to have lost it would hardly have been in the spirit of Rocky, and breathed of the dreaded 'downer'. Once again, what Stallone's image had been founded on – the fairy-tale of an underdog getting to the top – influenced the decision.

A sense of *déjà vu* hovered over the process. The original script brought Stallone's character and his son together, but had Father losing the championship. Stallone thought better of it and wrote a new ending where, not surprisingly, his character demolishes the competition. Both endings would be shot, both versions would be shown at sneak previews; the privileged first audiences would decide which would reach the screen.

Stallone looked at the quandary philosophically.

'In *Rocky I*, I got away with it, because no one really knew my image. If I lose here, it brings about a lot of concern. Not to me – I'd like to lose. But will it destroy the impact of the film's statement, which is about hard work paying off?'

In the end, Stallone didn't have to make the decision.

'There is no alternative ending,' declared Golan. Stallone would win the championship.

'What we have here,' said Stallone of *Over the Top*, 'is a sweet little love story.'

He played Lincoln Hawk (or Hawks – the screenplay never quite sorts out what its hero's name actually is), a sensitive trucker estranged from his dying ex-wife Christina (Susan Blakely, reunited with her co-star after *The Lords of Flatbush* and *Capone*) and wanting to re-establish his relationship with his squeaky-clean young son Michael (David Mendenhall). From her hospital bed, where she is awaiting heart surgery, Christina requests that Hawk collects Michael from his graduation at military school, though Michael is unwilling to leave with him. He asks his father for some identification, and is sharply reprimanded by his Commanding Officer. Together, Hawk and Michael truck towards the hospital where Christina's father Jason Cutler (Robert Loggia) displays an almost unhealthy devotion to his daughter and a manic hatred of his ex-son-in-law. Cutler tells Christina that Michael belongs to him.

In a roadside café, Hawk arm-wrestles and wins. That night, Hawk pulls the truck off the road and tells Michael they will sleep there. If Michael's neck should get sore in the night, he may use his father's shoulder for a pillow. Michael thanks him for the offer, but thinks he will manage without. As time passes, his head nestles into his father. Their friendship develops. In the rising sun, to upbeat music, they have fun working out together, and Hawk lets Michael drive the truck. In a roadhouse, Hawk persuades Michael to arm-wrestle a young punk, but Michael is defeated and, humiliated, runs out. His father catches him.

'The world meets nobody halfway,' he tells him. 'Do you understand what that means? If you want it, Mike, you gotta take it … As long as you lose like a winner, it doesn't matter, 'cos you did it with dignity.'

Michael goes back in and licks the punk, but later is abducted by Cutler's men, who have orders to bring him back to his grandfather. Hawk chases them in the truck and rescues Michael. Cutler's determination to nail the son-in-law he despises and get his grandson back hardens. Now the best of friends, Michael wants some answers from his father. He wants to know why he left home, but Hawk only stammers that he had his reasons, that he knows he made a mistake. They make it to the hospital only to be told that Christina has died on the operating table. Michael cries, runs off ('You've never been around when anybody needed you,' he screams at his father), and goes back to Cutler. At Christina's funeral, Hawk makes an unwelcome appearance in jeans and a black tee-shirt, puts flowers on the grave, and leaves. At night, he sits on the bonnet of his truck and broods against the fading light. He drives the truck to Cutler's and smashes it into his hall. Michael half wants to go back to his father, but is restrained by Cutler. The police arrest Hawk.

Cutler's lawyers tell Hawk they won't prosecute if he leaves the state and doesn't contest Cutler's bid for custody of Michael. Hawk is released and makes his way to the Las Vegas arm-wrestling championship. Michael escapes from Cutler and gets to Hawk, who wins the championship. Father and son are united. Cutler bites his lip as he looks on, nodding his head in generous realization that this is where Hawk and Michael belong – together.

All this was certainly quite different from Rambo, or Cobra, or Chuck Norris.

'Sly has had an image of violence,' Golan announced. 'That will change with this movie ... But I think we have enough to offer the public – action scenes, car chases, that kind of thing. But we will also give them sentiments – love.'

The most violent thing about *Over the Top* was the extent of the swing away from some recent Stallone movies that had seemed almost a celebration of violence. Of course Hawk, with his unspecified reasons for having walked out on his wife and young son, was a ready-made mirror image of the actor, again put through a plot devoid of romance. Christina is the palest of creatures, wanting only to forgive her errant husband and bring about the reconciliation with their son before she passes away. As Stallone heroines went, she displayed the ultimate passivity. The focus, when it is not rather arbitrarily shifted on to the sporting theme, is on the father-son relationship, but this is played out quite superficially. Father and son's joint goodness is as one-dimensional as Cutler's manic loathing of his son-in-law, and the often embarrassing dialogue between them undermines the film's possibilities even more.

Hawk is an articulate and feeling person – we know this because, early on, he sits quietly with his thoughts, silhouetted against the sky, a technique used later for the same effect in the monastery scenes of *Rambo III* – but there are no interesting edges to him. And there are reminders of *Rocky* everywhere. Like Rocky, Hawk is trodden down and has to pull himself up, perhaps via his own heartfelt advice to Michael about going for it and losing with dignity, which is a re-run of Rocky's advice to himself in *Rocky*, Mickey's advice in *Rocky II*, and Adrian's advice in *Rocky III*. Instead of the boxing match set-piece finale, there is the arm-wrestling set-piece finale. By a brilliant sleight of hand, the Stallone image was now so resilient that it could step across into another character, another sport, and yet play out all the same emotions, progress through the same moves, satisfy the old needs. The formula was obviously strong enough to withstand dissemination and re-shaping.

Steve Perrin of Columbia-Cannon-Warner arranged distribution of *Over the Top*. His philosophy was, if possible, to go for an opening that coincided with a holiday period: 'If we didn't go for instant appeal,' he said, 'the film would be dead.' He saw the film's target audience as between the ages of twelve and seventeen, but still the critics were allowed to make up their own minds at previews. By and large, they were not impressed.

Sally Rowland for *Films and Filming* cited 'Hawk's chillingly dead response to the news of his ex-wife's death' as typical of the star's performance, telling her readers that 'the film is not only mind numbingly crass but without a simple morality it is tame and thin … this latest Stallone vehicle attempts to place a human perspective to the *Rambo* genre and fails miserably.' *Daily Variety* said it was 'routinely made in every respect'. Kim Newman in the *Monthly Film Bulletin* struck a kinder note, deciding that 'as an example of by-the-numbers film making, *Over the Top* is not all that bad; as a Stallone vehicle, it understands its star presence far more than *Cobra* did. However, as a sports movie, it's distinctly half-hearted'.

Despite the protestations that *Over the Top* heralded the arrival of a softer, family-orientated Stallone – a return to the values of *Rocky* – both in his career and private life he was just starting off on what he would come to refer to as a jog through

Dante's Inferno. Between them, Brigitte and Rambo were about to traumatize him.

14 Jogging Through Dante's Inferno

'I think there was a lot of people around Sylvester – there still is – that really don't care about him, and it seemed like it was a constant war. I used to tell him – why don't you just take a look at the people that really care about you, and don't listen and don't go with what the others say, which was very difficult. It was sad, it really was.'

This particular evaluation of her marriage to Stallone was made by Brigitte in 1990, and was not quite all the story. The sadnesses, if they were to be apportioned, did not altogether neglect Stallone. From the very beginning of their marriage, Jacqueline was not the only person close to them to sense the temporariness of it all. It was only a matter of waiting for the bubble to burst.

The last piece of wedding cake had hardly been consumed before the deep-seated troubles began. Rambo and the Great Dane were the easy prey of gossip columnists, newspapers and Hollywood's aristocracy. Some of the rumours (so widely reported that they quickly gained credence) were simply incredible because they ran so completely against the image Stallone had promulgated in the cinema. To begin, he was credited with giving his wife a very considerable salary, which would be increased on an incremental basis each year. Sums of up to the equivalent of £300,000 a year were mentioned. If this was true, it belied an awful insecurity on Stallone's part, implying that only by making it increasingly financially attractive to stay with him would Brigitte's steadfastness survive.

For her part, Brigitte denied ever having been paid this 'salary', but certainly seems to have been absolutely unrestricted in her pursuit of luxuries. She would buy up whole collections of rich clothes: Valentino for evening wear and coats, Chanel for formal wear, or the creations of Azzedine Alaïa. Jacqueline spoke of her daughter-in-law running up vast bills on her husband's credit cards. Was it true that Brigitte had used up the whole of her first year's salary from her husband within only four months? It seems undeniable that Stallone was so in love with her that he was either oblivious to it, or even condoned it.

No sooner had Brigitte left the set of *Cobra* and joined *Beverly Hills Cop II* as the colourful villainess (where, some claimed, she revenged herself on Grace Jones, Dolph Lundgren's girlfriend, by giving a cruel imitation of her instead of delivering a proper performance) than Stallone was hearing stories about her relationships with the film's star Eddie Murphy and its director, Tony Scott. There was a brief separation between Stallone and Brigitte at this time, and press whispers of a break-up, but the marriage persisted, against what looked increasingly like colossal odds.

By January 1986 the one-time bodyguard employed by Stallone, Bobby Martini, was spinning ominous tales to the press about his ex-boss's marriage. The tabloid press warmed to Martini's reports of Brigitte's orgiastic shopping excursions to buy 'figure-hugging leather clothes', and a suggestive description of the couple's bed, which Martini said was 'black, round and leather-covered'. Some of his stories verged on the surreal. Brigitte's beloved little poodle, Polo, had been eaten by Stallone's bull-mastiff, but when a repentant Stallone had gone out and bought a replacement pooch for Brigitte, she complained that the creature had crooked teeth. Stallone had spent several hundred dollars on the new dog's corrective dentistry.

On a more personal level, Martini said that Stallone seemed jealous whenever Brigitte showed any signs of independence, and became particularly unhappy, for instance, when she showed interest in appearing in a non-Stallone film. Such an attitude had a reminder of his earlier attitude to Sasha, who had sacrificed so much to her husband's burgeoning career and later, when she had tried to establish herself as a career woman, had not exactly met with much encouragement from him. As for Sasha, Martini claimed she had tried to seduce him, and that he had then (bravely) told Stallone about the incident. Almost as a throw-away, Martini also let it be known that Brigitte was spending almost as much time with a close friend, Kelly, as with her husband. Events over the next months would suggest that this comment of Martini's had been more significant than even he, perhaps, had intended.

As excited press reports began to relate, Brigitte's fitness instructor, Kelly Sahnger, was a close personal friend. When Brigitte went shopping for jewellery or furs, Kelly would often accompany her. They attended parties together, where reports of their girlish laughter suggested two rollicking, healthy schoolgirls out of Elinor Brent-Dyer, although that respected author would have been amazed at one of their adventures. Brigitte decided to enlarge her breasts with a silicone implant and, as if to emphasize the sisterly fondness she had for Kelly, paid for her breasts to be similarly improved. The effect on Brigitte's already stunning appearance was extraordinary, accentuating even more the purely sexual aspect of the persona she presented to the world, and making the most determined attempt to match the adulated body of her husband. Photographers had been privileged to see Stallone and Brigitte relentlessly working out together in the gym, perfecting their bodies almost as if each was in homage to the other, but now Brigitte had surpassed human achievement, and, through the wonder of surgery, taken Kelly with her.

When the announcement of the marriage collapse came, it opened the floodgates of humiliation and public mockery on Stallone. Headlines screamed the news that Jacqueline had walked in on Brigitte and Kelly in bed together. It seemed the ultimate black joke about Stallone's super-macho image. Brigitte went on to say she had been upset about the rumours surrounding her relationship with Kelly, but within a few weeks of the marriage breakdown the two women were often to be seen together at parties, still giggling. Talking about her ex-husband sometimes brought on a fit of giggles. If Brigitte was heartbroken, she was suffering her pain quietly. She soon signed a lucrative contract to appear in an Italian television spectacular.

The divorce issued in September by the Los Angeles Superior Court gave Brigitte $3 million of Stallone's wealth, the pre-marriage agreement about divorce settlement having held up. Whatever the truth had been about her friendship with Kelly, Brigitte soon formed a new acquaintance. Mark Gastineau, a footballer for the New York Jets, was along the same evolutionary line as Schwarzenegger and Stallone, with a proud, arrogant sexuality. Six foot six inches of hairy brawn, and a life that declared itself almost null and void before her, proved irresistible to Brigitte, and the couple were eventually found enjoying the most romantic of lifestyles on a well-appointed ranch in Arizona.

After a cancer scare that thankfully proved a false alarm, Brigitte became pregnant. Gastineau gave up his successful career to tend her, waking her every morning and bathing her with warm oils. When the thought of Stallone intruded, her comments could seem ungrateful, condescendingly dismissive or downright crude.

'Forget about Rambo,' she said in the arms of her new lover. 'Mark is double the size. Everywhere. And I mean everywhere. Yeah. We are dealing with a Viking here. Extra, extra, extra large.'

It seemed she did not even dignify her ex-husband by his real name, as if the image of Rambo was the image she had expected him to come up to. It was a cruel progress from the young girl who had first fallen in love with the struggling, incoherent, sexually unsure Rocky.

In 1990, she was still giggling at the thought of him during a *Wogan* interchange she shared with Shelley Winters. By this time Brigitte was launching herself into the pop world with a song of which little was subsequently heard. Her film career seemed to be in limbo. Miss Winters assured her that she would be a sensation at the Actors' Studio, where her talents would be appreciated. She gazed at Brigitte's jeans and wondered why she could not afford a pair that had not been ripped.

Brigitte went on to explain to the audience that she had left Gastineau earlier that year, amid rumours of his having beaten her. She had given birth to their child in December 1989, and only a matter of weeks later their relationship had disintegrated. To the unsympathetic, it sounded like a re-run of Brigitte's marriage to Winding, even though Brigitte's intentions, that her love for Gastineau would last for ever, were no doubt completely true: they had sworn it by having each other's names tattoed, in a small cluster of flowers, on their buttocks.

The manner of Brigitte's departure, and the devastating speed of his marriage's collapse, at once had a deep effect on Stallone, who withdrew into himself and the making of the third Rambo movie. When he did comment on their relationship, it was often as a riposte to comments Brigitte had already made.

'The sex life wasn't that interesting,' he said later. 'Trust me! It was really quite normal and pedestrian. My God, if she was that fascinating I'd still be married ... I'm very naïve. I believe in the ethical aspects of love ... The people you love are those who can take you to the lowest depths.'

Looking back at this period in his life was, he said, like watching a play with someone else playing the lead; it simply didn't belong to him. In their own different ways, Stallone and Brigitte had paid the price of celebrity.

Stallone threw himself into *Rambo III*, but it was very far from being third time lucky. The film was the same song sung over, but the world was changing fast, sweeping out old concepts of international hostility and mistrust, introducing undreamed-of turn-abouts in destinies, emotions and hopes. Since the Germans had relinquished the position, the Russians had been the enemy of the West, the mighty machine that wanted only to crush the rest of the world, and now, with a few deft strokes of political genius, the scales had fallen from the West's eyes. The man who was about to alter the probable fate of the world was called Gorbachev, and Stallone had reckoned without him.

Rambo III might well not have been made if Gorbachev's influences had been guessed at the time of production, though Gorbachev had of course been dragged into *Rocky IV* to display a generous appreciation of Rocky's gifts. There seemed no reason why the latest Rambo adventure should not repeat the success of its predecessors, even if that success would be mainly commercial. At the bottom line, the philosophy of the new movie was simply to do for Afghanistan what the previous two had done for Vietnam, and if the Russians were seen as the real enemy in all the films, this was obviously their fault. What the latest Rambo adventure had certainly not taken on board were any criticisms (and there had been many) that the tone of the earlier movies had been so calculatedly jingoistic, hymns to the invincible nature of America's strength. *Rambo III* refused to throw any of this overboard. Its first shot was of the American flag.

Now, Rambo's deep thoughtfulness has found peace in a Buddhist monastery. His only recourse to violence is to win stick fights, but this is only done to raise money which he gives to the monks. Trautman is again the kindly Devil who tempts Rambo out of this haven, prompted by a government that again promises that even if Rambo co-operates with them, he will be on his own, that they will wash their hands of him should he be captured in action. Trautman tells him that over two million Afghans have been murdered by the Russians, who have employed chemical warfare. America has made inroads against these incursions, but has been unable to quell one pocket of Russian resistance, commandeered by the particularly brutal Zaysen (Marc de Jonge). Trautman intends to go in, and wants Rambo with him, but Rambo tells him his personal war is over, and he wants only the peacefulness of his present life. Where Rambo has merely been prostituting his strength for the worthy cause of the monastery, he is now asked to prostitute it for his country, but he refuses, until he hears that Trautman's mission has resulted in his capture. He resolves to rescue Trautman, the first American to be captured in Afghanistan, and begins his journey. Trautman tells his torturer that America has already had its Vietnam, and that Russia is now having its own. He refuses to reveal where the missiles against Russia are situated.

Rambo sees an Afghanistan hospital, which toughens his resolve against the enemy. An orphaned boy Tomask is fascinated by Rambo, and longs to be his partner. Rambo at once wins the respect of the rebels by joining them at their violent horse games, and makes his way into the Russian fort where Trautman is imprisoned. The boy creeps into the fort behind him. Rambo discovers Trautman, but has to escape without him. Trautman tells Zaysen that Rambo will have no mercy on him. Rambo sends the boy away, giving him the good luck charm he wears around his neck, and gets back into the fort. He and Trautman make their escape by helicopter, then make their way to the border.

They have almost reached safety when they are confronted by the massed forces of the Russian contingent. Zaysen tells Rambo to give himself up but, against all odds, Rambo effectively declares war on the Russians and begins to eliminate them in an orgy of killing. The rebels arrive on horseback to help him. The conflagration ends in a head-on collision between Rambo's tank and Zaysen's helicopter, in which Zaysen is blown to pieces. In the afterglow of battle, Rambo has become the saviour of the Afghanistan people. Asked to stay with them by the boy orphan, Rambo goes into one of his longest brooding thinks, but says he has to leave. As he drives away with Trautman, the two admit that they may be getting a little soft. The film dedicated itself to 'the gallant people of Afghanistan', a tribute that offered a sub-text of condemnation against the USSR.

Much of the making of *Rambo III*, filmed in Arizona, Israel and Mexico, happened in a vacuum for Stallone, and the shoot was fraught with personality, production and financial crises. The budget eventually exploded to a staggering $63 million. Even after Jacqueline had astrologically given her blessing to the cast and crew, there were constant firings, often because Stallone acted on his mother's advice that such-and-such a cameraman was unsuited to the movie. His co-star Marc de Jonge later claimed that 'although he wasn't producing the film, nor directing it, there was no doubting that he was in charge. When he wasn't happy, someone was fired. By the end of filming, more than thirty people had been fired'. Stallone, with the history of his marriage to Brigitte hanging over him, was also nervous at the possibility of an Iranian plot to kidnap him, and decorated himself with bodyguards.

The myriad explosions of *Rambo III*, the frightening horse sequence and the generalized killing in the movie also worried Stallone. There was one ghastly incident when Stallone and Crenna had to shoot a scene in a helicopter. The timed gas bomb that exploded beneath them unexpectedly threw flames through the helicopter, and the pilot dipped 2,000 feet to safety. Such dangers were part of the price Stallone had long paid for being in movies.

It was in Thailand that Stallone's resistance was at its lowest, however. The stick fight that opens the movie was filmed by the side of a stinking factory manufacturing soy sauce, and the heat was intense. Stallone had pumped up his heavily slicked body to almost grotesque proportions, and faced making the first scene of the film in which Rambo would conquer his adversary. And Stallone realized that this was, partly at least, what had gone wrong with Rambo. He did nothing but conquer. All battles were lost before him. Being all-powerful, there was never any question that he might be bettered, and this had brought about an attendant loss of public sympathy. Such a realization might have been staring him in the face for years, and even now seemed a somewhat simplistic criticism of Rambo, considering all the other faults his critics had awarded him, but it was progress of sorts; Stallone had put a question-mark over the progress of Rambo, and, consequently, over the direction his own life and career were taking.

Any dispassionate self-appraisal of his career at this point must have found him asking what had happened to the critically applauded actor he had been way back in *The Lords of Flatbush*, *Death Race 2000*, the first *Rocky*, even *First Blood*. Financial and popular success had, of course, happened, but the quality of his acting work since these films had been uneven, though one of his more recent efforts, *Over the Top*, had suggested he was still capable of real acting, even if he was still prone to dreadful lapses.

It seemed improbable that *Rocky* had ever been considered for an Oscar, and that for a brief period he had been greeted as a new angry young man of American cinema, as a force that would re-enliven what popular cinema had to offer. The likelihood of *Rambo III* ever being up for any sort of Oscar seemed remote, as did the prospect of any movie starring Sylvester Stallone. The reputation had been at once made and lost. His ambitions as a writer had been prescribed by the material he chipped away at, principally polishing and carrying on the lives of Rocky and Rambo. His directorial qualities had been generally ignored or complained about, from *Paradise Alley* on. And all this despite an almost consistent ability to bring in a commercial winner.

As for *Rambo III*, its fate was sealed when Gorbachev and Reagan began smiling at each other, and when Mrs Reagan frostily welcomed Mrs Gorbachev. As the Iron Curtain cracked, the thumping patriotism of *Rambo III* was exposed as political crudity of the most obvious sort, and Stallone was left with a picture that painted the Russians blacker than black when on the real world stage such perceptions were hectically being abandoned. Of course, it would always be possible for the film to be enjoyed while ignoring its political overtones, and enough Americans went to see it to earn the film $54 million. Across Europe, where Stallone's Rambo retained a fabulous potency, *Rambo III* would take $150 million. As with so many other Stallone pictures, the flop of *Rambo III* would be relative.

Rambo III, superbly directed by Peter MacDonald, made a good if glib job of explaining the plight of the Afghanistan, an argument here buoyed up by excellent supporting performances and the photography of John Stanier that makes us realize the despoliation of the breathtaking landscape. This, of course, goes some way to vindicating Rambo's own behaviour, and Stallone's (and his co-writer Sheldon Lettich's) viewpoint. The contemplative side of Rambo's character, lingered over in the early stages of the film and touched on at the close, is here beautifully expressed against a background of everything that is mystical and elemental – at the moment of his decision to leave the monastery and become an instrument of war, he is fixing a wheel.

True to the Stallone screen persona, we are also shown him thinking to himself against a fading sky, recalling similar moments in the *Rambo* and *Rocky* series, and *Over the Top*, but we never expect these thoughts to be presented. This deep characterization in shorthand has by now become a familiar part of the Stallone package, and is usually necessary – certainly in the *Rambo* series – at the beginning and end of each screenplay. The physical mayhem in between is thus given an introduction and a valediction.

Jerry Goldsmith's luxurious score is not far out by sounding as if the West is being won all over again, for what is being underscored is clearly meant to be a decisive triumph for the home country. Fortunately, Stallone's formula, otherwise in excellent working order, does not give us one of Rambo's emotional Niagaras as a finale; at the close of play Rambo simply seems reasonably content with what he has done, and ready to move on, though whether he is going back to the monastery or the barracks we have no clue. For some viewers, this lack of emotional collapse from the war-savaged Rambo may suggest that after all the killing he has no real conscience; that all the uneasiness, doubt and pain have been deadened. But this is to misunderstand or underrate the potency of the formula; the fact is that Rambo's vocal breakdown at the end of *First Blood* and *Rambo* will do pretty well for *Rambo III* also. Rambo is playing the same game with a different set of pieces for an enemy, and what matters ultimately is that the enemy has squared up to the mother country, though this message is diluted in *Rambo III* by our real understanding of the Afghan position.

The Russians of this film are the Nazis of the most blatantly propaganda entertainment, trapped at once by the old order (the

Commander has a photograph of Lenin on the wall) and the exigencies of technological warfare. True, there is a vague attempt to show that even Russians may be good deep down (two family photographs stuck in the Commander's mirror) but no other evidence is offered. When, halfway through the film, the war turns into a head-to-head conflict between the Russian commander and Rambo, we are also subliminally being offered philosophies that had recently permeated *Rocky IV*, where Rocky's fight against Drago represented the American and Russian war machines – the carrying on of a primeval justice. This is a trait that can be found running through much of Stallone's output, so common that it seems to be an inherited behaviour pattern.

The absolute male exclusivity of *Rambo III* also goes further than the other films in the series, and even the most intelligent critic could justifiably point at the only emotional relationships left available to the characters. And the more we have seen of Stallone's work, we feel this may actually be another aspect of the formula. We remember how Adrian is actually outside Rocky's relationship with Apollo Creed. When Rocky dances in the waves it is with Apollo, not Adrian. And in *Rambo*, the one female character had only existed to provide a brief obvious romance with our hero, and been snuffed out after one precious kiss from him. In these circumstances, perhaps it had been more honest, in *Rambo III*, to pretend the world had no women in it. There must have been at least a few moments during this period when Stallone wished such a Utopia might have existed.

The violence of *Rambo III*, when it came, was so detached but ceaseless that it seemed pointless, despite the worthy cause. More crucially, it began to affect Stallone himself. Through much of the *Rocky* series, the two *Rambo* movies, and *Cobra*, he had been made familiar with the old arguments about the crass, exploitative nature of his work. Critics began doing body counts of the *Rambo* films, delighting in the fact that each new movie upped its quota of body-bags. There were clear responses to such developments. The box-office upped its quota of money-bags.

Stallone made his own very physical response by improving the quality of his bodily equipment, and by the time he went into production for *Rambo III* he looked like two applicants for *The Incredible Hulk*. His muscles were now so pronounced, his biceps so splendid, his neck so tough and tightly veined, that he began himself to find his body almost risible. He looked, he said, 'like a berserker'; he joked that he couldn't get into his house.

Naturally enough, Stallone was often ready to defend the movie. In 1989 he said, 'I'm proud of (*Rambo III*) more than the others, because it dealt with the truth about what's happening in Afghanistan. It was the most responsible film I've ever made.'

But the violent tendencies of Rambo, and the success spiral on to which he had been catapulted, demanded a terrible price of the intellectual side of Stallone. It was easy and even justifiable for his more sensitive admirers to suggest he could only be churning out films of the quality of *Rambo III* for the money. It was the trap he had sworn, as the greenhorn star of the first *Rocky*, never to fall into, and he was totally enmeshed in it.

15 Transitions

Professionally and personally wounded, Stallone realized, after *Rambo III* and the devastation of his marriage to Brigitte, that something had to be done – on all fronts. Professionally, he looked back over his shoulder at the high hopes his early career had engendered in critics and audiences alike; the radiant notices he had won for *The Lords of Flatbush* and *Rocky*, and his own invigorating sense of discovery, in those early days, as a writer. Perhaps, indeed, all the real discoveries had been as a writer, not as an actor, for it could be said that he had never really intended to act. As he said, 'It was all by accident. I don't take credit for being this enlightened thinker about all this. It's like the Beverly Hillbillies. I was Jed Clampett – I fired a bullet into the ground and struck oil.'

However it had happened, nothing had succeeded like success, and the ongoing sagas of Rocky and Rambo were enough to prove it. For Stallone, however, it was becoming clearer that this simply wasn't enough, and the characters Rocky and Rambo had become had, in many ways, travelled a long way from his original conception of them. Audiences still wanted updates on both characters, however, and the studio bosses insisted that Stallone should keep coming up with the product. The débâcle of *Rambo III* – despite the fact that, physically, Stallone was at the peak of his career – had only proved to him how far he was from the quality and type of work he had hoped to be doing at this stage of his career.

His long-nurtured ambition to play Edgar Allan Poe still had the studios shaking their heads in polite disbelief. He had hopes of making a film about Puccini, but the idea strayed so far from the accepted image of Stallone that it remained forlorn. His script of *The Bozo*, the story of an evangelist, that Stallone had first worked on in the late seventies, also laid around unused.

Such unwillingness to back projects in no way meant that the studios thought Stallone's box-office power was declining – far from it – but these obvious 'departures' from the usual, predictable Stallone movies, desperately worried them. In the hugely lucrative contracts Stallone negotiated with them, the underlying agreement insisted on by the studios was that the star's films should be 'broad-based' – films that could without difficulty be perceived as action movies.

Mark Canton, production chief of Warner Bros, has admitted that if Stallone wanted to move into a very different type of film from that with which he is so closely identified, shaking off all the accumulated expectancies of Rocky and Rambo, that 'I'd have to give it some deep and long thought, and I hope I don't have to cross that particular bridge ... It would be highly unlikely that you'd do a departure film for the same type of budget ... The public has expectations of what a star should deliver.'

At least in delivering it Stallone could now expect anything between $12 million and $17 million per movie, a haul that would only continue to be brought in if, when all the talking was done, his films were what the studios wanted, for Stallone's supremacy by no means meant he could call his own tune – that has never been the way of Hollywood. By early 1990 he had contractually committed himself to making at least five more 'broad-based' films, spread over a period of six years, a schedule he hoped would allow him time out to pursue a more ambitious exploration of non-action films.

Now, he talked to quality directors about the future direction of Sylvester Stallone's career; to Stanley Kubrick (who liked the Poe film but declined to do it), to Mike Nichols, Sydney Pollack, Richard Donner, and others. Sometimes, even if the director was a good one, Stallone decided against the film. He turned down the leading role in *The Executioner*, to be directed by *The French Connection*'s director William Friedkin, on the grounds of it being too violent at a time when he was desperately trying to turn away from violence-based movies, but if Stallone was to travel on, he knew the best way forward could only be with the best of company, who could help bring about his rebirth. He realized the history he brought to every film he associated himself with, and knew the successes of earlier days would make his audience's acceptance of him in a different kind of role more difficult. Deep down, he may even have acknowledged the fact that the chances of his ever getting to do those serious roles he longed for were slight. 'The imagery that I bring would destroy the integrity of the film,' he confessed. Meanwhile, he had to make do with *Lock Up*.

If this new movie was supposed to mark the start of this metamorphosis, it didn't do so very wholeheartedly, for *Lock Up* did nothing to further Stallone's reputation or career. Though absolved from writing or directing it, the star's presence nevertheless permeated the whole movie, making it on one hand a hymn to the undimmable spirit of Mr Ordinary 'Good Guy' America, and, on the other, a hideously explicit exercise in audience gratification. The picture's authentic feel was in no small way due to its being filmed at the high security East Jersey State Prison, just outside New York, whose inmates included the very man on whom Stallone now claimed to have based much of the character of Rocky. The irony of the original Rocky languishing in jail while the man who had made him into a fictional superstar lived on in legend and wealth, may not have been wasted on Stallone, and would certainly have made a better story for a film than *Lock Up* did.

From the bulk of the prisoners, Stallone got a hard ride. They especially enjoyed taunting him by yelling obscene accounts of Brigitte's sexual exploits at him. The pain of his last few years was thus constantly being reawakened during the early stages of filming, and may have helped him evolve a theory about what *Lock Up* could be about. 'I think emotional pain is what audiences can relate to even more than physical pain,' he said, a recommendation that may have suggested something of the actor's own predicament. His obsession with time also figured. 'To me, a prison term is the end of your life,' he said. 'Our whole life is about time and you only have so much of it. And I don't want to waste my time doing things that aren't any fun when I could be painting, playing sport or being with a woman. With my personality, I couldn't take being locked away.' He had been once, briefly in the long-ago, for jay-walking.

In his first major screenplay, *Lock Up*'s main writer (of three) Richard Smith, presented the story of decent, clean-living Frank Leone, sent to prison because he takes justice into his own hands when the police refuse to act. Intelligent, feeling Leone (who has Paul Klee posters on the walls of his cell, caringly dusts off old family photographs and plays football in slow-motion with the neighbourhood kids), decides to break out of prison when the sadistic Warden Drumgoole (Donald Sutherland) refuses to give him compassionate leave to visit his dying father. Drumgoole – so unhealthily attached to his work that he has had a defunct electric chair lovingly restored to full working order – retaliates by removing Leone to a high-security hell-hole prison, where he embarks on a programme of breaking the man.

Leone's tender relationship with his family is played out against the brutalized prison scenes. As in *Rocky*, any hint of deeper feelings immediately has the film lapsing into sentimentality, using the old Stallone props – as we have seen with the lingering enjoyment of old family snaps, the humdrum and the unexceptionable somehow made wonderful by being shown in slow-motion, as when Leone's girlfriend (Darlanne Fluegel) falls into his arms, to the tinkling accompaniment of Bill Conti's score. And, in place of the *Rocky* set-piece training sessions, *Lock Up* settles for a sequence in which Leone and his cohorts rebuild a clapped out old car, to an up-tempo disco beat. Ultimately, of course, Leone forces Drumgoole to reveal his true colours (in the comfort of his own electric chair), and the cruelly punitive black warder Meissner (John Amos) magically transforms into an avuncular, gentle figure. This feeling that Shirley Temple's Blue Bird of Happiness has all the time been in Leone's back prison yard without him knowing it, gives the film a ludicrously unconvincing twist, and underlines the basic hollow quality of the movie.

Among the selection of easy philosophies the film offered, Leone's opinion that 'your body has to be in here but your brain doesn't' also unmasked the movie's determination to get mileage out of *Rocky*, with his inherited belief that the body and the brain were two quite separate factors – a belief that, in Stallone's career, can be clearly traced back to Stanley in *The Lords of Flatbush*.

The American critic James J. Mulay, for the incisive *Motion Picture Annual*, suggested that Stallone 'has yet to learn that the public is growing weary of his cartoonish action heroes and is moving on toward more human and realistic protagonists'. James Cameron-Wilson's decidedly backhanded compliment for *Film Review* was that in *Lock Up* 'Stallone gives possibly his best performance since *A Party at Kitty and Studs*'. More kindly, *Films and Filming*'s Martin Sutton admitted that there was still 'a certain giggy, visceral, leave-your-brains-at-home-buzz' to this latest effort, but regretted that 'Sly's messianic splendour begins to smack more and more of nostalgia for the cinemascope shoulders of Charlton Heston'. For whatever reason, *Lock Up* did only so-so business in the States, and was quickly forgotten elsewhere.

Stallone considered his next film, *Tango and Cash*, to be 'a perfect vehicle', and remembered working with his co-star Kurt Russell as so enjoyable that it was 'a crime, it was so much fun ... Terminal laughter'. Of all the actors he had appeared with over the years, he said by far the best experiences had been working with Russell and John Travolta. As for *Tango and Cash*, Stallone rather confusingly explained that 'My going too far into Supermanism has become a turn-off, and the audience is now clearly saying, "OK, Sly, give us something new, change the music, go back to where you came from." Which is what I'm doing. *Tango and Cash* taps a side of me that I have never shown before – somewhat debonair, irreverent and humorous.'

Again, though Stallone had no writing or directorial responsibilities on the movie, careful attention was given to presenting the Stallone persona as more sophisticated, nattily dressed, and urbane than before. In the opening sequence, there was even an attempt to deflate the Rambo image when Stallone's character Ray Tango referred to Rambo as 'a pussycat'. Tango was a hard-hitting Los Angeles cop, dressed more for Wall Street than the streets, incongruously matched with the more happy-go-lucky Gabe Cash (Russell), slouching through life in jeans and tee-shirts. The pair are framed for corruption by the vengeful, and delightfully mad, super-villain Perret (Jack Palance), and deposited – shades of *Lock Up* – in a high security penitentiary.

Their desperate attempt to escape, clear their names and nail Perret, provided the bones of a film that was fast-moving, stylish, but basically vacuous. As Cash, Russell got the girl (Tango's sister, played by Teri Hatcher), and got to play a brief scene in drag. One of the major disappointments of the picture was that amidst the frenetic fun Stallone was given no love interest.

The Russian Andrei Konchalovsky, whose more distinguished films included *Shy People* and *Runaway Train*, was credited as director, though he left the movie after 'artistic disagreements' before filming was completed, leaving its executive producer, and Second Unit Director, Peter MacDonald – who had already directed sizeable chunks of *Rambo: First Blood Part II* and *Batman*, and the whole of *Rambo III* – to close up on the production. Nobody should have been too surprised at such last minute substitutions on a Stallone movie.

Perhaps, at what was obviously a pretty crucial time in his career, *Tango and Cash* was a curiously ineffective choice for Stallone. Apart from the fact that here was a Stallone movie that was strong on comedy (the first to be so since the sad experience of *Rhinestone*), and that its star wore spectacles and well-cut clothes, some thought the mixture was much the same as before. But *Tango and Cash* did break new ground, suggesting that Stallone had indeed grown up, that he was not going to take Rambo as seriously as he had in the past, that he could indeed perform well a screenplay that was essentially a parody.

And in this version of a buddy movie, Stallone not only acknowledged that other, newer formulas were now spelling box-office success, but acceded that this success, so far as he was concerned, could be shared with another actor. His had not so far been a career distinguished by the starry company he kept on screen, a fact that to some extent had left him rather isolated as a respected performer. At times, in *Tango and Cash*, it seemed as if Russell's equal screentime appearance in the movie diffused Stallone's monopoly of stardom; indeed, there was a sneaky feeling that the film favoured Russell above Stallone. Nevertheless, Stallone obviously hoped the movie would help shake off some of the preconceptions about his persona and, despite some tawdry reviews, *Tango and Cash* certainly did better than *Lock Up*; perhaps the gentle transitions he was going through were working their magic.

The critic Nick Digilio, finding Stallone 'completely out of his element', declared that the film 'has to be seen to be believed … a wild and weird exercise in excess that also works as a satire of its genre … the plot is a recycled mess, the dialog (*sic*) is embarrassingly bad' – and Digilio went on to greet it as 'a very smart "dumb movie" '. For the *Monthly Film Bulletin*, Kim

Newman thought that 'Stallone and Russell play it like Hope and Crosby ... falling more or less in love with one another during their breathless adventure'. Iain Johnstone in the *Sunday Times* called it 'a crash-bang prison drama that looks more like a trailer than a film'.

There seemed little doubt that it was now time for Stallone to nail his talents to the mast. In 1990 he announced two forthcoming projects that promised to be quite outside the interest of what he had done before. Plans were announced for a movie, *Oscar*, in which he would play the son of Victor Mature, making a screen comeback after some twenty years of retirement. This coming together of two of cinema's most legendary he-men has a potential fascination before even a hint of the film's story leaks out. Subsequently, Mature was crossed out and Kirk Douglas pencilled in. There was also news of a comedy, to be filmed in 1991, in which Stallone would co-star with that substantial Hollywood property John Candy. The proposed juxtaposition of these two utterly dissimilar stars, suggests that Stallone is beginning to learn from the successes other stars have made – not least of all Schwarzenegger, who had made a hit of *Twins*, without damaging his predominantly muscular screen image. But despite the promise of a new model Stallone reaching the screens, it is obvious that, for a while at least, Rambo and Rocky will have to live on beside these new creations.

When filming on *Rocky V* wound up in mid-1990, and Stallone walked off the set, he insisted it was, at long last, the end of Rocky. He had in fact decided to kill Rocky off – a quiet, satisfied death, with Rocky gently resting his head on Adrian's shoulder, closing his eyes never to open them again – but the studios had refused to accept this proof of Rocky's mortality. Though it is perhaps unsafe to state that *Rocky V* is indeed 'The Final Bell' of the story (all along the way of the series, Stallone has often announced each sequel as positively the last), it seems unlikely that Stallone would want to revive the character again. A flagging box-office return, and the demands of his studio, may of course make a revival necessary, and the possibility has been left open. After all, dear old growling Mickey had departed this life in *Rocky III*, but was back in *Rocky V* for a dream sequence.

Meanwhile, there is a very real sense of Rocky (and Stallone) having come full circle in *Rocky V*, with Rocky's original director, John Avildsen, brought back to finish what he started, though in the event Stallone himself directed some of the second unit fight sequences. Now, Rocky is ageing, and brain-damaged; the years of fighting have taken their toll. He has to learn to achieve and find satisfaction and respect in taking another young hopeful – played by John Wayne's nephew, Tommy Morrison – under his wing. Rocky has found a new sort of immortality, the knowledge that his legend can live on through others, but not before he has almost lost Adrian and his son. Sage Stallone turned in an excellent performance as Rocky Jnr – some of the critics seriously suggested he was a better actor than his father – bringing the accumulated experiences of his real-life relationship with Stallone to bear. His father's comment on his son's achievement was 'There are moments when he isn't acting'.

Rocky V rather obviously trundled out the old Rocky messages about making it on your own, overcoming adversity and getting to the top of the heap, here summed up in the film's publicity phrase 'Go For It'. Now, it seemed to many a tired song sung over.

'When a character is on top, such as he was in *Rocky III* and *Rocky IV*, it's very hard to conjure up true grass-root, blue-collar proletariat emotion,' said Stallone, going on to claim that the new movie was 'very apropos to the mood of the country.' In fact, the film opened to rather disappointing business in the States, suggesting that public taste had moved on since Rocky had first lumbered into the public consciousness in the mid-seventies, and that Stallone's fictive hero had run out his story.

Now, when Stallone was seen publicizing Rocky's latest adventure, it was obvious that the gap between the character and his creator had widened hugely. When giving interviews, Stallone looked as much like a businessman as an actor – and was. He was still at pains to make it clear that Rocky was nothing more than an invention, that Sylvester Stallone was not Rocky, but rather a higher intelligence. Such an attitude had the uncanny effect of making Rocky seem even more hopeless and abandoned. Meanwhile, as the recent foray into Cannes had proved, Stallone's personal magnetism seemed undiminished. He walked into a Philadelphia Civic Centre overflowing with his fans to celebrate *Rocky V*, and was given an ecstatic welcome. How much of their rapture was directed at Rocky, and how much at Stallone, or even Rambo, must be something of a mystery.

Rambo's legend is quite another problem, as it seemed to get constantly washed up on the shore of the latest worldwide conflict. He had attempted the exorcism of his own horrors of Vietnam on his return to America in *First Blood*, then gone back to the real warfields in the sequel, and progressed to saving Afghanistan and blasting the Russians in *Rambo III*. Probably more than any other movie star, Stallone had been greatly affected by the extraordinary and rapid changes sweeping the world. At the time of writing, it might be expedient and good box-office tactics to pitch Rambo against certain factions of the Arab world, but – as Stallone knew to his cost after *Rambo III* – switches of political fortune could burn him badly.

One of the problems of the next *Rambo* may be in finding a serious, and socially acceptable, adversary. Stallone has suggested, perhaps not altogether light-heartedly, that when *Rambo* next appears it will be as a ruthless protector of the environment, a new all-Green Rambo, setting his superhuman talents against elephant poachers, or against the escalating destruction of the Rain Forests, or the industrialist polluters of the world's rivers. If this happens, perhaps Rambo will be better able to vocalize his philosophies, and – since killing, in any shape or form, is not a noticeably Green pastime – find an alternative to giving his opponents a quick ticket to Heaven. But, again, it will ultimately be the studios who show Rambo the way forward.

Back with the first *Rocky*, Stallone remembered life as being so much simpler.

'I was a hick then ... I was wearing a $60 three-piece denim suit from Poland, with flowers on the back. I thought I was really happening. I was still driving my four-cylinder Volvo, and I was happy.'

Now, his taste in clothes was impeccable. There could be no doubt that by 1990 Stallone had become probably Hollywood's best, and most expensively, dressed man. The clean line of his attire – often, in its sober greys and blacks showing an almost religious observance of top designer Gianni Versace – was matched by the cool, clean intellectualism of this man, now introduced almost anew, to his public. He wore spectacles, as he had done since adolescence, to face the world. He proudly announced that now he would always wear them. Photographers almost gasped as they detected grey hair at his temples – a sign of ageing which he had made no attempt to hide. He appeared on television interviews, looking devastatingly smart and surprisingly self-conscious. Being quizzed by Oprah Winfrey and her fawning audience of Stallone fanatics, Stallone at first seemed ill-at-ease, but eventually warmed to the occasion. A cheeky lady enquired about the state of his muscles, and was invited to come on down and feel them. The recluse of the time of *Paradise Alley* and *F.I.S.T.* was being expunged. Stallone knew he must be of the people. The public, the journalists, a few of the critics, and even his most ardent admirers, blinked, and saw a man who appeared to be witty, human and vulnerable, who cared about real issues, who could stand back and laugh at himself, and who once again wanted to communicate all this to the world. Perhaps, after a long time out in the cold, Stallone was coming back into the hearts of the ordinary people.

Beyond America, his reputation has never dimmed, and when he decided to show up for the 1990 Cannes Film Festival, he was the cynosure of attention. Crowds mobbed him with adoration. A handful of fans would quickly turn to a thousand, until he had to seek refuge in his hotel room. On such occasions, there was little doubt that it was Stallone the man, the movie actor, that set off such reactions, not remembrances of Rocky or Rambo. Every moment of his Cannes visit threw up a photo opportunity, not least a brilliantly staged reunion with his old rival Schwarzenegger, who alone was acknowledged to be the only possible true successor to the Stallone throne. Not that there even now seemed a real threat to Stallone's supremacy. In 1989, his annual income had been a staggering $63 million, with Schwarzenegger lagging behind at a mere $55 million. Despite not having made a truly successful film for some time, Stallone still belonged to the gods. At a party thrown during the Cannes Festival his name was spelled out across the sky in fireworks.

The quiet transitions affected by Stallone were nevertheless played out alongside the not inconsiderable violence of *Lock Up, Tango and Cash*, and *Rocky V*, with Stallone insisting that his audiences should differentiate between the man and the performances he was offering. Rocky might be brain-damaged, but his creator was a voracious reader, for whom no day would be complete without a dip into the works of Robert Frost or Edna St Vincent Millay, not forgetting John Dos Passos, Herman Melville, and the ubiquitous Poe.

Stallone's intellectualism spread over into his love of art, through which, over the years, he had built up an extraordinarily rich and colourful collection. It was a sore point with Stallone, however, that he was not perceived as being an art-lover, the owner of one of the most prestigious collections in the world. He felt slighted when people spoke of Madonna's art collection in the same breath. His knowledge of great artists was formidable, and he had a genuine appreciation of them, though he would frequently sell items from his collection. Towards the end of the eighties, his interest in maintaining so formidable a collection waned, possibly because, in the heady art world, he felt himself to be something of an outsider. Much of the collection was broken up. At various times, Stallone had owned works by Warhol and Degas, by Hockney and Magritte, by Rodin and Dali, by Douguereau and Bacon, such prizes sharing the wall with paintings by Stallone himself, their garish canvases hectic with thick colour and deep meanings.

His own works could dwarf those of the masters; one large canvas of his, bursting with life, was inscribed in Stallone's hand, 'For the eyes are the scouts of the heart'. And the arrangement of his collection could be startling; a Boyd Wood sculpture of two giant teeth tucking in to two violins, sitting beside an Old Master; Rodin's Eve sharing a corner with LeRoy Neiman's painting of Stallone as Rocky.

The concept of Time permeated many of his works, revealing his own preoccupation with it. Watches, of which he owned a great many, appeared with obsessive regularity on his canvases. Time, of course, had always been of paramount importance to Stallone. Now, perhaps stronger than ever before, there was a distinct feeling that it might be running out.

'Time is truly the enemy,' he said. 'It's not the great healer, it's the great stealer … Right now, my great effort is not to squander the time it will take to make the most important films that I wanted to do before. Artists die twice. First creatively. Then physically. The second one is the easiest.'

Conclusion: Past Magic

Lock Up, Tango and Cash and *Rocky V* had all pretty clearly displayed the sort of image Stallone had been obliged to show to the cinema public over the years, though each of these movies contained signs that he was trying to edge away from the sometimes crippling persona expected of him.

It must have been with a real sense of exasperation that Stallone looked on as Schwarzenegger managed successfully to negotiate comedy in *Twins* as well as almost corner the market in violent science fiction with *Total Recall*. At the same time Mel Gibson, another actor sometimes accused of having taken on some of Stallone's followers, was proving he could hit the box-office between the eyes by inaugurating the *Lethal Weapon* series, skirt through light comedy, and get to play Hamlet as well. There is no doubt that such breadth of activity is what Stallone longs to achieve and perhaps, ironically, it is only Rocky and Rambo that have prevented him from doing so.

This may be about to change. Rocky's story, we can hopefully believe, is over, but Rambo is due to make a reappearance, and any new style of acting career Stallone carves out for himself will have to make room for this, making Rambo's next outing an experience that won't undermine his creator's future. Perhaps this can only happen if Rambo regenerates as a sort of do-gooding, non-political, articulate hero, trying to live down the blanket condemnation *Variety* poured on to *First Blood*: 'there are enough nuts out there without giving them a hero to cheer for'. But how such a transformation will be carried through in a way that leaves the studio bosses, box-office and Stallone happy with John Rambo, is a tricky problem.

Dolph Lundgren, whose own career blossomed quite satisfactorily after Stallone had given him a break in *Rocky IV*, has offered his own, uncluttered view of Stallone's future.

'He knows exactly what people want to see on screen. The good guy is invincible and the bad guy's really bad with no redeeming qualities. I think times are changing now. The heroes as well as the villains will have to be more shaded, but I think Sly will go with the times.'

Others are equally hopeful that what lies ahead may be better, and more interesting, than much of what has gone before in Stallone's career. Jack Kroll of *Newsweek* has pointed out that 'for a long time James Cagney was not considered a serious actor, and Sly has done serious work in *F.I.S.T.* and *Paradise Alley* ... What Sly needs is to surround himself with really gifted, intelligent people he can't control ... He has to relinquish his control'.

For the director Milton Katselas, Stallone's major problem is that 'his sensitivity and delineation of character have been sacrificed to caricature. It's probably going to take time for him to satisfy his public while developing as an actor ... our best actors, like Dustin Hoffman and Al Pacino, are stage-trained'.

Susan Stotter, co-director at San Francisco's American Conservatory Theatre, is another professional who recognizes Stallone's potential – and the very fact that he is perceived as having so much of it makes its own curious comment on his already long and extraordinary career in films. Stotter claims that 'Stallone could be a serious actor – absolutely. He has tremendous sensitivity and charisma on the screen. He has great intelligence. He has glamour. I think there's a Macbeth in there, or a Brutus. Or a Mark Antony to Cleopatra.'

All this, of course, addresses Stallone the actor, but what of Stallone the writer and film director? The screenplays of the *Rocky* series and *Paradise Alley* represent his most significant achievements as a writer. Less spectacularly, he has also been responsible for, among others, *F.I.S.T.*, *Staying Alive*, *Cobra* and *Over the Top* – either solely or as co-writer. Looking back, it may be that there is not the recognition of so much potential in Stallone the writer as there is in Stallone the actor, but there are marvellous things in the best of his work (with *Paradise Alley* an often-overlooked prize example) that distinguish Stallone as a natural storyteller and born communicator.

For Stallone the director, the future seems less promising, but this is probably no more than he would wish for himself. He has had his very real successes as director – even the most grudging critic should realize the qualities of, say, *Rocky II* and *Rocky III*, and, again, *Paradise Alley* – but, since the indisputably feeble *Staying Alive*, he hasn't been behind the camera.

He is still, however, where he belongs: at the heart of popular movies. He is aware that for him success may, in a strange way, have come too soon, that he may have peaked too early in his career. Wherever that career leads on now, it is almost certain that Stallone will be remembered in the history of his industry for his creation of Rocky Balboa and John Rambo. For some, this would be achievement enough, but Stallone remains today what he has always been – a driven man. Physical and intellectual fitness are as important to him now as they have ever been.

His personal happiness must have been supported by a growing realization in the world outside that here was a rather gentle, sometimes awkward, clever man, who retained, or perhaps had recaptured, a genuine understanding of what real life was. Reports appeared in the press that he might start life again with Sasha, which, for the onlooker, would have made a perfect ending to the fairy-tale, proving that Stallone really is like good, dependable old Rocky. Time will tell. Meanwhile, he has said that nowadays he is better at being a boyfriend than a husband, a view apparently confirmed by his list of escorts since his parting from Brigitte, which includes model Naomi Campbell, Vanna White, Alana Stewart and heiress Cornelia Guest. At the time of writing, his companion is the twenty-one-year old Jennifer Flavin, known affectionately by associates as 'Flavin of the month'.

The couple do not live together. At the 1990 Cannes Film Festival the lovers posed for some sexually tantalizing photographs that offered another contradiction in Stallone's life; the pouting Flavin and Stallone seemed to look out defiantly on a world that was quite outside them. And Stallone can look out at that world with confidence, with the knowledge that his film stardom is bolstered by his place on the Carolco company board, and his ownership of the production company White Eagle. He also manages real-estate investments in Hawaii, California and the East Coast, oversees his film properties, has invested in a stable of thirty polo ponies, and juggles stockholdings.

Rocky, in *Rocky V*, had gone back to his roots, but for Stallone there can be no going back. Past magic cannot be recaptured, and now Stallone must find new songs to sing. It may be that he is on the brink of the most exciting period of his life and career, when all the promise and hope of the kid from Hell's Kitchen will come alive in a way that will satisfy his audiences and, more importantly, fulfil Stallone himself. If he continues to live out parables of his own life on film, we could all be in for an interesting experience.

Bibliography

Auster, Albert, and Quart, Leonard, *How the War was Remembered: Hollywood and Vietnam* (Praeger, US, 1988)

Bergan, Ronald, *The United Artists Story* (Octopus, 1986)

Bookbinder, Robert *The Films of the Seventies* (Citadel, New Jersey, 1982)

Douglas, Kirk, *The Ragman's Son* (Simon and Schuster, 1988)

Ebert, Roger, *A Kiss is still a Kiss* (Andrews, McMeel and Parker, New York, 1984)

Grobel, Lawrence, *The Hustons* (Bloomsbury, 1990)

Hall, William, *Raising Caine* (Sidgwick and Jackson, 1981)

Hirschorn, Clive, *The Universal Story* (Octopus, 1983)

Hirschorn, Clive, *The Warner Bros Story* (Octopus, 1979)

Kael, Pauline, *5001 Nights at the Movies* (Holt, Rinehart and Winston, New York, 1982)

Kael, Pauline, *When the Lights go Down* (Marion Boyars, 1980)

Leigh, Wendy, *Arnold* (Pelham, 1990)

Levy, Emanuel, *And the winner is ... the history and politics of the Oscar Awards* (Ungar, New York, 1987)

McGee, Mark, *Roger Corman: the best of the cheap acts* (McFarland, New York, 1988)

Medved, Harry and Michael, *Son of Golden Turkey Awards* (Angus and Robertson, 1986)

Milne, Tom (ed), *The Time Out Film Guide* (Penguin, 1989)

Morrell, David, *First Blood* (Barrie and Jenkins, 1972)

Motion Picture Annual, Cinebooks, (US, Various editions)

Naha, Ed, *The Films of Roger Corman: brilliance on a budget* (Arco, New York, 1982)

Peary, Danny, *Guide for the Film Fanatic* (Simon and Schuster, 1987)

Quinlan, David, *Quinlan's Illustrated Directory of Film Stars* (Batsford, 1986)

Stallone, Sylvester, *The Official Rocky Scrapbook* (Grosset and Dunlap, 1977)

Stallone, Sylvester, *Paradise Alley* (Putnam, New York, 1977; W.H. Allen, 1978)

Periodicals and journals consulted include *Empire, Films and Filming, 20/20, Films In Review*, the *Guardian*, the *New Yorker, Photoplay, Rolling Stone, Time Out, The Times* and *Village Voice*.

Filmography

A PARTY AT KITTY AND STUDS 1970 (re-issued as THE ITALIAN STALLION)

BANANAS
1971. United Artists (Jack Rollins/Charles H. Joffe). 81 minutes.
Director: Woody Allen. Producer: Jack Grossberg. Associate producer and editor: Ralph Rosenblum. Screenplay: Woody Allen, Mickey Rose. Photography: Andrew M. Costikyan. Music: Marvin Hamlisch. Stallone unbilled. Leading players: Woody Allen (Fielding Mellish), Louise Lasser (Nancy), Carlos Montalban (General Emilio M. Vargas), Natividad Abascal (Yolanda), Jacobo Morales (Esposito), Miguel Suarez (Luis).

NO PLACE TO HIDE (re-issued 1980 as REBEL)
1973. Robert Schnitzer. 78 minutes.
Director: Robert Schnitzer. Producers: Robert Schnitzer, David B. Appleton. Screenplay: Robert Schnitzer, Larry Beinhart. Additional Dialogue: Louis Pastore. Photography: Marty Knopf. Music: Joseph Delacorte. Stallone top-billed as Jerry Savage. Leading players: Antony Page (Tommy), Rebecca Grimes (Laurie), Vickie Lancaster (Estelle Ferguson), Dennis Tate (Ray Brown), Barbara Lee Govan (Marlena St. James), Roy White (William Decker), Henry G. Sanders (James Henderson), Jed Mills (Chuck), David Orange (Richard).

THE LORDS OF FLATBUSH
1974. Ebbets Field Film Co. (Columbia). 88 minutes.
Directors: Stephen Verona, Martin Davidson. Producer: Stephen Verona. Editors: Stan Siegel, Muffie Meyer. Screenplay: Stephen Verona, Gayle Glecker, Martin Davidson (additional dialogue: Sylvester Stallone). Photography: Joseph Mangine, Edward Lachman. Music: Joe Brooks. Stallone second-billed as Stanley Rosiello. Leading players: Perry King (Chico Tyrell), Henry Winkler (Butchey Weinstein), Paul Mace (Wimpy Murgalo), Susan Blakely (Jane Bradshaw), Maria Smith (Frannie Malincanico), Renée Paris (Annie Yuckamenelli), Paul Jabara (Crazy Cohen), Bruce Reed (Mike Mambo), Frank Stiefel (Arnie Levine), Martin Davidson (Mr. Birnbaum).

THE PRISONER OF SECOND AVENUE
1975. Warner (Melvin Frank). 98 minutes.
Director/Producer: Melvin Frank. Editor: Bob Wyman. Screenplay: Neil
Simon, from his stage play. Photography: Philip Lathrop. Music: Marvin
Hamlisch. Stallone nineteenth-billed as Youth in park. Leading players: Jack
Lemmon (Mel), Anne Bancroft (Edna), Gene Saks (Harry Edison), Elizabeth
Wilson (Pauline), Florence Stanley (Pearl), Maxine Stuart (Belle).

FAREWELL MY LOVELY
1975. Avco Embassy/Elliott Kastner/ITC (George Pappas, Jerry Bruck-
heimer). 97 minutes.
Director: Dick Richards. Producers: Jerry Bruckheimer, George Pappas.
Editors: Joel Cox, Walter Thompson. Screenplay: David Zelag Goodman,
from the novel by Raymond Chandler. Photography: John Alonzo. Music:
David Shire. Stallone eighth-billed as Jonnie. Leading players: Robert
Mitchum (Philip Marlowe), Charlotte Rampling (Mrs. Grayle), John Ireland
(Nulty), Sylvia Miles (Mrs. Florian), Jack O'Halloran (Moose Malloy),
Anthony Zerbe (Brunette), Walter McGinn (Tommy Ray), Jim Thompson
(Mr Grayle), Kate Murtagh (Amthor), John O'Leary (Marriott), Harry Dean
Stanton (Billy Rolfe), Joe Spinell (Nick), Jimmy Archer (Georgie).

CAPONE
1975. 20th Century Fox/Santa Fe (Roger Corman). 101 minutes.
Director: Steve Carter. Producer: Roger Corman. Associate producer: John
Broderick. Editor: Richard Meyer. Screenplay: Howard Browne. Photo-
graphy: Vilis Lapenieks. Music: David Grisman, Rudy Cipolla. Stallone
fifth-billed as Frank Nitti. Leading players: Ben Gazzara (Al Capone), Susan
Blakely (Iris Crawford), Harry Guardino (Johnny Torrio), John Cassavetes
(Frankie Yale), Peter Maloney (Jake Guzik), Frank Campanella (Big Jim
Colosimo).

DEATH RACE 2000
1975. New World Pictures (Roger Corman). 79 minutes.
Director: Paul Bartel. Producer: Roger Corman. Associate producer: Jim
Weatherill. Editor: Tina Hirsch. Screenplay: Robert Thom, Charles Griffith,
from story by Ib Melchior. Photography: Tak Fujimoto. Music: Paul Chihara.
Stallone third-billed as Machine Gun Joe Viterbo. Leading players: David
Carradine (Frankenstein), Simone Griffeth (Annie), Mary Woronov (Calamity
Jane), Roberta Collins (Matilda the Hun), Martin Kove (Nero the Hero).

ROCKY
1976. United Artists/Chartoff-Winkler (Gene Kirkwood). 119 minutes.
Director: John G. Avildsen. Producers: Irwin Winkler, Robert Chartoff.
Executive producer: Gene Kirkwood. Editor: Richard Halsey. Screenplay:
Sylvester Stallone. Photography: James Crabe. Music: Bill Conti. Musical
items: 'Take me back' (Frank Stallone), 'Gonna fly' (Bill Conti, Carol

Connors). Stallone top-billed as Rocky Balboa. Leading players: Talia Shire (Adrian), Burt Young (Paulie), Carl Weathers (Apollo Creed), Burgess Meredith (Mickey), Thayer David (Jergens), Joe Spinell (Gazzo), Jimmy Gambina (Mike), Tony Burton (Apollo's trainer).

F.I.S.T.
1978. United Artists/Norman Jewison (Gene Corman). 140 minutes. Producer/Director: Norman Jewison. Executive producer: Gene Corman. Supervising Editor: Antony Gibbs. Editor: Graeme Clifford. Screenplay: Joe Eszterhas, Sylvester Stallone, from story by Eszterhas. Photography: Laszlo Kovacs. Music: Bill Conti. Stallone top-billed as Johnny Kovak. Leading players: Rod Steiger (Senator Andrew Madison), Peter Boyle (Max Graham), Melinda Dillon (Anna Zerinkas), David Huffman (Abe Belkin), Kevin Conway (Vince Doyle), Tony Lo Bianco (Babe Milano), Cassie Yates (Molly).

PARADISE ALLEY
1978. Universal. (A Force 10 Production/A Moonblood Film). 107 minutes. Director/Screenplay: Sylvester Stallone. Producers: John F. Roach, Ronald A. Suppa. Executive producer: Edward Pressman. Editor: Eve Newman. Photography: Laszlo Kovacs. Music: Bill Conti. Song: 'Too close to Paradise' (Conti, Carole Bayer Sager, Bruce Roberts). Stallone top-billed as Cosmo Carboni. Leading players: Kevin Conway (Stitch), Anne Archer (Annie), Joe Spinell (Burp), Armand Assante (Lenny), Lee Canalito (Victor), Aimée Eccles (Susan Chow), Terry Funk (Franky The Thumper), Joyce Ingalls (Bunchie), Frank Macrae (Big Glory), Tom Waits (Mumbles), Frank Stallone Jnr. (Singer).

ROCKY II
1979. United Artists. 119 minutes. Director: Sylvester Stallone. Producers: Irwin Winkler, Robert Chartoff. Supervising Editor: Danford B. Greene. Editors: Stanford C. Allen, Janice Hampton, James Symons. Screenplay: Sylvester Stallone. Photography: Bill Butler. Music: Bill Conti. Stallone top-billed as Rocky Balboa. Leading players: Talia Shire (Adrian), Burt Young (Paulie), Carl Weathers (Apollo Creed), Burgess Meredith (Mickey), Tony Burton (Apollo's trainer), Joe Spinell (Gazzo).

NIGHTHAWKS
1981. Universal/Herb Nanas (Martin Poll). 99 minutes. Director: Bruce Malmuth. Producer: Martin Poll. Editor: Christopher Holmes. Screenplay: David Shaber, from story by Shaber and Paul Sylbert. Photography: James A. Contner. Music: Keith Emerson. Stallone top-billed as Deke DaSilva. Leading players: Billy Dee Williams (Matthew Fox), Lindsay Wagner (Irene), Persis Khambatta (Shakka), Nigel Davenport (Peter Hartman), Hilarie Thompson (Pam), Rutger Hauer (Wulfgar), Joe Spinell (Lt. Munafo), Walter Mathews (Commissioner).

ESCAPE TO VICTORY (US: VICTORY)
1981. Lorimar/Victory Company/Tom Stern (Freddie Fields). 120 minutes.
Director: John Huston. Producer: Freddie Fields. Editor: Robert Silvi.
Screenplay: Evan Jones, Yabo Yablonsky, from story by Yablonsky, Djordje
Milicevic and Jeff Maguire. Photography: Gerry Fisher. Music: Bill Conti.
Stallone top-billed as Hatch. Leading players: Michael Caine (Colby), Max
Von Sydow (Von Steiner), Carole Laure (Renée), Daniel Massey (Waldron),
Tim Pigott-Smith (Rose), Julian Curry (Shurlock), Anton Diffring (Boehm),
Pelé (Fernandez), Bobby Moore (Terry), Osvaldo Ardiles (Rey), Maurice
Roeves (Pyrie), Michael Cochrane (Farrell), Clive Merrison (The Forger).

ROCKY III
1982. United Artists/Irwin Winkler, Robert Chartoff. 99 minutes.
Director/Screenplay: Sylvester Stallone. Producers: Irwin Winkler, Robert
Chartoff. Editors: Don Zimmerman, Mark Warner. Photography: Bill
Butler. Music: Bill Conti. Stallone top-billed as Rocky Balboa. Leading
players: Talia Shire (Adrian), Burt Young (Paulie), Carl Weathers (Apollo
Creed), Burgess Meredith (Mickey), Tony Burton (Duke), Mr T (Clubber
Lang), Hulk Hogan (Thunderlips), Ian Fried (Rocky Junior).

FIRST BLOOD
1982. Carolco (Buzz Feitshans). 93 minutes.
Director: Ted Kotcheff. Producer: Buzz Feitshans. Screenplay: Michael
Kozoll, William Sackheim and Sylvester Stallone, from the novel by David
Morrell. Photography: Andrew Laszlo. Music: Jerry Goldsmith. Stallone
top-billed as Rambo. Leading players: Richard Crenna (Trautman), Brian
Dennehy (Teasle), Bill McKinney (Kern), Jack Starrett (Galt), Michael
Talbott (Balford), Chris Mulkey (Ward), John McLiam (Orval), Alf
Humphreys (Lester), David Caruso (Mitch), David Crowley (Shingleton),
Don Mackay (Preston).

STAYING ALIVE
1983. Paramount (Stigwood/Stallone). 96 minutes.
Director: Sylvester Stallone. Producers: Robert Stigwood, Sylvester Stallone.
Screenplay: Sylvester Stallone, Norman Wexler, from characters created by
Nik Cohn. Editors: Don Zimmerman, Mark Warner. Photography: Nick
McLean. Music: Johnny Mandel, Robin Garb, Bee Gees, Frank Stallone.
Stallone in non-speaking cameo. Leading players: John Travolta (Tony
Manero), Cynthia Rhodes (Jackie), Finola Hughes (Laura), Steve Inwood
(Jesse), Julie Bovasso (Mrs. Manero), Charles Ward (Butler), Frank Stallone
(Carl).

RHINESTONE
1984. Twentieth Century Fox/Howard Smith, Marvin Worth. 111 minutes.
Director: Bob Clark. Producers: Howard Smith, Marvin Worth. Screenplay:
Phil Alden Robinson, Sylvester Stallone, from story by Phil Alden Robinson.

Editors: Stan Cole, John Wheeler. Photography: Timothy Galfas. Music: Dolly Parton, Mike Post. Stallone top-billed as Nick Martinelli. Leading players: Dolly Parton (Jake), Richard Farnsworth (Noah), Ron Leibman (Freddie Ugo), Tim Thomerson (Barnett), Steven Apostle Pec (Father), Penny Santon (Mother), Russell Buchanan (Elgart), Ritch Brookley (Luke), Jerry Potter (Walt), Billie Joe (Jesse Welles).

RAMBO: FIRST BLOOD Part II
1985. Tri-Star (Buzz Feitshans). 93 minutes.
Director: George P. Cosmatos. Producer: Buzz Feitshans. Executive producers: Mario Kassar, Andrew Vajna. Screenplay: Sylvester Stallone and James Cameron, from story by Kevin Jarre. Editors: Mark Goldblatt, Mark Helfrich. Photography: Jack Cardiff. Music: Jerry Goldsmith. Stallone top-billed as Rambo. Leading players: Richard Crenna (Trautman), Charles Napier (Murdock), Steven Berkoff (Podovsky), Julia Nickson (Co), Martin Kove (Ericson), George Kee Cheung (Tay), Andy Wood (Banks).

ROCKY IV
1985. United Artists. 91 minutes.
Director/Screenplay: Sylvester Stallone. Producers: Irwin Winkler, Robert Chartoff. Editors: Don Zimmerman, John W. Wheeler. Photography: Bill Butler. Music: Vince DiCola. Stallone top-billed as Rocky Balboa. Leading players: Talia Shire (Adrian), Burt Young (Paulie), Carl Weathers (Apollo Creed), Brigitte Nielsen (Ludmilla), Tony Burton (Duke), Michael Pataki (Nicoli Koloff), Dolph Lundgren (Drago), Rocky Krakoff (Rocky Junior).

COBRA
1986. Warner Bros/Cannon (James D. Brubaker). 87 minutes.
Director: George P. Cosmatos. Producers: Menahem Golan, Yoram Globus. Editors: Don Zimmerman, James Symons. Screenplay: Sylvester Stallone, based on the novel *Fair Game* by Paula Gosling. Photography: Ric Waite. Music: Sylvester Levay. Stallone top-billed as Marion Cobretti. Leading players: Brigitte Nielsen (Ingrid), Reni Santoni (Gonzales), Andrew Robinson (Detective Monte), Brian Thompson (Night Slasher), John Herzfeld (Cho), Lee Garlington (Nancy Stalk).

OVER THE TOP
1986. Cannon (Golan-Globus). 93 minutes.
Director: Menahem Golan. Producers: Menahem Golan, Yoram Globus. Editors: Don Zimmerman, James Symons. Screenplay: Stirling Silliphant, Sylvester Stallone, from story by Gary Conway, David C. Engelbach. Photography: David Gurfinkel. Music: Giorgio Moroder. Stallone top-billed as Lincoln Hawk. Leading players: Robert Loggia (Jason Cutler), Susan Blakely (Christina Hawk), Rick Zumwalt (Bob 'Bull' Hurley), David Mendenhall (Michael), Chris McCarty (Tim Salanger), Terry Funk (Ruker), Kelly Sahnger (Cashier).

RAMBO III

1988. Carolco (Mario Kassar/Andrew Vajna). 102 minutes.
Director: Peter MacDonald. Producer: Buzz Feitshans. Editors: James Symons, Andrew London, O. Nicholas Brown. Screenplay: Sylvester Stallone, Sheldon Lettich. Photography: John Stanier. Music: Jerry Goldsmith. Stallone top-billed as John Rambo. Leading players: Richard Crenna (Trautman), Marc de Jonge (Zaysen), Kurtwood Smith (Griggs), Spiros Focas (Masoud), Sasson Gabai (Mousa), Doudi Shoua (Hamid), Randy Raney (Kourov), Marcus Gilbert (Tomask).

LOCK UP

1989. White Eagle Productions/Carolco Pictures. 109 minutes.
Director: John Flynn. Producers: Lawrence Gordon, Charles Gordon. Editors: Michael N. Knue, Donald Brochu. Screenplay: Richard Smith, Jeb Stuart, Henry Rosenbaum. Photography: Donald E. Thorin. Music: Bill Conti. Stallone top-billed as Frank Leone. Leading players: Donald Sutherland (Warden Drumgoole), John Amos (Meissner), Sonny Landham (Chink), Tom Sizemore (Dallas), Frank Macrae (Eclipse), Darlanne Fluegel (Melissa), William Allen Young (Braden), Larry Romano (First Base).

TANGO AND CASH

1989. Warner Bros/Guber-Peters. 102 minutes.
Director: Andrei Konchalovsky. Producers: Jon Peters, Peter Guber. 2nd Unit Director: Peter MacDonald. Supervising Editor: Stuart Baird. Editors: Hubert De La Bouillerie, Robert Ferretti. Screenplay: Randy Feldman. Photography: Donald E. Thorin. Music: Harold Faltermeyer. Stallone top-billed as Ray Tango. Leading players: Kurt Russell (Gabe Cash), Jack Palance (Yves Perret), Teri Hatcher (Kiki), Michael J. Pollard (Owen), Brion James (Requin), Geoffrey Lewis (Police Captain), James Hong (Quan), Robert Z'Dar (Face).

ROCKY V

1990. United Artists/Star Partners III. 104 minutes.
Director: John G. Avildsen. Producers: Irwin Winkler, Robert Chartoff. Editors: Michael N. Knue, John G. Avildsen, Robert Ferretti, Trevor Jolly. Screenplay: Sylvester Stallone. Photography: Steven Poster. Music: Bill Conti, Stallone top-billed as Rocky Balboa. Leading players: Talia Shire (Adrian), Burt Young (Paulie), Sage Stallone (Rocky Jnr), Burgess Meredith (Mickey), Tommy Morrison (Tommy Gunn), Richard Gant (George Washington Duke), Tony Burton (Tony), James Gambina (Jimmy).

Index

A-Team, The, 98
Actors' Studio, 16, 27, 159
African Queen, The, 90
Ali, Muhammad, 45–6, 49, 84, 91, 98, 115, 140
Allen, Woody, 31, 119
Amos, John, 170
Andrews, Julie, 93
Angeli, Pier, 52
Anton, Susan, 85–6, 130
Antonowsky, Marvin, 128
Apprenticeship of Danny Kravitz, The, 104
Archer, Anne, 72
Ardiles, Osvaldo, 90
Arnold (book), 134
Assante, Armand, 71, 74
Attack (see *Nighthawks*)
Avildsen, John G., 48, 49, 53, 55–6, 80, 81, 174

Badham, John, 114
Bananas, 31
Bancroft, Anne, 38
Bartel, Paul, 41–2
Batman, 172
Baxter, Warner, 116
Beatty, Warren, 30
Bee-Gees, The, 113, 118
Berkoff, Steven, 125, 126
Best Little Whorehouse in Texas, The, 120
Beverley Hills Cop II, 149, 150, 157
Bianco, Tony Lo, 63
Big Bad Mama, 41
Birth of a Nation, 78
Blakely, Susan, 40, 152
Bloody Mama, 41
Bloom, Jake, 48
Blue Angel, The, 149
Bodyguard, The, 119
Bogus Kingdom, The, 31
Borgnine, Ernest, 52
Bovasso, Julie, 117
Boyle, Peter, 63
Bozo, The, 167
Brando, Marlon, 12, 61, 74, 111, 119
Brent-Dyer, Elinor, 158
Broadway Danny Rose, 119
Brooks, Joe, 35
Browne, Howard, 40
Butkus (dog), 13, 38, 51, 56

Cagney, James, 179
Caine, Michael, 90, 92, 94
Campbell, Naomi, 180
Canalito, Lee, 71, 74, 115
Candy, John, 173
Canton, Mark, 168
Capone, 40–2, 152
Capone, Al, 40
Carradine, David, 42
Carter, Jimmy, 12
Carver, Steve, 40
Champ, The, 53
Champion, 25
Chaplin, Charles, 56, 71, 73
Charles, Ezzard, 49

Chartoff, Robert, 46–8
Chayefsky, Paddy, 52, 56
Church of the New World Unity, 97
Cincinatti Kid, The, 59
Clark, Bob, 120
Clay, Cassius (see Ali, Muhammad)
Cobra, 146–9, 154, 157, 165, 179
Cochrane, Michael, 92
Cohen, Marvin, 151
Columbu, Franco, 126
Comedy Man, The, 83
Conan the Destroyer, 134
Conti, Bill, 93, 102, 170
Conway, Kevin, 63, 67, 72
Coppola, Francis Ford, 48, 112
Corman, Roger, 39–42, 47
Cosmatos, George Pan, 124, 147
Cotton Club, The, 112
Coward, Noël, 95
Crenna, Richard, 106, 107, 109, 124, 162
Crosby, Bing, 173
Cry Full and Whisper Empty – in the Same Breath, 31
Czach, Sasha (see Stallone, Sasha)

Dante, Joe, 42
Davenport, Nigel, 87
Davidson, Martin, 33, 35
Day of the Locust, The, 49
Dean, James, 12
Death of a Salesman (stage), 25, 33
Death Race 2000, 39, 41–3, 163
Delta Force, The, 150
Dennehy, Brian, 63, 105, 106, 109
Dennis, Patrick, 11
Desire Caught by the Tail (stage), 27
Diers, Marianne, 133
Dietrich, Marlene, 149
Dillon, Melinda, 62, 67
Dr Strangelove, 41
Dog Day Afternoon, 39
Donner, Richard, 168
Doors, The, 118
Douglas, Jerry, 29
Douglas, Kirk, 25, 106, 173

Eastman, George, 21
Eastwood, Clint, 12
Eccles, Aimée, 72
Edna the Inebriate Woman, 104
Eliot, T.S., 69
Escape to Victory, 81, 90–6, 104, 119
Eszterhas, Joe, 59, 60, 66
E.T., 100
Evans, Robert, 112
Executioner, The, 168
Extension, The, 30

Fair Game (see *Running Duck*)
Farewell, my Lovely, 39
Farmer, Francis, 119
Farnsworth, Richard, 121
Fat City, 90
Fiddler on the Roof, 59

189

Finch, Peter, 57
First Blood, 25, 37, 104–11, 119, 124, 125, 128, 130, 136, 163, 164, 175, 178
F.I.S.T., 39, 59–67, 69, 70, 76, 78, 80, 85, 86, 141, 176, 179
Flavin, Jennifer, 180
Fluegel, Darlanne, 170
Flynn, Errol, 19
Fonda, Henry, 12
Fonda, Jane, 119
Ford, Gerald, 12
Fortune and Men's Eyes (stage), 27
42nd Street, 42, 116
Frank, Melvin, 38
Frazier, Joe, 98
French Connection, The, 168
Friedkin, William, 168
Funk, Terry, 72

Gable, Clark, 12
Gambina, Jimmy, 49
Garcia, Andy, 119
Garlington, Lee, 146
Garner, James, 91
Gastineau, Mark, 158–159
Gazzara, Ben, 40
Gere, Richard, 112
Gibson, Mel, 14, 178
Glecker, Gayle, 34
Globus, Yoram, 150
Godfather, The, 49, 112
Godfather II, The, 39, 49
Godfather III, The, 119
Golan, Menahem, 150, 152, 153
Goldengirl, 85
Goldsmith, Jerry, 164
Gorbachev, Mikhail, 140, 142, 160, 163
Gorney, Karen Lynn, 114
Gosling, Paula, 146
Grant, Cary, 12
Graziano, Rocky, 52, 61
Grease, 115
Great Escape, The, 91, 93
Green Berets, The, 105
Griffith, Chuck, 41
Grimes, Rebecca, 36
Guardino, Harry, 41
Guest, Cornelia, 180

Hair (stage), 29
Happy Days, 35
Hatcher, Teri, 171
Hauer, Rutger, 87, 88–9, 149
Hell's Kitchen (see *Paradise Alley*)
Hemingway, Ernest, 30
Hercules, 21
Herd, Richard, 62
Herzfeld, John, 26, 31
Heston, Charlton, 171
Hitchcock, Alfred, 114
Hitler, Adolf, 95
Hoffa, James Riddle, 59, 60
Hoffman, Dustin, 179
Hogan, Hulk, 98
Hope, Bob, 99, 173
Horses, 32
Huffman, David, 62
Hughes, Finola, 116, 117
Hunchback of Notre Dame, The, 26
Huston, John, 90, 92, 94, 95

Incredible Hulk, The, 165
Indelible Shadows (book), 95
Indiana Jones and the Temple of Doom, 128
Ingalls, Joyce, 76–7, 130
Insdorf, Annette, 95
Inwood, Steve, 117
Ionesco, Eugene, 26
Italian Stallion, The, 29

Jesus Christ Superstar, 59
Jewison, Norman, 39, 59, 60, 64–7
Johnson, Don, 151
Jones, Grace, 157
Jonge, Marc de, 161, 162

Kassar, Mario, 104
Katselas, Milton, 179
Kennedy, Edward, 12
Key Largo, 90
Khambatta, Persis, 88
Kilmer, Val, 118
King, Perry, 34
Kirkwood, Gene, 46, 48
Klute, 30
Kojak, 38
Konchalovsky, Andrei, 172
Kotcheff, Ted, 104, 106
Kovacs, Ernie, 57
Kovacs, Laszlo, 67
Kubik, Larry, 46
Kubrick, Stanley, 168

Labofish, Jacqueline (*see* Stallone, Jacqueline)
Lancaster, Vickie, 36
Laurentiis, Dino de, 134
Leibman, Ron, 121
Leigh, Wendy, 134
Lemmon, Jack, 38, 48
Let My People Come (stage), 29
Lethal Weapon, 178
Lettich, Sheldon, 164
Levy, Emmanuel, 52
Life at the Top, 104
Lion in Winter, The, 86
Liston, Sonny, 49
Little Me (book), 11
Lock Up, 39, 169–71, 172, 176, 178
Loggia, Robert, 152
Lords of Flatbush, The, 33–8, 40, 42, 43, 119, 152, 163, 167, 170
Lovers and Other Strangers, 27
Lumet, Sidney, 39, 55
Lundgren, Dolph, 13, 136–8, 141–2, 157, 178

MacArthur, Douglas, 62
MacDonald, Peter, 163, 172
MacDonald, Richard, 67
McQueen, Steven, 60
Macrae, Frank, 72
Mace, Paul, 34
Madonna, 177
Maltese Falcon, The, 90
Man Who Loved Cat Dancing, The, 86
Man with the X-Ray Eyes, The, 48
*Martini, Bobby, 150, 157
Marty, 52, 56
Mason, Jackie, 48
Massey, Daniel, 92, 95
Mature, Victor, 37, 173

Melchior, Ib, 41
Mendenhall, David, 152
Meredith, Burgess, 49, 50, 56
Merrison, Clive, 94
Miami Vice, 151
Milland, Ray, 48
Miller, Arthur, 25
Mineo, Sal, 27
Mr Toad Goes West (stage), 18
Mitchum, Robert, 12, 39
Moore, Bobby, 90, 91
Moore, Dudley, 86
Morrell, David, 104, 106, 109
Morrison, Jim, 118
Morrison, Tommy, 174
Much Ado About Nothing (stage), 96
Muppet Show, The, 85
Murphy, Eddie, 149, 157
My Wicked, Wicked Ways (book), 19

Napier, Charles, 124, 125
Nataro, Ray, 97
Neagle, Anna, 40
Nelson, Gary, 86
Network, 56
New York, New York, 46
Newman, Paul, 47, 52, 60, 61
Nichols, Mike, 168
Nicholson, Jack, 60
Nickson, Julie, 125
Nielsen, Brigitte, 13, 133–8, 141–50, 155–60, 162, 167, 169, 180
Nighthawks, 86–9, 90, 104, 149
Nine to Five, 119
Nixon, Richard, 59
No Place to Hide, 36–8, 110, 119
Norris, Chuck, 37, 150, 153

Oh Calcutta! (stage), 28
Official Rocky Scrapbook, The, 47
Oliver, Jane, 45, 58–9
O'Neal, Ryan, 47
Oscar, 173
Osman, Alan, 97
Osman, Bernice, 97, 102
Over the Top, 141, 150–4, 163, 164, 179

Pacino, Al, 12, 39, 41, 60, 119, 179
Page, Antony, 36
Palance, Jack, 171
Pals, 119
Paradise Alley, 13, 19, 43–4, 67, 70–5, 76, 78–9, 80, 81, 85, 86, 93, 115, 117, 119, 163, 176, 179, 180
Paradise Alley (novel), 69–70
Parton, Dolly, 119–22
Party at Kitty and Studs, A, 28–9, 143, 171
Passing of the Third Floor Back, The, 109
Paul of Ethiopia, Prince, 24
'Peace in our Life' (song), 130, 150
Pelé, 90, 92
Perez, Tony, 46
Perrin, Steven, 154
Picasso, Pablo, 27
Pigott-Smith, Tim, 81, 94
Pinter, Harold, 26
Poe, Edgar Allan, 30, 111, 167, 168, 177
Police Story, 38
Poll, Martin, 86–7, 89
Pollack, Sydney, 168

Polo (dog), 157
Porky's, 120
Porky's II, 120
Prisoner of Second Avenue, The, 38
Puzo, Mario, 112

Quayle, Anthony, 31

Raging Bull, 46
Rambo: First Blood Part II, 37, 108, 120, 124–30, 147, 149, 150, 164, 165, 172
Rambo III, 108, 127, 154, 160–7, 172, 175
Reade, Walter, 27
Reagan, Nancy, 163
Reagan, Ronald, 12, 128, 163
Rebel (see *No Place to Hide*)
Red Sonja, 134, 141, 150
Redford, Robert, 47
Reds, 30
Reeves, Steve, 21, 37
Return of the Jedi, 128
Reynolds, Burt, 47, 120
Rhinestone, 19, 119–23, 172
'Rhinestone Cowboy' (song), 121
Rhodes, Cynthia, 116, 117
Richards, Dick, 39
Righteous Brothers, The, 145
Roach, John, 43, 70
Robinson, Andrew, 145
Robinson, Phil Alden, 119, 121, 123
Rocky, 13, 19, 28, 43, 45–61, 64, 67, 68, 69, 70, 74, 76, 78, 81, 83, 84, 85, 88, 89, 90, 91, 94, 100, 101, 102, 104, 105, 113, 119, 130, 136, 139, 142, 143, 151, 154, 163, 164, 165, 166, 167, 170, 175, 179
Rocky II, 37, 80–5, 86, 96, 100, 101, 136, 154, 180
Rocky III, 37, 49, 97–102, 104, 115, 120, 136, 138, 141, 154, 173, 174, 180
Rocky IV, 37, 115, 118, 136–43, 148, 150, 160, 165, 174, 178
Rocky V, 143, 173–75, 176, 178, 180
Roeves, Maurice, 91, 92, 96, 103
Rollerball, 39, 41
Roosevelt, Theodore, 62
Rose, Billy, 15
Ross, Diana, 98
Rossi, Lucca, 134
Runaway Train, 172
Running Duck, (novel), 146
Runyon, Damon, 69, 74
Russell, Kurt, 28, 171–73
Russians are Coming, The Russians are Coming, The, 59

Sad Blues, 31
Sahnger, Kelly, 150, 157–8
St. Valentine's Day Massacre, The, 39
Santoni, Reni, 148
Saturday Night Fever, 113, 114, 117
Save the Tiger, 48
Schatz, Thomas, 12
Schnitzer, Robert, 38
Schomberg, A. Thomas, 101
Schwarzenegger, Arnold, 14, 37, 39, 134, 158, 173, 176, 178
Score (stage), 28–9
Scott, Tony, 149, 157
Shaber, David, 86
Shakespeare, William, 96, 103

Shavers, Ernie, 98
Shaw, Tom, 92
Shire, Talia, 13, 48, 49, 52, 53, 56, 119
Shy People, 172
Silliphant, Stirling, 151
Simon, Neil, 38
Singin' in the Rain, 83
Smith, Maria, 35
Smith, Richard, 169
Somebody Up There Likes Me, 52, 61
Sound of Music, The, 93
Spinell, Joe, 50, 74, 101
Stallone, Frank, 15–22, 56
Stallone, Frank Jnr, 17, 18, 20, 56, 113, 130, 150
Stallone, Jacqueline, 13, 15–17, 19–25, 26, 28, 30, 43, 56, 80, 96, 131, 137, 144–5, 156, 158, 162
Stallone, Sage, 57, 174
Stallone, Sasha, 13, 26, 31, 38, 43, 45, 47, 56, 57, 67, 69, 76–7, 81, 84–6, 95–6, 130–2, 143–4, 157, 180
Stallone, Seargeoh, 84, 130–1
Stanier, John, 164
Star is Born, A, 78
Star Wars, 64
Starrett, Jack, 107
Stay Hungry, 39
Staying Alive, 27, 113–18, 123, 179, 180
Staying Fit (book), 115
Steiger, Rod, 63, 65, 67
Stein, Jack, 85
Stewart, Alana, 180
Stone, Oliver, 118
Stoolie, The, 48
Stotter, Susan, 179
Straight, Beatrice, 57
Streetcar Named Desire, A, 111
Streisand, Barbra, 60, 78
Summer, Donna, 144
Superman II, 100
Suppa, Ron, 43, 70
Sutherland, Donald, 170
Sydow, Max Von, 90, 93, 94, 95

Tango and Cash, 28, 171–3, 176, 178
Teamsters' Union, 59, 60
Temple, Shirley, 170
Tero, Lawrence, 98
They Shoot Horses, Don't They?, 46
Thom, Robert, 41
Thomerson, Tim, 122

Thompson, Brian, 146, 149
Till Young Men Exit, 31
Tomlin, Lily, 119
Total Recall, 178
Touch of Evil, 31
Travolta, John, 113–19, 144, 171
Twins, 173, 178

Vajna, Andrew, 104
Veidt, Conrad, 109
Verona, Stephen, 33–5
Victoria, Queen, 40
Victory (see *Escape to Victory*)

W.W. and the Dixie Dancekings, 48
Wagner, Lindsay, 88
Wald, Jeff, 58
War and Peace (novel), 69
Washington, George, 52
Wayne, John, 12, 104–5, 174
Weathers, Carl, 49, 50, 83, 98
Weintraub, Jerry, 112
Weiss, Larry, 121
Welles, Orson, 56
Wenger, Cliff, 127
Wepner, Chuck, 45–6, 115, 140
Wexler, Norman, 114, 118
White, Vanna, 180
Wilbur, Claire, 29
Williams, Billy Dee, 87, 89
Williams, Tennessee, 111
Willis, Bruce, 14
Winding, Julian, 134, 135
Winding, Kaspar, 134, 135, 159
Winfrey, Oprah, 176
Winkler, Henry, 34, 35
Winkler, Irwin, 46, 47, 48, 144
Winters, Shelley, 159
Winterset, 49
Wise, Robert, 52
Wogan, 159
Wolf, William, 30

X (see *Man with the X-Ray Eyes, The*)

Young, Burt, 49, 50, 55, 56
Young, Gig, 27
Young, Rhoda, 26

Zimmerman, Don, 119, 120